TRICKS OF THE MIND

DERREN BROWN

TRANSWORLD PUBLISHERS
61–63 Uxbridge Road, London W5 5SA
a division of The Random House Group Ltd

RANDOM HOUSE AUSTRALIA (PTY) LTD
20 Alfred Street, Milsons Point, Sydney,
New South Wales 2061, Australia

RANDOM HOUSE NEW ZEALAND LTD
18 Poland Road, Glenfield, Auckland 10, New Zealand

RANDOM HOUSE SOUTH AFRICA (PTY) LTD
Isle of Houghton, Corner of Boundary Road & Carse O'Gowrie,
Houghton 2198, South Africa

Published 2006 by Channel 4 Books
a division of Transworld Publishers

Copyright © Objective 2006

The right of Derren Brown to be identified
as the author of this work has been asserted in accordance
with sections 77 and 78 of the Copyright, Designs and
Patents Act 1988.

A catalogue record for this book is available
from the British Library.
ISBN 9781905026265 (from Jan 07)
ISBN 1905026269

All rights reserved. No part of this publication may
be reproduced, stored in a retrieval system, or
transmitted in any form or by any means,
electronic, mechanical, photocopying, recording,
or otherwise, without the prior permission of
the publishers.

Set in 11/15pt Century Old Style by
Falcon Oast Graphic Art Ltd.

Printed in Great Britain by
Clays Ltd, Bungay, Suffolk

5 7 9 10 8 6

Papers used by Transworld Publishers are natural, recyclable products
made from wood grown in sustainable forests. The manufacturing processes
conform to the environmental regulations of the country of origin.

To Mum, Dad and Bro.

CONTENTS

PREFACE

Some time last spring I thought I would visit Her Majesty's Fish in the aquarium, which sits beneath the gently disappointing London Eye not far from our production offices. At the time I had just had a fish-tank installed at home and was looking for sea-monsters with which to fill it. Tentacled, multi-limbed, slithering creatures which are entirely at home only when attacking submarines or James Mason were what I was after, and the thought of visiting a place where such things as giant octopodes (I notice that Microsoft is not only unhappy with the correct plural, but also allows *octopi*, which those of you who delight in annoying others will know is in fact wrong) might glare at me through toughened and confusingly-focused glass struck me as far too exciting for words. As it turned out, Zone Twelve of the Aquarium was irksomely short on invertebrates of any sort, and the highlight of the afternoon proved to be looking at an enormous American lady squashed against the glass from the opposite window of the shark tank.

I was, throughout my tour of largely similar fish, doing my best to read the little plaques next to each tank, which told me and other curious visitors the name, feeding habits and musical tastes of whatever was diving, swimming or floating upside-down inside. About halfway through this fabricated subterranean labyrinth, my conscious mind suddenly latched onto an oddity. I realized that underneath the descriptions of the various natant ichthyoids there was a translation of what I presumed to be the same information *in Braille*. For a while this seemed quite natural, and then I caught myself wondering: on average, how many blind people a year visit the London Aquarium? Now I don't wish to sound insensitive, but I imagine the number must be negligible.

I would welcome any answers from blind people to a couple of questions that have been bugging me since. Firstly, *how do you know where the Braille sign is located?* This must be relatively straightforward in such things as lifts, but what about in an alien environment? If alone in a train toilet, how does one find Braille instructions for the use of obscured or unusual soap dispensers or toilet flushes? That sounds like an unpleasant and even unhygienic search to be undertaking while bumping around somewhere near Didcot Parkway. My second concern, clearly, is if a blind visitor found the Braille sign in the Aquarium, of what earthly use would it be? Aside from possible fleeting strokes of a passing stingray in the 'touching pool', the London Aquarium seems to be an experience ill suited to visitors with severe visual challenges. It occurred to me that the Braille signs, if located, would at best provide the blind visitor with no more to take with him from his afternoon than a list of fish. *A list of fish.*

Upon leaving the Aquarium, both taken aback by the exit route through McDonald's and still disappointed by the poor show on the squid front, I was stopped by a young chap who wanted to say hello and ask me a few questions about what I do. We chatted for a while, and then he asked if there was a book available that could teach him more about the various skills I employ to entertain and sexually arouse the viewing few. Now I have been asked by many of you, sometimes with a politeness that reflects favourably upon your upbringing but all too frequently with a rudeness and an icy stare that makes me want to harm your children, if there is such a book that can throw some light on the fascinating and highly-paid areas that inform my multi-award-winning and massively enjoyable body of work. You hold in your hands, or in the case of some of you your feet, the answer to that question. I have tried to cover all my main areas of interest in relation to my shows, bring them all together like naughty children and bundle them into a hygienic and unobtrusive book-like format that can be inserted quite comfortably to allow the reader to confidently roller-skate or play tennis.

Over the years I have met many people during the inevitable mingling that occurs when I leave my apartment and dart across the street to buy a bread or a bag of milk, just like ordinary bloody people. From listening carefully to you when you talk, I can tell that some of you are bright and witty, people I would happily show around my home, whereas others of you would seem to require professional care. Many of you approach what I do with a dose of intelligent scepticism and a sense of fun; others of you might read the *Daily Mail*, live with more than three cats or regard *Trisha* as serious journalism. Of course, this second group generally includes those permanently outraged people who write letters of complaint to newspapers and broadcasters of television shows – a particular madness that leaves me dumbstruck. Dumbstruck, that is, not only by the madness itself, but also by the fact that such people are often encouraged to call in to or vote in television or radio debates of real complexity, and are treated as a vital voice of democracy. Uninformed strong opinions – and I particularly include religious ones, which for some reason get special treatment – are of course mere clusters of prejudices and no more appropriate than mine, yours or anyone else's are on topics we don't understand – as worthless as my opinions on hockey, Noel Edmonds or rimming.

So, taking on board the wide range of people who might watch my shows, I have tried to pitch this book to the intelligent reader with a layman's interest in things mind-related. Some of those things I feel passionately about and others are drier subjects: I just offer my thoughts at the level at which they occur in my enormous round bearded head. The subjects covered are diverse, and some are a little more academic in tone than others. Equally, I have rejected the option of writing an anaemically 'light' introduction to exciting mind-feats, which would make for easy reading and quick writing but would undoubtedly be misleading, and instead incorporated a level of scepticism where I feel it is important. This comes from a desire to make the contents of the book as worthwhile and unpatronizing as possible ('patronizing', of course, means 'to talk down to people').

I do hope that you are inspired to delve further into one or more of the areas to which this book will introduce you; if not, it should make an excellent and inexpensive bath-toy for your least favourite child. I would love to feel that this book can give you information you can apply practically, or use as a springboard for further useful discovery. That would be my aim. I would hate you to leave with just a list of fish.

PART ONE

Tricks of the Mind

DISILLUSIONMENT

DISILLUSIONMENT

The Bible is not history.

Coming to terms with this fact was a fiddly one for me, because I believed in God, Jesus and Satan (ish). And one aspect of believing in those things and meeting once a week with like-minded people is that you're never encouraged to really study the facts and challenge your own beliefs. I always imagined that challenging my beliefs might make them stronger.

It will be hard for many of you to reconcile the image you are most likely to have of me from the high-definition image that graces your stylish front room or caravan – e.g. 'handsomely mysterious' (*Nuts Literary Supplement*); 'certainly not at home to Mr *or* Mrs Smug' (*Manchester Evening Scrotum*) – with the revolting vision of my late teenage self: a bouncing, clapping awfulness who could think of nothing more rewarding than to try to convert his unspeakably tolerant friends to the sanctimonious life he knew as a believer. For all you unsanctimonious believers out there, I'm sure I did you a disservice. Picture, if you require a good vomiting, a whole herd of us being encouraged to display the Pentecostal gift of 'talking in tongues' by a self-styled pastor, with the proviso that if we ceased babbling because we thought it silly then that was indeed the Devil telling us to stop. Envision, as a secondary emetic, me telling a non-Christian friend that I would pray for him, unaware of how unspeakably patronizing such an offer might sound. I would delight in being offended, and puff up with pride at being outspoken and principled. And this the unpleasant result of a childhood indoctrination followed by years of circular belief to support it.

In the last years of the eighties, the rising phenomenon of the New Age movement became a *bête noire* to my rather rabid pastor and many others like him. We were warned that Satan himself encouraged interest in crystals and psychic healing, and that witchcraft alone could explain the growing number of alternative bookstores popping up in Croydon. I was convinced, and accepted such things as tarot cards as profoundly dangerous. For those of you who find this laughable, please don't think for a moment that plenty of modern churches don't confidently talk of demons as real, if invisible, creatures, populating such sinful environs as student bedrooms and heavy metal music shops. Part of this man's job – a 'pastor', remember – was to convince ordinary, innocent people in his care that such things were true, so that they'd be frightened enough to cling more closely to this religion in which that still small voice of loveliness had been drowned out by a desire for sensationalism.

In the early nineties, however, a small event happened that was to prove to be my own domestic Damascus experience. A Domestos experience, if you like. I was living in Wills Hall, a student hall of residence at Bristol University that comprised mainly a quadrangle (which, as with quadrangles everywhere, we were not allowed to traverse; for grass, when grown in a rectangle, is always sacred) surrounded by old buildings reminiscent of an Oxford college. In fact, the story goes, Mr Wills, the tobacco giant of the twenties, had these and other buildings built in that grand style to create an

Oxonian environment for his son who had failed the Oxford examination and had to study in Bristol. (Take heed, any of you students who feel the victim of undue parental pressure. Consider yourselves lucky that your father didn't build the university especially for you.) Any road up, I came down to breakfast late one afternoon from Carsview, the studenty, pretentious name I had given my room, to see a poster in the entranceway of my building. (If English Heritage is already thinking of a plaque, it was Block A.) A large black eye printed onto yellow card advertised a hypnotic show and lecture, to be performed and delivered that night in the Avon Gorge Room of the Students' Union. I had never attended such a thing, and it sounded more fun than the regular evening ritual of drinking fruit tea and deliberating the correct use of *Kafkan* over the less preferable *Kafkaesque*, before heading back to my room for a gentle wank.

The formal demonstration, given by a hypnotist called Martin Taylor, was followed by an after-show session back at a student's house, where he continued to hypnotize the more suggestible of us in return, I remember vividly, for a Cornish pastie and overnight accommodation. There was nothing of the Rasputin about him; indeed he was chipper, blond and open about how it all worked. As I walked back late that night with my friend Nick Gillam-Smith, I said that I was going to be a hypnotist.

'Me too,' he said.

'No, I really am,' I insisted.

I found every book I could on the subject and began to learn. There were student guinea-pigs every day to try it out on, and later college gerbils, who proved even less responsive. The exact sort of rugby bloke who had left me feeling terribly inferior at school now proved the ideal subject for this new skill I was learning, and the feeling of control over such people was terrifically appealing. I began to perform little shows around the university, or would hypnotize friends in bars so they could get drunk on water.

I had not been to church with any regularity for a couple of years, but was still a believer. I was amazed to hear from my Christian friends that by hypnotizing people I was ushering in demonic forces. At one show, the membership of the Christian Union sat at the back of the audience and talked loudly in tongues in an attempt, I presume, to exorcize the evil being perpetrated on stage. On another occasion, one Sunday near Christmas, I walked into the big student church to be greeted with 'What's he doing here?' from someone on the back pew. Nice.

I was confused. If God created us, then presumably the human mind is the pinnacle of creation (second only to Amazon.com and Philip Seymour Hoffman). And I certainly knew that I had a better idea of how hypnotism worked than these people. Still, one can't judge an entire religion on the unpleasant behaviour of a few individuals, so I shrugged off these reactions. Indeed, I was unsure of where to take the hypnosis myself. I had hired myself out for a stag night, and I knew that coming on after lesbian strippers and making grown men dance ballet was not my future. So one afternoon, spent as a true flâneur browsing through remainder bookshops in town, I came across *Mark Wilson's Complete Course in Magic*, an exciting and impressive-looking tome whose top hat and white gloves depicted on its glossy cover promised to teach me all I needed to know to become a competent conjuror. Never one to arrive at an acumen regarding a set of printed pages bound along one side, based purely upon my discernment of its sheathing, ho ho, I set about the task of studying its secrets and learning the esoteric switches, shifts and moves it taught to see whether between us we could succeed.

The slow-creeping obsession of magic, from interest to hobby to grounds for divorce, brings with it an unavoidable fascination with trickery and fraudulence in the world of the paranormal. The tradition of magician-debunkers is almost as old as the debunkees they pursue, and will probably always tag along behind the unavoidably more sensational and popular line of psychics and spiritualists, the exposers embittered and bored by the fact that desperate people seeking easy answers are rarely interested in being told that those answers are lies or that the seekers might be being exploited and manipulated. This, coupled with my love of suggestion and the techniques of the hypnotist, led to an interest in how we might come to believe in such things as paranormal ability, and how we might be convinced by the apparent efficacy of the various New Age practices, which were becoming hugely fashionable among white middle-class people at the time, who presumably felt vaguely guilty about being white and middle-class. Certainly it was clear enough to render the worries of 'ushering in demons' as frightened nonsense. The world of the paranormal is, I feel, a fascinating and at once depressing and oddly life-affirming mixture of self-delusion, placebos and suggestion, charlatanism and exploitation. But there is certainly no need to talk of demons.

I discovered that world of delusion through a love of illusion, and it is my delight in and curiosity for the possibility of real magic that leads me to want to see how these things work. Some people may express their affection for the notion of magical abilities and spiritual planes by embracing such ideas with no desire for evidence other than their own conviction; others (like me, who always took toys apart when I was little) want to see what such ideas are made of.

What struck me about the people I knew who did believe in the paranormal was that they had a clearly circular belief system. Essentially, one believes X so strongly that all evidence that does not support X is ignored, and all events that fit in with X are noticed and amplified. For example, a good friend who worked as a psychic healer told me how she had healed a chap at a party who had badly scalded his arm after a boiler had burst in front of him. Her account of it seemed impressive: she had laid hands on him for a while, and the pain and blistering had subsided very rapidly. So as we had mutual friends, I asked someone else who had been at the party if the story was true. He laughed. Yes, she had indeed laid hands on him, but only after they'd packed his arm in ice and snow for over an hour. My psychic friend had not wished to mislead me; she had simply filtered out the snow-packing as unimportant in the story. Indeed, the episode was confirmation to her of her abilities, and it fuelled her belief.

The more I came up against this sort of thing, the more I became concerned that I, as a Christian, was falling into exactly the same trap. Was I not indulging the same sort of circular belief? Remembering prayers that had been answered, and forgetting those that weren't? Or deciding they had been answered but in a less obvious way? What separated my belief from the equally firm convictions of my psychic friend, other than the fact that hers were less mainstream and therefore easier to poke fun at? Weren't we both guilty of the same comforting nonsense? Surely I was being a hypocrite.

It's a question I still ask of intelligent Christians, because I would dearly like to hear a well-formed answer. One can be a true believer in anything: psychic ability, Christianity or, as Bertrand Russell classically suggested (with irony), in the fact that there is a teapot orbiting the earth. I could believe any of those things with total conviction. But my conviction doesn't make them true. Indeed, it is something of an insult to the very truth I might hold dear to say that something is true just because I believe it is. Surely if we have a belief in a cosmological process we are happy to live by and express to the point where we will endure public ridicule, we should want it to have its roots in something outside our own unreliable convictions. Some sort of evidence outside what we happen to feel is right. Now, we can all appreciate that we get things wrong some of the time, and are sure of things we later find out were mistaken. Our level of personal conviction about a subject bears no relation to how true it is in the outside world. For some things this distinction isn't terribly important. The appreciation of a painting or a piece of music, for example, or even falling in love, is all about our subjectivity. But to decide that the entire universe operates in such and such a way, let alone to go to war because we are so convinced we are right that others must agree with us or die, that surely should demand a higher level of argument than 'It's true because I really, really feel it is'.

So to avoid my self-directed charge of hypocrisy, I thought I would look at the outside evidence. It's actually rather straightforward to do this with Christianity, although the believer is not usually encouraged to do so by his peers or pastors.

Not only is the believer encouraged not to question or challenge his faith, but, to use Richard Dawkins' apt expression, any rational inquiry is expected to 'tip-toe respectfully away' once religion enters the room. It is dangerous to question from within, and rude to question from without. We are allowed to question people about their politics or ethics and expect them to defend their beliefs, or at least hold their own in any other important matter by recourse to evidence, yet somehow on the massive subject of God and how he might have us behave, all rational discussion must stop the moment we hear 'I believe'. This, despite the fact that religion can be, as we see in these current days of religious violence from East and West, a murderous preoccupation rooted in the ethics and ignorance of the early centuries when its scriptures were being formed.

Moderate religious people may of course express distaste for such violence, pretending that the clear calls for grotesque and violent behaviour in their sacred book aren't there and cherry-picking the 'nice bits', but they are still guilty of not opening up the subject of belief to rational discourse, and in doing so are part of the machinery that leads to all the ugliness caused by fundamentalism.

To me and my erstwhile fellow Christians, it all rested on whether or not Christ really came back from really being dead. If he was actually resurrected as it says in the Bible, then it's all true, regardless of what one thinks of Christians and their behaviour. If he didn't, then it's all nonsense, and Christianity is a delusion.

It all centres on that one question, and the burden of proof, of course, must lie with the Christians who claim it; it's not up to the rest of us to prove a negative. To their credit, they do appear to tackle this head on. There is a popular argument among defenders of the Faith that revolves around disproving possibilities other than Jesus' resurrection. If Jesus (who we can safely say was a historical figure, even though a far more pedestrian one than the man presented in the Bible) didn't appear again after his death, then the Romans need only have produced the body to end the new religion. It would have been over in a week. If the body had been stolen by the apostles, or if the apostles knew he hadn't really come back to life, then it makes no sense for those first evangelists to have been persecuted and killed for proclaiming the new faith.

There are plenty of arguments like this, but all are based on the notion that we can take the New Testament stories as accounts of real events. But to decide that the Bible is history, one must ignore the vast amount of impartial biblical research that shows it really isn't – in other words, to decide that one's personal conviction means more than clear evidence. We cannot value personal conviction when we are looking at to what extent the story stands up as fact. Such things must be put to one side; only evidence must be of interest. And the evidence shows very clearly that the stories of the New Testament were written in the first couple of hundred years after the historical Jesus died. These stories then continued to be edited and revised for political and social needs for most of the first millennium. Jesus was one of many teachers at a time of massive social upheaval and tension, and inasmuch as one can separate his words from those later put into his mouth, he taught a mix of a much-needed social vision ('The Kingdom of Heaven') and personal stoicism. After he died, and after the Kingdom of Heaven hadn't arrived, his followers formed communities that were persecuted or ridiculed; they needed stories and legends to inspire them and give them credence. So they created them: as was customary, words and actions that fitted present needs were put into the mouths and lives of historical figures and then read as history. Inspiring figures were enormously bent, stretched and rewritten so that their 'lives' would fit what they had come to stand for. Although the Gospels are attributed to individuals, they were written largely by communities. Great and powerful stories were told, changed and rearranged over several generations.

I have a layman's interest in this sort of scholarship, coupled with a personal desire to back up my disbelief in the way I expected I should be able to back up my belief when I had it. When I realized that the accounts of Jesus were just tales, I had to accept that the resurrection could not be argued from those very sources as fact, which unavoidably led to the conclusion that nothing separated my 'true belief' from anyone else's 'true belief'. Nothing lay between my nonsense and everyone else's nonsense. I just believed because I always had done, and because it had come to be a very important psychological crutch, if I can use that word.

The brave or intelligent Christian who is interested in questioning blind faith would be well advised to read Richard Dawkins' book *The God Delusion*. I mentioned Dawkins to a Christian friend who said, 'Oh, he's always banging on about religion'. Not a moment's thought to what Dawkins' arguments might be or whether they might hold up, which I thought was a shame. For me, after so many years of trotting out adolescent 'proofs' of God's existence, I found this work enormously valuable for putting them into perspective. Sadly, I imagine many Christians will be more concerned with stopping others from reading Dawkins' book than being brave enough to read it themselves, perhaps even with an eye to strengthening their own belief.

Now, perhaps – if you have not already set fire to this book in outrage – you are wondering why such things matter. We all find nonsenses to believe in; it's part of being alive. Besides, you have bought this book for other reasons: such talk of religion neither induces sexually attractive persons to succumb to your raging, tumescent will, nor does it help you with your physics revision. We are indeed quite fascinatingly diverse, and if we were all to think the same there would be no need for so many television channels. But consider this: is it not better to make informed decisions than ill-informed ones? Would you knowingly accept lies sold to you as truth? Does 'tumescent' mean 'erection'?

TRUTH AND LIES

Inasmuch as I do very much hope to improve you no end by introducing you to some skills and topics I personally find fascinating, we must first consider the rather embarrassing question of how honest I'm going to be with you when discussing my techniques. Some areas of the gutter press and of my own family seem convinced that amid the wealth of unmistakable candour, even-handedness, incorruptibility, rectitude and probity that has characterized my work to date, there might lie the occasional false or disingenuous datum designed to throw the careful seeker off course. Well, as my great-grandmother once said: rectitude and probity, my arse.

The shows that shove themselves into your living rooms each week, or which trickle down from the ether into your hard-drive during the night, are openly described by none other than me, at the start of what we in the industry call 'episodes', as a mixture of 'magic, suggestion, psychology, misdirection and showmanship'. The routines-stunts-tricks-gags I perform sometimes rely on magical principles, sometimes on psychological ones. For example, *Séance*, if you were embarrassingly kind enough to watch it or even take part in its 'interactive' element, believing it to be live, appeared to involve some form of spiritual activity, but was clearly a series of tricks mixed with suggestive techniques to get the desired results. If you found yourself spelling out the correct name of the deceased on your Ouija board at home, then that was the result of a trick (to make you think of the right name) followed by suggestion (to have you unconsciously move the glass around the table to spell it out). It was the same process with the participants on the show. On the other hand, *The Heist*, which was the last special to air at the time of writing, was unique in that it contained no tricks and no fooling of the viewer. There were a few 'tricks' employed during the two-week filming, designed to convince the participants that they were learning amazing new skills, but they were not included as they seemed to detract from the openness of the process. Had the final armed robberies not worked – though I had no doubt they would – I had a *very* vague plan B and C up my sleeve to ensure that the show would come together in some form. But I didn't need to go down those routes. (Let's just say that I had *a lot* of dancers tucked around corners, waiting for a signal.)

There are certain rules we stick by to preserve integrity in the process of making the television show. And I imagine that the rules are self-evident. They have evolved from having tried different approaches to achieve the effects I am after, and also from becoming better known, which brings with it new priorities. For example, I have never used stooges in my work. To use a stooge is to have an actor playing the part of the person who is taking part in the trick or supposedly having his mind read. He or she plays along and pretends to be amazed. TV and stage magic are no strangers to the use of such a ploy, but to me such a route is artistically repugnant and simply unnecessary. And I can't imagine what it would cost to silence such people after the event. Secondly, I would not want any participant to watch the show when it airs and see a different or radically re-edited version of what he understood to have happened. Again, this would be a ludicrous move, given that there will always be journalists ready to listen to the views of aggrieved participants. I enjoy what I do, and I value people enjoying themselves when they take part, so their overall experience is paramount to me.

The type of performance I upsettingly force upon you has its roots in a craft called 'mentalism', which in turn is rooted in magic and conjuring. Many mentalists (such as me, though I've never liked the term) started out as magicians before turning, as it almost amusingly were, mental. However, while most magicians are fairly recognizable and conform to a limited set of types, mentalists are fewer and further between and can be radically different. The skills are harder to acquire, and personality is paramount. Many cross what to me is an ethical line and become tarot-readers and 'psychics'. Some talk to the dead. Some work in churches, both spiritualist and mainstream Christian. Some remain entertainers but routinely claim real psychic abilities. Some debunk those that do. Others host seminars of a motivational-weekend-team-buildership variety and sell their abilities as 100 per cent finely tuned psychological skills. The real skills at work may be pure conjuring, or they may rely on knowing how to tell people what they want to hear. They might be harmless, entertaining, useful or inexcusably manipulative. They might be driven by profit, ego or heartfelt altruism.

My response when making the shows has been to move into as honest an area as possible, while still retaining the necessary sense of drama and mystique. While I was a little bolder in my claims at the very start of my career, I had no desire as I became more successful to pretend that I was something I was not. So now I clearly frame both live and TV shows as that mixture of psychology and trickery, and concentrate on making them as entertaining as possible while avoiding any direct claims that are untrue. Of course the result is necessarily ambiguous, but I hope that's half the fun.

The issue of honesty ties in with an inherent problem with any form of magical entertainment. Unless the performer is an out-and-out fraud, claiming to be absolutely for real, there exists in the bulk of any audience an acceptance that some jiggery-pokery must be at work. Now this experience of being fooled by a magician should be made pleasurable and captivating by the performer, otherwise he has failed as an entertainer. However, he is entering into an odd relationship with his audience: he is saying, in effect, 'I'm going to act as if this were all very real; but you know, and I know that you know that I know, that it's really a game.' To an extent, we (as an audience) will play along with that game as long as we are rewarded by an entertaining show. Also, the game involves us putting up with a character that is, in effect, showing off. The vast majority of magical performances contain an implication of 'I can do something you can't'. While this may apply to pretty much any performance, such as that of a musician or a dancer, it is far more blatant within magic, and we know that magic involves cheating. (Also, magic rarely hides its cleverness in real beauty or drama. It's too often ugly and theatrically vapid.) Perhaps for these reasons we are less prepared to remain in awe of the abilities we perceive a magician to have.

Magic, I feel, more than most performance types, requires genuine self-deprecation on the part of the performer, and classically it is one area where we never find it. How many magicians can you honestly say are particularly likeable characters? Or who didn't become annoying after a promising start? Any you genuinely don't think would benefit from a hard smack? (You may include this author, of course.) The magical performer, aware of the fact that there is deception at the heart of his craft, might then compensate for that embarrassing truth by developing an on- and off-screen personality that is rather self-important. By doing this, he is further stretching his audience's preparedness to play along with him fooling them. If he becomes insufferable, they will quickly respond with derision. They will try to make the self-styled big man as small as possible. Witness our response to Blaine's box stunt, which was more fun and interesting then *no* box stunt, yet was perhaps a little misjudged in its self-important tone. Compare this with the sheer brilliance of *Derren Brown Plays Russian Roulette Live*, which eclipsed the American's dangling incarceration and won the hearts of the British public.

As regards the issue of self-importance, I do think that the honesty question is fundamental. There is something so delicious, so deeply satisfying, in arriving at a combination of influences and techniques that form the method behind a great trick or stunt, a joy perhaps not dissimilar to that of a composer or a painter when he finishes a piece he is happy with. Yet that delight is something a magician is not allowed to communicate to that body wearily referred to by the cognoscento as the 'lay' public, as he gazes down from the dizzy ecclesiastical heights of thaumaturgy. Primarily this is because one might expose a secret that in turn would undo the very amazement one had successfully produced. So the magician, who beneath all his posturing is still a child at heart, hides that rather more appealing side and makes a pretence of solemnity and an art of self-apotheosis. The result is a lie, and a thin one that all but the most gullible of spectators will eventually see through.

I have always liked the idea of communicating that excitement and delight in the utilization of obscure, devilish and esoteric principles, both honest and dishonest. It's a primary driving force behind my work. This book will therefore be a genuine attempt to offer an introduction to those areas I love. For reasons of space, practicality and retaining some mystery I cannot explain everything here; so in return for not being impossibly open, I promise to be entirely honest. All anecdotes are true, and all techniques are genuinely used.

Read on, you splendid thing.

PART TWO

Tricks of the Mind

MAGIC

A COIN TRICK

Go and get a coin. Go on. Place it on the table, about four inches or so from the edge nearest you. Now, using your right hand if you are right-handed, pick it up; but rather than trying to lift it straight from the surface of the table, slide it naturally back towards you with your fingertips, and let your thumb contact the underside as it reaches the table edge. As you pick it up, make your hand into a fist around the coin, bring your arm up and hold it there.

Got it? Do it a few times, and note the feeling of the movement. Be relaxed and natural. Good. Now, this time, as the coin reaches the edge of the table, pretend to pick it up using exactly the same series of movements but let it fall into your lap instead. Your thumb doesn't really contact it, and the continuing movement of the fingers just push it off the table. Then, as before, make a fist as if the coin was still there, and bring your hand up.

Blow on your hand, and open it. The imaginary fool sat opposite you is delighted: the coin has vanished. He believes you have special powers: you can rest. Now, be good enough to do this a few times until that moment of letting the coin drop is as relaxed and natural as picking it up normally. Alternate between really picking it up and only pretending to, until the two sequences look and feel the same. If you can try it in front of a mirror, you will be amply rewarded. Especially if you are as 'impishly beautiful' (*Penge Herald*) as I am.

This is an elementary coin sleight, but it is barely magic. Let us take this now comfortable sequence and make it more effective. In doing so, there is much to be learned about what makes magic *magical*. Firstly, why put a coin down in order to pick it straight back up again? Who other than a seriously retarded individual would enact such an absurdity? Such odd behaviour does rather detract from a convincing moment of magic. If you remove a coin from your pocket, place it on the table near you, then immediately pick it up to show it's gone, then clearly the action of putting it down and picking it up was somehow special and necessary, and its very unnaturalness suggests to the spectator that some derring-do must have occurred. Compare this, say, with the situation where the coin was there already. If you are just picking up a coin that happened to be in place on the table, that becomes immediately much better. So perhaps you might hunt for something in your pocket a little earlier, removing a coin or two to facilitate the search. They get left on the table, forgotten and unimportant, one of them in the correct position for the trick. Now you *have* to pick it up to do anything with it, so we start off with a much more natural set of circumstances.

Good. Now, there is another issue to be solved. The coin is there on the table; you apparently pick it up and make a fist; you open the fist and it's gone. Because the chain of events is so short and easy to reconstruct, it is more than possible that an astute observer (and many magicians underestimate how astute people are) could work out the trick. *If it has gone from your fist then perhaps it was never in your fist, so you can't have picked it up. Must have gone somewhere else. Aha! Somehow slid off the table.* And if they dive over the table to search your lap area for concealed currency, you're in a right pickle, and must resort to violence to keep them from lifting the dark veil of your art. So, we have to upset their chain of events so they can't reconstruct so easily. This time, instead of making a fist around the imaginary coin, fake putting it in your *other* hand after you've supposedly picked it up (i.e. your left, but feel free to reverse all of this if you're left-handed), and then closing *that* fist around it. Do it with the real coin a few times to see how you perform this motion normally, then do exactly the same thing *sans* the coin. And if you read through that a few times, I fully imagine that the use of the word *sans* will become both unnecessary *and* irritating.

By the silly act of pretending to put a coin that isn't there into your left hand, and curling your fist around it, you have now made it much more difficult for the observer to reconstruct events. Blow on the empty left fist and show that the coin has vanished. If they think that the coin was never really in the left fist (a decision they will have to arrive at once they have been roused with smelling salts and violent slapping), then the only explanation is that you must have retained it in the right fist. But they can see that the right fist is empty too. They will be too busy pondering this conundrum to work their way back to whether or not you even picked it up.

Good, but still not great. How great would it be if they were convinced they saw the coin in your right hand before you put it in the left? Then there really would be no solution for them. So, this time, before you pass the 'coin' across to your left hand, mime showing it at your fingertips. Hold it up for half a moment, as if you're fairly displaying it between your thumb and first two fingers. Now, anyone studying your fingers will see that there's nothing there. But if you make it a quick and casual gesture – a swing of the hand up in the air as you say, 'Watch . . .', and then back down again to pass the coin to your left hand – then they will, once you are relaxed and you time it just right, swear that you showed them the coin in that hand.

That is an extraordinary thing. And imagine the delight that comes from knowing you got away with it.

Now, when the right hand retreats after apparently passing its coin to the left hand, move your attention to the left hand but don't show your right to be empty. Keep it well over the table, and hold it in a loose fist, as if you could still be secretly retaining the imaginary coin in it. Now you are toying with them. You are going to create a false solution: that you palmed the coin away in that right hand. Blow on your left and show it empty. Hold your position for a second to register the climax of the trick, then innocently open both hands as you say, 'It's bizarre, isn't it?' You have given them a moment to hang their only explanation on the surmise that you must still have the coin in your right hand, then removed that one possibility from them.

Still not finished, though. Much of the experience of magic happens *after* the trick is over, when the spectator tries to reconstruct what happened. This is why we've already made it difficult for him. But there's more we can do: we can plant the seeds of false memories, and at the same time cover any worries you may have about not performing the sleight correctly. Earlier I suggested that you take out a couple of coins and place them on the table. Let's say Coin A is a little further towards the centre of the table, too far to do the sleight. Coin B, however, is nearer you and in position for the trick.

Look at both coins, and hover your hand a little over both, as if you are deciding which one to use. This secures in the spectator's mind the image of two coins fairly on the table. Decide on Coin A, and pick it straight up off the table. Don't slide it back, just pick it up. All attention will be on you and the coin. Place it fairly into your left hand, and make a fist around it. Squeeze it and toy with it a little. Open your left hand for a moment, look at the coin and close it again. You're having trouble, though your spectators have no idea what you're trying to achieve. Give up and drop the coin out of your hand onto the table, away from Coin B. Make a self-deprecating remark – 'Right, that didn't work, sorry.' The spectators' attention will dissipate, and you should relax too. As you relax (allow your body to slump back a little which will cue them to relax with you), go into the trick by apparently picking up Coin B.

You are now performing the sleight when the spectators are paying the least attention. Their eyes may still be directed at you, but for the vital moment they are off-guard. As long as you can make them relax in this way, you'll get away with anything during this vital 'off-beat'. Once Coin B is apparently in the left hand, sit forward again and build up the tension. The trick is now so much more convincing. Moreover, you have, by unsuccessfully going through the trick once with Coin A, given them some snapshots that will confuse them later in their reconstruction. They have seen a coin being picked directly up from the table. They have seen a coin clearly in your left fist. Later, they will confuse what they saw the first time with what they saw the second time. No-one should remember that you picked up the second coin in a slightly different manner.

There is still more. How are you *apparently* making the coin vanish? For all these precautions and convincers we have woven into your little performance, is there not something rather cheap and amateurish about blowing on your hand and then immediately showing it empty? It's here that you actually create the magic. The magic happens not from what you do, but from what the spectator perceives. And it has its home not in the fact that the coin vanishes (that's the *result* of the magic), but *how* it vanished (that would be the magic part). So how about this: when the coin is apparently in your left hand, toy with it a bit. Move it around. That's not something any sane person would do unless there really were a coin there, so it really cements the illusion. Act as if you have to get it into some special place in your hand in order to make it disappear. Needless to say, you don't verbalize this, you just act *as if.* Concentrate: making a coin disappear isn't easy. Perhaps it even hurts a bit (this small touch is a dramatic and rather powerful idea suggested by the always brilliant Teller). Maybe (another great modern magician, Tommy Wonder, emphasizes the importance of this sort of 'silent script' for magic) your hand isn't quite warm enough and that's making it more difficult. Maybe the fact that you've just eaten makes it very hard to make it fully disappear. There's probably no need to blow on your hand now, or if there is it's just for show. But not yet . . . wait . . . hang on . . . there it goes . . . I can feel it . . .

And when it goes, does it pop? Get very hot? Does it disappear or somehow melt into the hand? Would it be interesting to vanish the coin and then ask the spectators if they can still see it, as if they might have only hallucinated its disappearance? How many different ways could you play with this to see what gets the best reaction?

Any tension you feel the first few times you do it will be relieved by two things: firstly, your muscles will learn how to perform the series of moves as fluidly as possible, with the minimum of effort; and secondly, the reactions you will get, so out of proportion to the act of slipping a coin off a table, will delight you so much that in no time you'll be showing everyone. And to tell them how it was done ('Pathetically, I just slipped the coin off the table') would be to take away their amazement and replace it with disappointment. Try that once: you'll see that they switch from thinking it was a great piece of magic to, at best, an average trick.

A CARD TRICK

While out getting hopelessly soused, smashed, sloshed, sottish, Scottish, sow-drunk or sizzled during one of your regular saturnalian Saturday nights, bring out your packet of pasteboards and offer the following piece of whimsy to your well-oiled companions. The trick is perhaps not really 'magic'. Indeed, it falls into a slightly unpleasant area of conjuring known as the 'sucker trick', which delights in exposing the spectator as a fool. Still, it should earn you a few free drinks.

Pick upon the dunce or besom-head you wish to victimize, and have him shuffle the cards. It is worth making sure that you do not pick a skilled card-shuffler or closet croupier: if he performs anything other than a basic overhand shuffle (avoid anyone who riffles the two halves of the deck together), have him pass the deck to someone else for 'further shuffling'. Unless you happen to have caught either Dame Fortune or her unusual sister Mistress Providence during moody lady-time, you should find that this one move brings forward a suitably unimpressive shuffler.

Take the deck back from this unsuspecting clodpate and turn it face up in your hand. This means, in case the esoteric idiom of the thaumaturge eludes you, that you make sure you are looking down at an actual card face on the top, rather than the back of a card. However, the very nano-second that you have seen this card, turn away and spread them a little in your hands, to show the assembled halfwits and harlequins the faces of the deck. 'They are all different, obviously, and well mixed now,' you say, to justify this sequence which has afforded you a glimpse of that first card.

Turn the deck face-down before turning back around, and place it neatly and squared-up on the table. You have given the impression that you have not seen any of the cards, and while this is not terribly important at this point, it will help to create the surprise later. Do remember the bottom card you glimpsed: this is your 'key-card', and your ability to recall that card later will make all the difference between you seeming as much like a turnip or twerp as your friends, or looking literally as clever as Jesus.

Now, tell the gullible mooncalf or merry-Andrew sat in front of you to cut the deck into two while you look away. Mime the action of removing a pile of cards from the top of the deck and placing it to your right of the remainder. You do want him to place his cut-off top half to your right, but in case he places it to the left, make a note of the position of the deck on the table, so that when you turn back in a few moments you will be able to tell which half is which, in case of any confusion.

Turn away and let the lean-witted Punchinello do as you so patiently told him. Tell him to remove the card he cut to (the top card of the bottom half) and have a good look at it. As he does so, turn back round and casually pick up the original *bottom* half of the deck (from which he would have just taken his card). This should be the pack of cards to your left. Normally, if you don't turn completely away, you can tell peripherally that he has placed it down correctly. Either way, do ensure that you are picking up the bottom half. The card on the underside, or 'face', of this half is of course the card you have remembered, but you'd be a fool to have to double-check.

Hold this half above the other half (the original top half that he cut off), and tell him to replace the card. Without telling him to do so, you can make it clear that he is to place the card back between the two halves. It will seem a very natural thing to do, as he has just removed it from the middle of the deck and now appears to be putting it back in the same place. In fact, rather excitingly, his card is now next to the key-card. It is this secret fact that is soon to win you victory over the dumb-clucks and dunderheads and secure you the intimate favours of any creature on this earth.

Now, although it is vital that these two cards stay together, you are now very bravely going to ask the Tom-noddy to shuffle the cards. What's that? Won't that undo all our clever machinations? Have I separated myself from my senses? How could such a thing work? Am I simply mad? Perhaps at this point you are ripping these pages from their binding in blood-red boiling anger, incontinent with rage at the wasted effort you have put into learning this so far; already dialling the ladies and gentlemen at both the Fourth Chanel and the *Daily Mail* to insist that this volume is torn from the shelves of WHSmith and simply never aired on Radio One. I merely say: bear with me. Cease all activities that are not entirely tantamount to bearing with me, and let me explain. It is for this reason alone, if you will just simmer down for a second, that you have chosen a poor shuffler. As long as he once more gives the deck a simple overhand shuffle, you can rest assured that the two important cards – your glimpsed key-card and his selection – will remain as a pair. You can subtly hurry him along and stop him from shuffling too thoroughly by extending your hand after a few moments and casually saying, 'Great – just so we don't know where the card is.' Also, asking him to 'mix them a bit' rather than 'shuffle' very often helps too.

Take the deck back when he is done, and say that you are going to deal the cards face-up onto the table, and he is to try not to react if he sees his card. Hold the deck face-down, and start to deal cards from the top, turning them over one at a time. Make a rough pile on the table as you do so. You are – and I'm sure I don't need to tell *you* – watching out for your key-card. The moment you deal that key-card, the *next* card will be the very card the Charlie sat before you is thinking of. However, bat not an eyelid, and keep dealing past the chosen card, making sure that you continue to make such a rough pile on the table that the index of the actual chosen card remains visible to you. Our imprudent friend will of course be gloating with that quite specific smugness of one who believes his card has been mistakenly dealt past.

Stop whenever you feel the moment is right, and proudly state the following: 'I bet you a pint/glass of wine/warm water with a slice of lemon/million pounds that the next card I turn over will be your card.' Look like you are poised to turn over the next card from the deck. Have the cockle-brained halfwit agree to the deal, then reach forward, remove the chosen card from the pile, and turn it over. Climb onto the table and roar for applause before triumphantly urinating on the group.

There are a couple of afterthoughts regarding this trick which might be of use to you – crumbs from the table of a showbiz pro. Firstly, when you take the deck back after shuffling, just before you start dealing, take a look at the bottom (face) card of the deck. This can be easily done by tapping the deck on the table to square it, and just glimpsing the bottom card. It is conceivable, though very unlikely, that this card is your key-card. If indeed you do recognize it to be so, it means that the actual chosen card is on the *top* of the deck – the very first card you would deal. If this happens, you can remedy the situation by having someone cut the deck before dealing. This will allow you to proceed with the trick as explained above, as it will bring the two cards back together in the middle of the deck. Alternatively, it does allow you to segue into a much more impressive trick instead. If you see that key-card on the bottom, I would suggest placing the deck face-down on the table and talking some nonsense about how when we choose a card we develop a kind of relationship with it, and that in something as random as a shuffle it is possible for us to express that affinity by unconsciously controlling it. If you feel like really lying, you could tell them that in a series of tests it's been shown that particularly intuitive people will actually shuffle a card they're thinking of to the top of the deck without realizing it. Have them accept the seeming unlikelihood of such a statement, then sit back and let them take as long as they want to reach forward and turn over the top card for themselves.

Secondly, dealing the cards to random positions on the table rather than into a pile offers you other opportunities to make this even more dangerously impressive. Let's imagine that you deal past the key-card and you see that the selection is a four of hearts. Unless you are unfortunate enough for the selection to reveal itself near the end of the deck, you can now join up the scattered cards into a '4H' as you deal, and continue dealing. If you don't feel you have enough cards left to do this convincingly, it doesn't matter; the scattered dealing will just seem a mysterious part of the secret. But if you do manage to casually deal the cards into a giant representation of the selection, then you have what we like to call a 'kicker ending': after turning over the correct card, you can point out the arrangement on the table, which gives the impression that you knew the card from the very start.*

PERCEPTION IS EVERYTHING

The fascinating, frustrating and wonderful thing about magic is that none of the years of practice you might put into it mean anything of themselves. For many years I took great pleasure in coming up with card tricks, many of which relied on fairly complicated sleights. I'm

*I offered to teach this trick to one of the inmates at the Young Offenders' Institution where we filmed the very first item on the very first *Mind Control* show. 'It's good stuff to learn,' I said, pleased that although we'd clearly been offered the least frightening and most pleasant guys in there, I was fitting in okay and felt cool. 'You know, it's always good knowing a couple of card tricks – just to impress your mates down the pub,' I added, riding the youth-wave of my coolness. 'Yeah,' he answered, 'Only, like, I don't go down to the pub much, 'cos I is in prison.' I also heard that the wardens ration out the washing-up liquid in case it is used wrongly.

rather out of practice now, and have lost some interest too, but for a long time it was something of a passion. The magic community is bursting with hobbyist performers who spend long hours perfecting complicated flourishes and sleights, which is not in itself an ignoble path to follow, but such obsession has very little connection with the magician's ability to create the experience of magic in an entertaining way. If one wished to be a comedian, one would need to start performing on stage to give oneself that title. There are plenty of people who like telling jokes after dinner, but none other than the most arrogantly self-appraising would call himself a comic. With magic, the very role is pretence, and any child who can search endlessly for your card in a special deck from a toyshop can call himself a magician. One's own level of technical expertise may separate the professional from the hobbyist, but it is not the stuff from which magic is made.

This is because magic isn't about fakes and switches and dropping coins on your lap. It's about entering into a relationship with a person whereby you can lead him, economically and deftly, to experience an event as magical. That experience has something to do with a rather child-like feeling of astonishment, but also contains an adult intellectual conundrum. It exists only in the head of the spectator; and though your skills may have led him there, it is not the same as those skills. It inhabits an experience the spectator has; it is not to be found in the method the magician employs. Hence the overriding importance of presentation. One famous and wonderful magician, Eugene Burger (a giant among close-up conjurors), has said that he could spend the rest of his life just learning how to perform three or four tricks.

For example, it is an interesting maxim in conjuring that much of the magic happens after the trick is over. Returning to our coin trick, we planted images in their minds designed to confuse their later reconstruction of what happened. *Didn't I see the coin in his hand before it vanished? I'm sure he picked it straight up off the table: I saw it.* But there is more to it, and the psychology is interesting. When our imaginary spectator is amazed at a trick, he has been charmingly fooled into experiencing something impossible. He has an emotional reaction of astonishment that is greater and more overwhelming than the knowledge in the back of his mind that he must have been fooled. Indeed, so contagious is his own amazement that the knowledge that he has been fooled is neither here nor there. If anything, he'll feel admiration for the person who fooled him for doing so brilliantly. Amazement, like bewilderment, is a state that brings with it a heightened suggestibility, so immediately the baffled spectator will absorb any suggestions given him by the magician, all of which will be designed to make the feat seem even more impossible. The fooled spectator will do everything he can to enhance how wonderful the trick was.

This is worthy of note. Rarely is there any sense of challenge, anger or resentment at being tricked, although there will always be irritating magicians who will court that reaction, and spectators with issues regarding control who will always respond in this way. Some form of unspoken contract exists between the performer and the spectator which permits the deception.

However, the spectator *has* been fooled, which means that he is in something of a dilemma after the event. If the trick has hit home, he'll want to talk about it with friends, in the same way one instinctively wants to share anything amazing by enthusiastically telling anyone who'll listen. As we know, in an attempt to infect the other person with our excitement regarding an event, we tend to give a less than balanced account of what happened. We focus on all the factors that contributed to our amazement, ignore those that might detract from the wonder we wish to convey, and generally try to paint a vivid and colourful story, albeit one prone to exaggeration. This ties in with how people report apparently psychic experiences, which we'll look at later.

However, balanced with this desire to communicate his enthusiasm and inspire it in others, the spectator is also aware that the person to whom he is describing the trick might be laughing a little at him for being duped. Anyone who has tried to convince someone to join a pyramid scheme will know that feeling. So, in order not to be seen as an easy target, the person describing the trick will often exaggerate the factors that made it impossible. For example, he'll insist that the magician never touched the deck of cards, that he himself thoroughly shuffled them, or that he definitely saw the coin in the magician's hand moments before it disappeared. Interestingly, it's not the case that the spectator is merely making these things up to impress other people: he will normally believe them himself. Proof of this is that if asked by the magician immediately after the trick to recap exactly what happened, he'll normally supply similar exaggerations, denials and insistences that he will report to a friend. Although, of course, time is the friend of this developing hyperbole and selective amnesia.

If you understand this very reliable law, it is easy to plant all sorts of seeds within the performance of a trick, or in the moment following the climax when the spectator is at his most suggestible, to ensure that the magic trick ties itself up neatly after the event to form the memory of something that is genuinely impossible. Realizing this, and utilizing the principle, allows enormous fun to be had. For example, in a card trick I used to perform, it was important that the deck was in a special order at the start. However, later on it was safe for the spectator to shuffle them. At this point I would give him the deck for the first time and say, 'Shuffle the deck again, but this time do it *under* the table.' Immediately he is concerned about the slightly awkward process of shuffling them blindly without dropping any, and has not questioned the little word 'again', which was slipped in. It can be helped along with the words 'It's not as easy, is it?' while he shuffles. He is unwittingly accepting the suggestion that he has shuffled them before, and that makes it very easy for him to misremember what happened. If he then relates the trick as having begun with him shuffling the deck, he'll confirm that to himself and develop a lovely false memory, and the trick becomes impossible ever to work out.

There are many more psychological principles one must instinctively absorb to perform this sort of close-up magic as beautifully and deftly as possible. I am less interested in stage magic illusions, as while it is more demanding to pull off a top-class performance on stage, the interpersonal element tends to be fixed and prescribed, and in this sense it's less interesting than the close-up situation. One principle really hit home while I was performing at a restaurant table in Bristol many years ago. I had been working on a long and involved card trick where three chosen cards would disappear from the deck, turn up in obscure places such as my shoes and inside the card box, and go through a series of vanishes, changes and appearances in this way. I thought it would be a great climax to have each of the three cards appear under each spectator's drink, and I had spent many hours at home in front of a mirror working out a clever sleight to get the three cards palmed and fed under the glasses at suitable moments. Normally one can get away with this sort of thing once, but three times seemed a rather tough call.

Now, there is a law in physics, I trust you remember, which states that for every action there is an equal and opposite reaction. For example, if I were to repeatedly punch Robert Kilroy-Silk full in the face, or push a rolled-up copy of the *Daily Mail* very far into his bottom, he would react by begging for mercy and probably crying. His reaction would be in direct proportion to how much I was hurting him, or something. Equally, it can apply to the psychological grammar of magic. If you are watching a half-decent magician perform a trick for you, you are probably watching very carefully to catch him out. You'll watch his every move like the proverbial hawk, determined not to miss anything. By doing so, you are unwittingly playing into exactly those hands you are studying so intently. This is because for every unit of concentration, there must follow an equal and opposite unit of relaxation. Remember the business with your new coin trick where you tried it first with Coin A and failed? The more they watch you, the more they will relax and stop paying attention when they think the trick is over. When you fail to make the first coin disappear, the spectators relax, and you then perform the sleight.

Conjurors understand this principle, and during my years as a conjuror, the act of performing a trick like this became rather like a game. Firstly, invite concentration; then supply a sense of closure, or climax, or failure; next, perform the sleight-of-hand or moment of trickery as both you and the spectator relax. The spectator will never suspect that he is being manipulated in this way, and even if he does, then there's very little he can do about it. One of the mistakes a novice magician makes is to tense up and lean forward when he performs a sleight. The more experienced performer knows the value of relaxing across a reliable off-beat to render his moves invisible. For this reason, very often the more attentive a spectator is, the easier he is to fool. Scientists have many times been fooled in the laboratory by charlatans posing as psychics for the same reason. The more you watch, the more you'll miss.

It was this principle that provided an unexpected answer in the restaurant that night. I reached what would normally have been the end of the trick, which involved producing the three cards from inside the card box after they had seemingly disappeared from my hands. I fanned them, and tossed them down on the table. Both my verbal and non-verbal language signified a clear end to the trick. They reacted very nicely by physically moving back and applauding. Their crescendo of concentration had peaked moments before (*The cards have gone again? But I was watching . . . where could they be? Must try and catch him out . . .*), and with the final production they were happy to be overwhelmed and to give up. And in their enthusiastic reaction, they became inattentive to my actions on the table. It takes effort to concentrate, and there's only so much effort you can apply before you want to stop and relax. At this point I took the three cards and, smiling and thanking them for their attention, reached across and pushed one under each of their drinks. Not a furtive move, just relaxed, casual and unhurried. As I did this, I also let three other cards drop face-down on the table from the balance of the deck, to replace the three chosen cards that had been there before. Because these were face-down, the group would presume they were still their cards. Not one of the party seemed to notice my actions, or the exchange.

I returned to a relaxed, sat-back-in-the-chair posture myself, then said something along the lines of, 'One more time . . . watch.' I sat forward, picked up one of the three face-down random cards, and placed it into the deck. I picked up one of the remaining two, then swapped it for the third one and placed that in the deck. I was keeping them focused on the cards again, and the meaningless switch of the second for the third card helped convince them that I was using the same three chosen cards: why would I worry about the order in which I was returning them if they weren't the same three? I replaced the final card, squared the deck up and held it in a slightly unnatural position, to raise their suspicion and invite them to watch me closely; I may even have shuffled awkwardly to maintain their focus on the deck. Then I turned it face-up and spread it across the table, being careful not to go near their drinks. I pointed out that their cards had gone. They looked for them in the spread, and in doing so again their attention was still directed to a limited area of the table and away from their glasses. I sat right back to put as much distance between me and them as possible, then asked them to look right at me. I said to them calmly and clearly, 'Each of your cards is now right in front of you, under each of your drinks.' It was nice to watch their faces for a moment as they processed that information before looking.

Years of practising sleight-of-hand and secret moves that might have allowed me to secretly slip a card under a glass without being noticed had gone out of the window. I had just put them there quite openly, right in front of them. I had made no attempt to hide my actions. You start to live for moments like that.

Much, if not all, of conjuring relies on the performer creating a false trail of events that clearly leads to a particular climax. Very little is hidden: most sleights and 'secret' moves happen right out in the open, but the spectator pays no attention to them. It seems that the magician creates a very strong sense of A leads to B leads to C leads to D, where A is the start of the trick and D is the impossible climax. All of these stages are punctuated clearly, and there should be no confusion along the way. In fact, it's one of the rules of great magic (according to Dai Vernon, the father of modern close-up conjuring) that tricks should be very simple in plot. One of my considerations when putting my own performances together is making sure that you, the witty and sexually attractive viewer, can recap to your inattentive friends (who perhaps due to illness did not watch my show) exactly what I did in a few simple words. While it is tempting to pile on extra coincidences or outcomes along the way, much is lost if the whole thing doesn't feel simple and direct. So, A, B, C and D should be plotted on a simple direct line. In a magic trick: A (he asked me to shuffle the deck) is followed by B (I took out a card and put it back in the deck), which leads straight to C (he made the deck disappear) and D (and then I found my card in my own pocket). A miracle! Missed along the way are the seemingly insignificant moments that fall between A, B, C and D: the moving of the spectator into position at the start (as perhaps a card is loaded into his pocket); the quick check of the deck made by the magician after it was shuffled (allowing him to secure the duplicate card in the deck which he then had to force on the spectator); and the magician's first failed attempt to find the card, or even his wrapping of the deck in a handkerchief, before vanishing the deck (which enabled him to spirit the pack away into his pocket or some other receptacle). These details are irrelevant to the main thrust of the story, and may easily be forgotten as the story of the trick is told.

For all these reasons, it is generally the most disinterested spectator who is hardest to fool. When I performed this kind of magic for groups at parties, it was the peripheral punters, stood on the sidelines with folded arms, half in conversation with each other, who were the danger. If they were not paying attention, I could not bring them into the game. They watched less, but they saw more.

To pursue an interest in conjuring magic is to open the doors to obsession. Generally one begins early (I came into it at a relatively late age), most probably as an unconfident child. Few kids seek to learn a skill specifically designed to impress people unless they feel less than impressive themselves. As things develop, there are magic shops and magic clubs, lectures, books and props, and the potential of meeting unusual, even hypnotically grotesque characters. The protégé delights in learning new sleights, and eventually spends so much money on his new hobby that he is tempted to try to earn a little something with it. Unfortunately, he will have been exposed to predominantly appalling magic, and will have learned only to ape the mannerisms and performance styles of his mentors. Many people I know have had the strange experience of chatting to a perfectly pleasant young man who turns out to be a magician. Curious to see what he can do, they accept his offer to 'show them something', and are surprised to see him, as if someone had pressed 'Play', transform into a quite unlikeable caricature, changing his speech pattern, making rude comments about what they are wearing, cracking weak, unpleasant and soulless gags and utterly disengaging them from the situation. Sadly, the ability to perform magic naturally, and with any charm, is perhaps the most difficult thing to learn.

It is, however, an obsession that can connect one with an underworld of seedy, smelly old men, crooked gambling and highly guarded secret skills. I think these are good things. Relentless egos, terrible outfits and terrific bitchiness make for a diverse, colourful and sometimes frustrating fraternity. The intrigued reader is advised to contact his local magic shop, order a dozen decks of cards and a recommended introductory text, and get started.

TRICKS WITH SUGGESTION

When giving a live show, there are moments that provide enormous private enjoyment for the performer. One such moment for me was telling the audience at the end of a touring show's first act that the second half would involve the use of a Ouija board. Ostensibly I was giving any members of the audience who might object to such a thing the chance to leave during the interval, but of course the real purpose was to heighten the drama of the evening.

Many people will scoff at notions of the supernatural but still refuse to use a Ouija board. This is perhaps because we have heard tales of bad experiences with the board, and we don't know how to explain them; they seem less easy to dismiss than someone who says she has psychic ability. Somehow the notion of ushering in malign forces still hovers around the board like the very spirits we are supposedly toying with.

We will save discussions of supernatural belief for a later chapter, but for now it might comfort some of you to know that I used the board seriously over about a hundred nights of performing the show, and at no point did anything unexpected occur. Yes, the glass moved, and yes, words were spelled out. Yes, the volunteers from the audience who had their fingers on the glass (I didn't touch it) swore that they weren't moving it themselves. And no, not a single piece of trickery was involved in making that glass move. And yes, with a couple of thousand people a night focusing their energy on spiritual forces entering the room and moving the glass, one could safely expect *something* untoward to happen if it could. And no and yes, it never did, although it looked like it did every night.

There is a simple but intriguing explanation for how the Ouija board works. Those of you who prefer to believe that spirits move the glass are of course welcome to your beliefs, but the actual principle behind it is not speculative, or a narrow-minded refusal to accept 'evidence' of spiritual activity. It works perfectly reliably in all sorts of situations, and can easily be shown to be the guiding force behind the magic of the Ouija. The answer lies in a fascinating principle called 'ideomotor movement'. From understanding this fully, we can use it to perform many other supposedly 'spiritual' feats, and achieve many seemingly inexplicable phenomena without the use of trickery.

The principle works like this. If you focus on the idea of making a movement, you will likely end up making a similar tiny movement without realizing it. If, undistracted, you concentrate on the idea of your hand becoming light, you'll eventually find that you make tiny unconscious movements to lift it. While you may be consciously aware that these movements are happening, you are not aware that you are causing them. In the same way that a nerve repeatedly firing can cause a twitch that feels outside your control, so too an ideomotor movement (from idea + movement) will feel that it is happening outside your control. Certainly some people are more susceptible to it than others; indeed it seems vaguely to go hand in hand with hypnotic susceptibility, but it is a very common thing that we all experience in one way or another. For example, you may have caught yourself involuntarily kicking at an imaginary ball while watching a football match, or making sudden brief empathetic movements as you follow characters in a film.

This principle was first used to explain some spiritualist phenomena after a fascination with the occult spread like wildfire through America and the UK in the late 1800s. The movement of spiritualism, with its trappings of dark séances, floating tambourines and ectoplasm, had grown from the activities of some upstate New York sisters by the name of Fox who in 1848 freaked out their mother by creating spirit rappings in their house. They became local celebrities, and the fad for contacting the dead soon spread. By the time they owned up to the hoax, it was too late: the spiritualist movement was too powerful and autonomous for their confession to make any difference. In turn it grew into what we now think of as modern spiritualism, or the mediumship we see on TV or in certain churches, which is based on less-easy-to-disprove 'readings' rather than floating objects in the dark but still dates back to the same hoax.

The precursor to the Ouija board was table-tipping. The attendees at the séance (the 'sitters') would position themselves around a table and wait for the spirits to communicate. With their fingertips resting on the surface of the table, they would feel the supposedly inanimate piece of furniture come to life and start to spin and rock. It is a very dramatic demonstration, although one that is rarely seen today outside private séances in the old style. I used it in an episode of *Trick of the Mind*, and was delighted to see that it works as effectively with a modern audience.

How is it possible for people to move a table around without realizing? Surely it is less fantastical to accept a spiritual explanation? Not at all. If a few people are convinced that the table will move (that's the skill: convincing them that it will happen), they will after a while begin unconsciously to push it. And bear in mind that a light table on a polished floor can move as easily as a glass on a Ouija board when pushed by a handful of people. It may be heavier, but we're not talking about *lifting* it. Towards the end of the nineteenth century, an investigator carried out a simple experiment to see whether the movement of the tables in these séances was really due to spirits or just these unconscious movements from the sitters. He laid a sheet of glass on top of the table and had the sitters place their fingertips on that. Spirits were summoned to move the table, and everyone waited to see what would happen. The reasoning was simple: if the table still moved, then the movement was coming from the furniture; if only the glass moved on top of the table, then it clearly came from the sitters' fingertips. Not surprisingly, when the spirits were summoned to move the table, the glass slid around and the table didn't budge an inch.

My interest in the Ouija board was heightened when some friends brought a home-made version over one evening. It was suggested that we 'give it a go', and immediately I felt like a doomed teenager in a bad American horror film. Coupled with my excitement was a clear theoretical understanding of ideomotor movement and how it was supposed to operate, so I was interested to see how things would work out. Doug, one friend, was convinced by its efficacy and it was he who was pushing for us all to be impressed by it. I suggested that we contact my grandfather who had died a few years before, and ask for proof that his spirit was coming through; but I added that I myself should not place my fingers on the glass, as I might prove guilty of making the tiny unconscious movements needed to spell out the details we were hoping to see. Doug, however, insisted that the person who knows the deceased needs to have his fingers on the glass. A convenient point, I thought, and I joined in with the others, though I decided to do nothing to influence the movement of the glass. We solemnly asked whoever could hear us to bring us into contact with my deceased granddad.

The glass was placed between two circles, one with a 'Yes' written inside, and one with a 'No'. Around them, in a large circle, were written the letters of the alphabet. With four of us each with two fingers on the glass, we asked our first question under Doug's instruction: 'Is there a spirit present?' We were told to start the glass moving around in a little circle, and wait for it to start to move over to the 'Yes' or 'No'. Now, at the time, we were all rather focused on the exciting possibility that the glass would start to pull one way or the other, and missed the clever psychology of the situation. Clearly, a move to 'No' would be rather ridiculous, a textbook error on the part of the spirit which would cause him no end of embarrassment in the Happy Summerland. So there we were, moving the glass around in a little circle, expecting and waiting for it to move a little to the left into the 'Yes' circle. Of course it eventually did.

Doug, now excited, urged me to ask a question. 'Tell us your name,' I asked. None of the guys present knew my grandfather's name, so I was ready to become a believer if it was spelled out. After ten seconds or so of stillness, the glass started to move slowly, seemingly pulling our fingers with it across the makeshift board. It rested for a moment on the 'R'. Then it started again, shifting across to the 'U'. Now picking up speed, it zipped across to 'P', then 'E', 'R' again, and 'T'. Rupert. Then it stopped. We all let go. It was impressive stuff.

'That's amazing!' Doug exclaimed. 'As soon as you asked for it to spell a name, I thought of Rupert. I knew that was the name before it even spelled it!'

'That'll be it, then,' I said. 'My granddad's name was Fred, not Rupert.'

Doug had expected it to move towards the 'R', and had provided the movement needed. Once he saw that he knew what was coming and *expected* it to continue to spell that name, and as each move to each letter convinced him more (and made him push it more), the impetus increased as the suggestion involved became more intense. We tried a similar thing without him, and the movement was much more sluggish.

Still he wanted to persevere, so I suggested we contact a woman who I said had died in the area recently. In fact she was a complete fabrication, and I invented some details about her that we could use to check for proof. Sure enough, we had no trouble contacting her even though she never existed, and had all the details verified even though they were never true. When I told the others that she lived in Clevedon, the glass spelled out exactly that. It took only a tiny suggestion from me that there might have been some foul play for accusations of murder to come through the board. When the direction of movement of the glass was expected – for example, when spelling out the ends of words already recognizable from the first few letters – the speed of the glass increased. There were times on stage during the tour when the randomly chosen volunteers were clearly quite suggestible, and this speed picked up to the point that the glass would occasionally overshoot its mark and drop off the table. In a domestic setting, this is the sort of thing that can be exaggerated over time as the story gets passed on and retold, into a version where the glass flings itself from the table and smashes against a wall without being touched.

For those of you who saw the first live show and remember that the board spelled out such things as the name and seat number of a person in the audience *while the letters were mixed up and concealed*, and quite rightly cannot see how this can be settled by the above explanation, you'll just have to take my word that no spirit forces were involved and pure sneakiness was at work.

Ideomotor movement is so reliable that it can be used for a series of impressive 'psychic' demonstrations. I shall offer a few of my favourites here.

The Pendulum

The pendulum is a favourite means of divination of the New Age community. By dangling a weight on a chain or string and watching its movements, a pregnant mother is supposed to be able to tell the sex of her foetus. Indeed some would say that all sorts of events can be thus foretold.

Like many things held dear by that community, a paralysis of reason prevents its members from looking at what really makes the pendulum work, so they fall prey to all sorts of romantic nonsense associated with it. In fact, the pendulum is a perfect demonstration of ideomotor suggestion, and you should try this now if you have never come across it.

Go and make yourself a pendulum this instant. You'll need to tie or attach a small weight (a couple of keys on a ring will work, but a heavy finger ring is ideal) to about eight inches of string (or thread, or a necklace chain). Sit or stand comfortably and hold the top of the string so that the weight hangs down. Let it rest still, and make sure that your hand, elbow and arm are able to move freely.

Now focus on the weight. Imagine it is able to move through the sheer force of your will. Tell it with your mind to start swinging back and forth – that is, away from and back towards you. Imagine it doing so, slowly at first, then picking up speed. Watch it and wait for the movements to actually start. Will it to move. Bear in mind that the only thing that will stop this from working is if you decide that it's not going to happen, so be patient and *expect* the weight to start swinging. You can imagine something pulling it, or a force around it, or whatever helps. There is no force, of course, but such thinking might lubricate your imagination. As you notice the movements, instruct it to swing more and more. Watch as the arc increases with your command. Then, after it has swung for a while, tell it to slow down and come to a rest. Wait for it to stop.

Now do the same thing, but tell the pendulum to swing from side to side. Will it to do so, and it will. Watch as your mental commands translate into actual movement of this inanimate object. Then, as it swings, imagine it reverting to a forwards and back motion. Mentally instruct it to change direction. Watch it change right in front of you from one axis to another. Wait for it to swing away and towards you as it was before.

Now will it to swing in a clockwise circular motion. Wait for it to do so. You should absolutely feel that this is happening outside your control. If you're not having much luck, leave it and try it later. Otherwise, have it swing in a circle, and tell it to make the circle larger and larger. When it is comfortably doing this, instruct it to trace a much smaller circle and watch as the circumference decreases. When the circle is small, you can tell the pendulum to change to an anti-clockwise swing, and it will, after it struggles for a few moments with its own momentum.

Some patience and experimentation with the pendulum will reward you with an astonishing demonstration of auto-suggestion. You are of course unconsciously moving it yourself, a fact to which anyone watching your hand will testify. Amazingly, your movements might be quite large and you still won't notice that you're making them. Once you can make it work comfortably, you might want to try using it as a New Age believer might. Here you decide that a swing in one direction means 'yes', and in the other means 'no'; a circle, perhaps, could represent 'maybe', or some other option. Now ask the pendulum a question to which you know the answer. Give it a while to start moving and you should find it gives the correct response. Excellent stuff, but nothing magical. You are merely making it move in the direction you expect. If you ask it a question to which you do not know the answer, you may get a movement, but there's no reason to think that it's the correct one.

Can a woman use it to tell the sex of her baby? This rests upon the question of whether you believe that a mum-to-be unconsciously knows the gender of the child she's bearing. If mothers do have some special unconscious knowledge, then quite possibly the pendulum might yield a correct answer. Unfortunately, there's no evidence to suggest that they *do* have such unconscious knowledge. Indeed it seems unlikely, as if it were true it would be unnecessary for so many mums-to-be to request scans that tell them whether they are housing a boy or a girl. Now, of course, plenty of mothers will insist differently. The problem is, it's a fifty-fifty chance, and a new mother is very likely to remember if her hunch was correct. In fact, it will seem to her to be evidence of a very special bond with the child, so she's unlikely to want to step back and look more objectively at the situation. Around half of all mothers who had a hunch would be able to tell you that they were able to predict the sex of their child, and that's an awful lot of mothers.

Whether you use a pendulum or rely on a mother's intuition, it's clear that you're more likely to attach importance to a successful correlation between prediction and baby gender than an unsuccessful one. In other words, if you're wrong, you forget about it, whereas if you're right, it seems that something extraordinary has happened. This benefit of hindsight and the pitfalls of such beliefs are subjects we'll look at later. It's lovely to think that a mother *does* know, and it may be that she does, but until someone surveys a large number of expectant mothers and sees if significantly over half of them can guess correctly, there's no way of knowing. Meanwhile, especially seeing as we'd have probably cottoned on by now if expectant mothers could reliably tell the sex of their baby, there's no reason to think that mothers-to-be have such an ability, and therefore no reason to think that the pendulum can offer any special insight. Certainly, as is sometimes done in cases where the value of the pendulum is *really* misunderstood, there is no sense at all in someone else (such as a New Age therapist) holding the pendulum over the stomach of the expectant mother. At best that will betray only what the person holding the pendulum thinks the gender might be.

Pendula, table-tipping and Ouija boards are all fascinating and potentially spooky manifestations of the ideomotor suggestion. The next technique is a favourite of mine and is related to this type of phenomenon. Some aspects are easy to master, others are very difficult. Practise, and you will give a very strong impression to the uninitiated that you can read minds.

Muscle-reading

Reading the biographies of obscure, forgotten mentalists and similar performers ranks high on my list of an evening's preferred solitary pursuits, a step above checking the taxidermy for moths and a notch below scouring the net for novel and fulfilling erotica.

One largely forgotten individual discovered in these memoirs was J. Randall Brown, born outside St Louis in 1851 (his story is told by Denny Laub in a tiny specialist magazine called *Minds*, quoted later by a charming and successful performer called Banachek in his book on muscle-reading). Brown (no relation) found out at school that if a classmate hid an object, he could find it by having the classmate touch his forehead and concentrate on its location. From these beginnings, this shy man pioneered a fascinating new form of entertainment that was soon to catch on across the country. On a trip to Chicago, Brown demonstrated his skill in a public house in front of some newspaper reporters who happened to be present, and immediately became a sensation. Soon he was hiring venues to demonstrate his mind-reading, sometimes posing as a scientist. He would turn up in a city, gather together local dignitaries and reporters and give a demonstration. Afterwards, he would ask them to place an invitation in the local papers for him to give a public performance.

One Dr Beard (I swear these names are not made up) challenged Brown to undergo some tests, which though proved inconclusive raised the accusation that Brown was not reading minds at all, but instead picking up on the tiny muscular cues given off by his subjects. Brown responded to this by trying 'non-contact' versions of the stunt, in which he and the subject held on to opposite ends of a wire, sometimes hundreds of feet long.

Brown's fame passed, and he was buried in an unmarked grave in 1926. Before he died, he may have taught his ability to his assistant, Washington Irving Bishop. Bishop is one of my favourite characters from this tradition. Aside from his furthering of muscle-reading, Bishop also came up with the concept of the 'blindfold drive' in 1885. This involved him racing a horse and carriage at top speed through the streets blindfolded in search of a hidden object. In modern times this stunt is sometimes re-created using a car by performers with an eye for publicity and sensation, perhaps most notably in 1966 by the awesome giant of the profession, David Berglas.

I confess I have always had an admiration for the ability of many of the great magicians and mentalists of history to create legends around themselves. Both Berglas and Chan Canasta, two modern heroes of mine, have inspired great and probably apocryphal tales, such as when the team behind *This Is Your Life* suggested Canasta as their next victim, only to have the great Polish 'psycho-magician' call them moments later in the middle of their meeting to apologize and say he couldn't make the date. I have dined with Berglas, who, scribbling on a Marriott napkin, set out his much-coveted system for guaranteed profit at the roulette table. The napkin, covered in numbers and now rather incomprehensible, is framed in my office, making a mockery of the many magicians who think the system is a myth. It certainly exists, and one day I hope to find a trustworthy enough mathematician to confirm that it really works.

When he visited the UK, Bishop adopted the policy of making out he was enormously wealthy, to the point that he would donate his smaller fees to charity. This rather grand approach, of course, led to his being able to charge stupendous fees for getting involved in specialist projects. Eventually, though, he fled our shores after being sued for £10,000 by a famous magician for libel, following the latter's objection to Bishop's claims of real psychic ability.

Even Bishop's death at the young age of thirty-three is shrouded in controversy and sensation. Bishop would sometimes dramatically swoon at the end of a performance, and he said that he was subject to cataleptic fits that might make him appear dead. He warned that he should be carefully examined before any autopsy or burial was carried out. When he did die, his mother claimed that he had been killed by the autopsy carried out on what she held to be his still living body. What a thought.

To learn the basics of muscle-reading, first be prepared to try and fail a few times. It does work better with some people than others, but as long as both you and your subject approach the task with openness and receptivity, you should soon enjoy real success.

Gather together seven or eight objects and scatter them on a table that is large enough for the items to be well spaced. Invite a friend to think of one of the objects, and make no attempt to second-guess which you think he might go for. Now, standing next to him, tell him to hold out his hand. Then take hold of his wrist. I don't find it makes much difference if you hold his right or left wrist, but it is important that you are comfortable and have room for movement.

You must now give him some important instructions. Tell him to mentally guide you to the chosen object. He is to tell you, *in his mind*, to move left, right, forwards, backwards or to stop, and to focus his thoughts entirely on telling you these things. He is to say nothing out loud, but he must give very clear instructions in his head.

You must act as if you are merely holding onto his wrist for telepathic reasons. However, in reality you are using the sensations that come from his hand to guide yourself to the correct object. When first practising, hover his hand over the table, in the centre of the objects. As he concentrates, gently nudge his hand one way then the other. You are feeling for resistance. If he is mentally instructing you to move in a particular direction, he will naturally provide tension when you try to push his arm a different way. So you must take your cue from the path of least resistance. You must be constantly open to this physical feedback, and aware that at any moment he could be signalling you to change direction. You should find that after a while you can successfully find your way to the correct object every time.

Once you understand and can work with this principle, the next stage is to try it in a much larger space. Have your friend think of a large object in the room you are in. Take his hand again, but this time you will make it look as if you are pulling him across the room to the object, rather than guiding his hand to whatever he has chosen. So position yourself a little in front of him, and extend your free hand forward as if you are groping for which way to go. Feel for the same signals in the hand, and let him guide you in the same way by offering a path of least resistance. Often I will hold onto the right wrist with my left hand, and then, when needing to check a signal, tense my left arm a little so it is rigid. Then I can sway my whole body in different directions while continuing the instructions for him to command me which way to go. This often gives a clearer signal than just using your hand to move his.

With some subjects, it will feel after a while that they are taking you straight to the object. Instead of just avoiding resistance, you will actually feel them tug you in the correct direction. These more suggestible types can make the whole thing amazingly easy. If you keep an eye on the subject's feet, often they too will tell you which way to turn by subtly moving in the desired direction. And as with a Ouija board, where you can specifically tell the sitters not to move the glass or planchette and they still will, you can also emphasize to your muscle-reading subject not to give you any clues. Because the resistance and movements are unconscious, it really won't make any difference as long as he's focusing his efforts on the mental instructions.

It is possible to turn this into a real performance piece, although it can suffer from being difficult to pace. The modest American performer known as the 'Amazing Kreskin' famously has his performance fee hidden somewhere in the auditorium and muscle-reads the person who hid the cheque in order to find it. The deal is that if it isn't found, he doesn't get paid. Although I have never seen him perform this (and to be honest, I'm unsure how interesting to an audience the drama would be of the performer maybe not getting paid), I have seen other muscle-readers at work. I suspect that problems with speed and maintaining tension make this difficult to pull off as a real audience-pleaser, and perhaps for that reason it is rarely performed. But as a private, impromptu demonstration, it can be very effective.

If you want to practise this skill without fear of failure, try adapting the card trick you previously learned. After the card has been returned to the deck and the deck has been shuffled, spread the cards face-up on the table. Look for your key-card and note the card *above* it which will be the selection. Spread the cards messily on the table, and make sure that the selection can be seen. Look away, ask your participant to note where his card is, then have him mix the cards further. Now, close your eyes, turn round, take hold of his wrist and hover his hand over the table. Try to locate the card through the muscle-reading process, feeling for which direction you should move in order to reach it. When you think you have it, open your eyes and visually check that you are correct. Either way, bring his hand down onto the correct card. If you have stopped nowhere near it and this means shoving his hand across the table before it lands on the chosen card, it will play as a joke: it will look as if you had indeed worked out the correct card but were pretending to be wrong, you clever sausage.

PART THREE

Tricks of the Mind

MEMORY

MEMORY

Imagine if you will, or apprehend if you won't, that you are out shopping one rainy Monday or Thursday afternoon, and you quite literally pop into your friendly local high-street out-of-town clothes-store in search of new duds and toggery with which to sheathe your fiddle-fit bodyshell. You see a dazzlingly fabulous cardigan for sale, of unquestionable quality and exquisite design. As you delight in all things floccose, its perfect pocket ribbing and flattering unisex diamond accents prove an irresistible combination and in a state of some discomposure you hunt for a price-tag. Reduced to a mere thirteen Great British pounds sterling and twenty-eight bright new penceroonies! A fucking bargain. Grabbing the glittering Guernsey from the rail with one hand and groping for your wallet with the other, you elbow rudely past the elderly, the infirm and the sheer lazy to get to the till point and secure the cut-price lammy as your own.

Now – and here I must insist that you bring to bear upon the proceedings the full force of your self-control – how would you feel were the gum-chewing shop assistant to then try to charge you not the advertised price of £13.28, but an outrageous higher price, such as £52.17? You would confidently show her the clear and unambiguous price-tag and insist upon paying the lower amount. Yet the girl does not listen; she fecklessly, juicy-fruitily repeats the higher price. You look over to where the disputed item had hung and spot a large sign bearing the legend 'Special Offer: this cardigan reduced to £13.28!' Triumphantly you point the placard out to her and again make to hand across the advertised price. Still this otiose dullard blandly repeats the higher price, obviously oblivious to the proof of her palpable howler.

Now call me the world's leading handsome mind-reader, but you are probably thinking at this point that you are indeed legally justified in insisting on the lower price. If that is so, you are very wrong indeed. She can in fact charge you anything she likes. Allow me, my beautiful but ill-informed bitches, to explain. We are talking here about contracts, and at what point they become binding. A contract needs an offer and an acceptance. Once you can show that both these criteria have been present, a contract would appear to have been formed. To believe that the price-tag is legally binding, one would have to take that advertised price to be the *offer*, and then presume that taking the item to the till constitutes *acceptance*. However, that would then contractually bind you to purchasing, and you would not in that case be allowed to return it to the shelf, or to change your mind. Equally, if a brochure were to advertise goods at a certain price, and we saw this as an offer, and were you then to order a vast quantity of them (an acceptance), we would be contractually obliging the company to supply this enormous number to us. This clearly cannot be right, as they should surely be allowed to apologize and say that they have only a limited number in stock.

So the law regards price-tags and the like as mere 'invitations', unbinding precursors to the making of an offer. In fact the offer is made later by the customer, when he approaches the shop assistant and indicates what he wants to buy. When the assistant accepts his offer and a price is agreed, the contract is made.

Of course, it may not be in the shop's interest to insist on the higher price. Probably for the sake of goodwill they will let you have it at the lower. But you cannot insist. You cannot find a wrongly labelled item on the shelf and then insist on buying it at that price if the assistant notices the discrepancy. It is only the fact that most people working in shops as assistants probably also misunderstand the law and feel they are somehow bound by price-tags that this presumption has been perpetuated.

Now, this sphincter-looseningly fascinating nugget of contract law was first decided by the 1953 case *Pharmaceuticals Society of Great Britain* v. *Boots Cash Chemists*. This fact helps all of us to derive particular satisfaction from getting away with it in Boots. The case was one of hundreds I had to learn about for the various law courses I took at university. Despite some excellent tutors and lecturers, I had overall precious little interest in the subject, though some of the thought exercises and counter-intuitive intricacies, like the above, I found enjoyable in their necessary pedantry. When it came to examination time, then, I was faced with the task of learning a long, long list of cases, each containing some important principle which was arrived at (the 'ratio'), the name of the case, and the year in which it was decided. I knew there was no way of learning them by rote, and I had no desire to become one of the few students who spent their every waking moment, and several of their sleeping ones, in the library, hidden among piled-up copies of *Hansard* or *Clarkson & Keating*, trying to push more dry information into their cerebra.

Instead, I wanted to find a way to memorize these long lists and chunks of information that was efficient and sensible. I played with techniques I had used for my A levels (in the face of similar disgust towards anything other than the most civilized revision schedule), and with a bit of imagination found a way of committing maybe two hundred useful cases to memory without anything one could seriously think of as effort. Since then I have practised and developed these sorts of memory skills through studying the work of committed experts. I will share here what I believe to be the most effective techniques, and those with which I have had most success teaching others. They can be used for remembering shopping lists, tasks and speeches; revision purposes; remembering names at parties and meetings; as well as for performing powerful memory stunts for those you wish to impress. It matters not how rich or poor you feel your memory is at this time, you will find these techniques invaluable.

STARTING POINTS

There is very little evidence to suggest that the popular idea of a photographic memory really holds. While there are a few savants who are able to hold in their minds very complex, highly detailed after-images of a scene ('eidetic memory'), it typically does not hold for long, and tends to be prone to subjective distortions rather than being photographically perfect. Moreover, most of the studies on extraordinary memories seem to show that these seemingly gifted individuals instinctively use rich mnemonic strategies of the kind I will teach you here.

Another myth worth busting is that we 'only use 10 per cent of our brainpower'. While it is certainly the case that pretty much all of us have it in us to use our minds more powerfully, statistics such as this are meaningless. We use different parts of the brain to achieve different things at different times, and never has any serious study arrived at a figure like this, let alone defined what 'brainpower' might actually mean. Also subject to popular exaggeration is the idea that the right and left sides of our brain are distinctly different, and that by tapping into our imaginative right hemisphere we are able to learn, draw and achieve creative success with ease. While there are some differences between the two hemispheres – for example, the left side of the brain is used for language – there are far more similarities.

Some time ago I attended a weekend course on photo-reading. It promised to give me powerful unconscious abilities to absorb the content of a book at immense speed, and then to recall the information easily. About ten of us took part, and I knew most of them, as well as the instructor himself, who was a keen trainer of NLP (neuro-linguistic programming – a subject we will relish later). I thought something might be amiss when we were taught the first stage of photo-reading, *previewing*. We were told to pick up a book and look over the back cover where we would find a taste of what the book contained; our unconscious minds would then start to get a sense of whether or not the book would interest us. Right. I thought perhaps that might count as a fairly conscious process, but I stowed my scepticism neatly to one side and continued to listen. Next, we were told to have a look at the list of chapter headings, which would allow us to get a sense of the framework of the book and to begin to create an unconscious map of its contents. I was delighted to find that I had already been carrying out the first important stages of photo-reading every time I picked up a book. Maybe I was going to be a natural.

For the next stage I had to relax, imagine myself as receptive, hold the book in front of me and riffle through the pages before my eyes, making no attempt to read or remember anything. Then I was to turn the book upside-down and do the same backwards. This, I was told, completed the photo-reading system. Wow! I was excited.

My unconscious, I was informed, now had the *entire* book stored in its dark recesses; all I needed to learn now was how to retrieve that information. This was to take a little more practice, but was essentially simple. Now, to impress the group, I had brought with me a book on Wagner* to use, so I was to 'retrieve' the book's contents as follows: I should ask myself a question the book should be able to answer; then I should riffle slowly through the book again. My unconscious, knowing where the answer lay, would alert me to the correct page and the information would jump out at me as I passed it. Do read that again if necessary.

Everybody seemed happy with this process, and presumably with the idea of paying the £300 the trainer normally charged for this horseshit. I put up my hand and asked, 'Erm, I don't want to seem rude, and perhaps I'm missing something, but aren't you just showing us how to *look something up in a book?*' It was explained to me that perhaps I was already using these techniques unconsciously myself, perhaps due to having spent time at a university where I had to read and absorb a lot of books. People without tertiary education, it would seem, do not know how to skim through a book looking for a piece of information.

Bizarrely, everyone else in the group, many of them university-educated themselves, still seemed happy to go along with this system that taught *nothing*. Because I pushed the point, the trainer offered to prove that the unconscious stores the entire contents of the book during that riffling process. He said that if I closed the book and asked on what page a certain answer or piece of information could be found, my mind would produce the correct answer by telling me the page number. Excellent! That was more like it, and I was ready to take back my cynicism. He offered to try it with one of

*Amusing no-one but myself, I had selected a book by John L. DiGaetani called, I kid you not, *Penetrating Wagner's Ring*.

the other guys who said he was really benefiting from the system, and he had him photo-read my Wagner book in a few seconds. Then the trainer opened the book, looked at the text and asked my fellow student to tell him on what page he could find the answer to a particular question (I cannot remember the question he suggested, but it is pretty irrelevant). I eagerly awaited my neighbour's answer. He closed his eyes for a moment and answered '143'. The trainer, looking at the number of the correct page, was elated. It turned out that although the actual page number itself was quite different (e.g., 172), the test had been a triumph (i.e., the 1 was correct, the 4 and 3 clearly constituted the number 7, and the 2 was very close to a 3).

What more proof could a man need?

Possibly a room full of people armed with too much belief and not much experience with books might decide that such a course works wonders for them. A couple of convoluted successes like the above might send enough people away with a deluded sense of their new ability to give them some satisfaction for a while before they stop making the effort to fool themselves.

Other courses are less esoteric. Classic speed-reading involves learning to read a page without bothering to look at every word. Generally the student is taught to train his eye to follow his finger as it moves down the centre of each page, allowing his peripheral vision to take in enough to make sense of the page's contents. While there is nothing wrong with this in itself, if one wants to skim through a book, don't be misled into thinking that you are retaining any sort of super-memory of the book. Speed-reading, as it is taught in books and on courses across the world, is just learning to skim. Nothing more.*

Rather than being like a special muscle that needs training, memory is far better thought of as a set of processes. Generally

*I'm reminded of the Woody Allen line, 'I just speed-read *War and Peace*. It's about some Russians.'

when we 'try' to remember a lot of information, we don't work with those processes very well. We become tense, for example, and we try to over-fill our short-term memory by pushing too much information into it. We seem capable of mentally processing only around seven units of anything at a time; after that we start forgetting bits of information in order to store new ones. If we come across a string of information that contains more than seven or so units, we instinctively want to break it down into smaller chunks. You have probably had the experience of hearing a clock chime the hour, then afterwards asking yourself how many times it struck. Up to about seven chimes and we can recall the sound; after that, we have no chance. A line of poetry that contains more than around seven beats needs to be broken into two lines. We regroup digits in phone numbers to make them roll off the tongue in easy chunks of three or four. For the same reason, if we try to hold on to more than about seven items at a time in our heads, we get stuck and confused. With the methods here, you will be able to store a vast number of pieces of information without ever trying to remember several things at once.

I have not invented any of the following techniques, but I use them all. I offer you systems that are tried and tested, but with my own thoughts and tips from my experience. Please try out the techniques as you are invited to, even if you have never thought about improving your memory. They really are fun, surprising and immensely useful, and it takes very little effort to play along as you read them. At the risk of over-stressing the point, if you merely read through them without applying yourself at all, they will seem only daft and unworkable; whereas if you do try them for yourself, the next pages could excitingly transform aspects of your life.

You'll need a pen and paper.

THE LINKING SYSTEM

If I were to be stopped in the toilet by any one of you and asked for the names of the British royal dynasties throughout history in chronological order, I would be more than happy to answer, 'Norman, Plantagenet, Lancastrian, York, Tudor, Stuart, Hanoverian, Windsor.' I learned this when I was six because I went to a very odd primary school.

Imagine the opening scene of *Oliver Twist* but with less singing. The school was an anachronism: set in middle-class Purley, it was run according to the Victorian principles (remember her from *Dallas*?) held dear by Miss Routledge, the headmistress, a strapping lesbian octogenarian in blazer and tie who, as I remember, ate nothing but boiled eggs which she constantly spilled down her sloping, uni-mammarous front. This terrifying old woman with a man's haircut routinely doled out corporal punishment and bellowed at children until they wet themselves; and following her rules we all used dip-pens and ink-wells until the last year of school, wore short trousers, and were neither allowed to run in the playground nor talk during lunch. Each morning we would learn a new wild-flower, and each lunchtime we would pay twopence for cup-a-soup, dished out by her moped-driving erstwhile lover (I like to think) Mrs Morton, aged perhaps seventy. Fees were £50 a term – a ridiculously low figure, even at that time – and I think the money went entirely on boiled eggs and dry cleaning.

It certainly wasn't spent on books. The books we used were old-fashioned to the point where the pages should have been turned with special tongs. I would not have been surprised to find that my old geography book contained hand-drawn maps with 'There be Beasties here' written in the sea. Our maths textbook, for example, was written according to the old monetary system of pounds, shillings and pence, which, I hasten to add for fear you may think me too old, had been superseded some years before. We were told to ignore the shillings and just work with the pounds and pence. My brother, nine years younger than me, attended the same school, and Routy was still ruling over it then, although well into her nineties. I kid you not when I say that not only was he using the same maths book, but when I looked inside his copy with its torn pages and overpowering aroma, I saw that high up on the list of crossed-out names of children who had used and owned the book previously, there were the half-forgotten names of my own classmates.

One more memory: during one of Routy's morning lectures we were taught – presumably from some half-absorbed Freudian text mingled with old-wives' wisdom – that little girls loved their daddies best, and little boys loved their mummies best. Picture us, aged between six and ten, filing out from the hall past our feared headmistress, each in turn being asked which one of our parents we loved best. If we answered wrongly – and dwell upon this with me for a moment as we both consider what strange things we took for granted as children – we got a smack. I remember vividly a girl in front of me, one of the youngest, crying and screaming that she loved her mummy best, while Routledge roared, 'WHAT ARE YOU, A LITTLE BOY??!' and whacked her too hard on the back of her legs in front of the whole school with the full unquestioning force of her Victorian, Sapphic rage.

Despite the fact that none of the teachers was qualified but merely followed her system; despite all learning being by rote to the extent that we had to learn our little paragraphs for each subject word for word and were penalized in exams for any deviation from the exact wording; despite my getting the slipper eleven times and being called a 'dirty slum-boy' for writing 'poos' with chalk on the tarmac outside the entrance to Lower Prep; despite the token fees and the textbooks that smelled of must and old piss, she got almost all of us into decent secondary schools. And when I went to visit her a few years later in her flat above the school, she suddenly seemed smaller, oddly like Arthur Mullard, bewilderingly sweet and entirely gracious.

And alongside learning to write with dip-pens, we also learned to memorize the families of kings in chronological order. She had us repeat the following sentence: *No Plan Like Yours To Study History Well*. Each word in the sentence could be transformed into a royal family. *Norman, Plantagenet, Lancastrian, York, Tudor, Stuart, Hanoverian, Windsor*. The list might be misleading for all I know, but I won't ever forget the order of royal dynasties as taught by Routy, even though I haven't spoken that list out loud for perhaps twenty-five years.

This was the first time I came across mnemonics. Later they would take me comfortably through a dull university degree and transform much of my approach to learning.

There now follows a list of twenty random words. Before we go any further, I'd like you to give yourself thirty seconds to try to learn as many of them as possible, in order. Be good enough actually to try this, because I really want you to see how quickly you're going to improve with minimal effort. A pen and paper will help you check your results. Go on. I'll go check my emails.

1 : telephone
2 : sausage
3 : monkey
4 : button
5 : book
6 : cabbage
7 : glass
8 : mouse
9 : stomach
10 : cardboard
11 : ferry
12 : Christmas

13 : athlete
14 : key
15 : wigwam
16 : baby
17 : kiwi
18 : bed
19 : paintbrush
20 : walnut

Good. Now, put the book down for a moment and try to recall them in order. Write them out if you have pen and paper at the ready. Do it now.

There you go. I hope you joined in. Relax and forget about them now, and put away your piece of paper. Now, possibly you're a clever bugger who knows the technique I'm going to teach, and remembered pretty much all of them. Well, in that case, feel free to skip ahead, or join in with the others anyway. No-one likes a smart-arse.

A few more of you may have tried making up a story using the words. That can work well, but you will find a far better technique in the pages that follow. Certainly the vast majority of you would have found the task rather difficult, and would have been really struggling to recall the words correctly by the halfway stage.

I know I told you to relax and forget about them, but now I'd like you to try to recall them again. After that, I'd like you to try to list them backwards. Just try, now. I won't ask you to go to any effort again.

I'm presuming you found that impossible. You have just tried very hard to learn the whole list and failed. What you could remember was more difficult to recall a minute or so later. And backwards recitation was presumably out of the question. The following technique is simple and easy, and if you approach it with a spirit of playful curiosity, you will be able to have someone write down a list like this, calling out the words as they go, and you won't need to try to learn anything, because by the time they have finished, you will have them all memorized. You can have them do the same with fifty words, which requires no extra effort on your part. You will be able to recite the list backwards from memory as easily as forwards, and still remember the list forwards and backwards *days* afterwards.

Here's the technique in a nutshell: we're going to take each word and find a visual link with the word next to it. Not just any picture that happens to link them, but one that involves the following criteria:

1. The picture should be *vivid*. That means you need to take a moment to clearly see the picture in your head once you have decided upon it. Also, let yourself emotionally engage with it for a moment. If the picture is amusing (many of them will be), look at it and find it funny. If it's disgusting, actually find it repulsive. Some people don't think they can visualize anything, and get very sweaty when asked to do anything like this. If you think you're one of those people, don't worry. There's no proper 'visualization' involved. This is easy.
2. The elements of each picture should *interact*. Picturing A and B stood next to each other won't do the trick. If A could be made of B; or if A could be forced into B; or if A could smack, bugger or dance with B, that's much better.
3. The picture should be *unusual*. If you have to link 'man' and 'cup', for example, you may be able to vividly imagine those two interacting, but the picture may be too normal, such as 'a man drinking from a cup'. The picture will be more memorable if the man is trying to drink from a giant cup, or is sucking the cup into his face, or if there is a tiny man in a cup trying to get out before the tea gets poured in.

With this in mind, let's return to our list. I typed simple words at random, so aside from constituting a fascinating glimpse into my shoutingly advanced psyche, they should serve as good as any to demonstrate this technique. I shall give here the pictures I find myself wanting to use when I link the pairs together. For now, read through my linking images without substituting your own, unless you are sure that yours conform to the criteria above. Notice also how each image makes you feel. Is it funny? Disgusting? Dangerous? Actually take a second to feel that response and really picture what I describe to you; it will help enormously with what follows. Don't just skim them, otherwise you'll have to come back and do it again.

Telephone/Sausage: Trying to dial an old-fashioned phone using a flaccid, uncooked sausage. It feels revolting and cold to the fingers, and is utterly impractical to work the dial. I can maybe get the dial around a little way, but then it just purrs back into place.

Sausage/Monkey: Watching footage from a wildlife documentary of a monkey, in the jungle, cooking a sausage over a barbecue. These are rare monkeys, and this is the first time they have been filmed. Next to him he has a selection of dips.

Monkey/Button: You no longer have to spend valuable time doing up your own shirt buttons. You now have a trained monkey to do such things. You stand there in your socks and he does up all the buttons with his clever simian fingers.

Button/Book: It's a book entirely about buttons, and in order to open it you have to unfasten a line of big colourful buttons down the side. Hugely impractical marketing gimmick. Makes opening it really irritating.

Book/Cabbage: Opening up a book to have a quiet lunchtime read, only to find that the cover and all the pages have leaves of rotten stinking cabbage stuck to them. The stench is terrible, and the pages are ruined. Someone has played a stupid joke on you, and now you've got fetid cabbage juice all over your fingers.

Cabbage/Glass: A beautiful but enormous cabbage, realistically created out of glass. The artist is proudly showing it off, flicking it with his fingers and making a 'pinging' sound. Everyone's standing around with glasses of wine appreciating it. Personally you think it's ridiculous and ugly.

Glass/Mouse: You go to drink a glass of wine, to find that the wine has gone and there's a tiny mouse in the bottom of the glass. The mouse is clearly drunk, and is wearing a party hat with streamers over his shoulder. A party blow-out extends limply from his mouth, and he's hiccuping bubbles, like a seventies cartoonist's depiction of a drunkard.

Mouse/Stomach: Unfortunately I can think only of that urban myth unfairly surrounding Richard Gere some years ago. If you're not familiar with it, then imagine your tummy full of squeaking mice, which then stream out of your navel like the rats out of Hamelin.

Stomach/Cardboard: A pregnant lady covering her stomach with cardboard from old boxes. Taping it around her, until she is enormous. Now she feels protected.

Cardboard/Ferry: Image of a big P&O ferry sinking in the sea because in a spectacularly misjudged move to save money, the entire boat was manufactured out of cardboard. People are escaping from dinghies, unaware that they are made not from rubber but from ordinary paper.

Ferry/Christmas: A little ferry sat on top of a Christmas tree, perhaps at a school for the hard of hearing. Little steamers, windows, everything. Tinsel around the hull.

Christmas/Athlete: It's you and all the relations you normally spend Christmas with, running around a race-track in the snow with party hats and crackers trying to beat Kelly Holmes to the finish-line. Your nan is doing superbly, racing ahead in her coat, hat and bag, giving the double-gold winner a run for her money.

Athlete/Key: The winning athlete is given a four-foot-long golden key on a ribbon as a prize. She tries to hold it up for the audience as the National Anthem plays, but it's extremely heavy, and she wishes she could have just had an ordinary medal.

Key/Wigwam: A key hangs unnoticed from the headgear of a Native American Indian who is unable to get into his wigwam to go to the loo. Hugely frustrating for him. You can picture him, all red-faced. See the key glinting in the light as he searches for it.

Wigwam/Baby: Latest New Age fad: put your baby to sleep every night in a wigwam. Dream-catcher included. Imagine a giant baby asleep inside, snoring, making the sides of the wigwam suck in and blow out.

Baby/Kiwi: A baby shoving green furry kiwi fruit into its mouth. One after another. A huge pile of them waiting to be eaten. Green kiwi juice all down its bib. Throwing up kiwi vomit. He loves kiwis, the little tinker.

Kiwi/Bed: Tucking up a little kiwi for the night in a big king-size bed. Pulling the covers almost over it, then sitting next to it and reading it a story about the Little Kiwi, until it falls asleep.

Bed/Paintbrush: You've changed your décor and the bed no longer matches. So rather than buy new covers, you paint them the same colour as the walls. Sloshing paint over the entire bed, watching it go hard and uncomfortable.

Paintbrush/Walnut: Not owning a nutcracker, you're forced to try and smash open a great big walnut with the end of a paintbrush. Trouble is, you're using the brush end, which isn't working, and there's paint splashing everywhere. It's a mess, but you really want that walnut.

There you have it. Now, presuming you haven't been wasting your time and my time and everyone else's time, and did actually read that through properly, turn the book over and start going through the list, starting with 'telephone'. If you didn't picture each one, go back through them and do that first. Then see how many you can recall without looking. Let each word take you to the next one. If you get stuck on any, check the images above. You'll probably find it wasn't vivid enough the first time for you, in which case feel free to change it in a way that helps more. And notice how much easier it is to get so much further. *And* this is only the first time you've tried this technique. *And* I didn't tell you to try to memorize anything. Off you go.

Once you've done it correctly, and you feel all excited, now *really* surprise yourself by going through the list backwards. *Walnut* . . .

You are working with your memory's tendency to store vivid images much better than dry information. Rather than trying to learn something by rote, you are letting it sink effortlessly into your longer-term memory, by making it appealing to your brain. Once you've got the idea, have a friend call out a list of random words as he writes each one down. Take a moment after each word to cement an image before asking him for the next one. It's easiest to ask for nouns, which are simple to picture, but a more abstract noun like, say, 'anger' can easily be turned into an image, such as an angry shouting face. Rather like 'Christmas' here being represented in terms of a Christmas tree or the relatives you associate with it.

And if you thought you couldn't visualize, congratulations, you've just been doing it.

Uses of the Linking System

Now there's nothing wrong with just showing off with this in front of your friends. If you want to impress them even more, as I said, try it with a longer list, but before you recite the words, make a big deal about needing to look at the list for three seconds. Take the list, stare at it blankly, but don't do anything other than remind yourself of the first word. Then hand it back and begin reciting. This 'three-second' ploy, though unnecessary, makes the trick oddly *more* impressive than not looking at it at all, as your audience will believe that you learned the whole list in three seconds. They'll forget that you also had the time as the words were being called out, and in time (if we think back to our discussion on selective memory and magic) they may even remember that the words were written down without being called out. Possibly over-egging the icing on the lily, but you might like to try it.

The linking system is invaluable for remembering shopping lists and tasks. If you have a list of things to buy, entertain yourself by finding images like this which connect the items on the list and see how well you do without referring to a piece of paper.

I use linking techniques all the time if there's one important thing I mustn't forget. For example, if I know that when I get home I have to call one of my few remaining friends, I'll link an image of that person to the walk up to my front door. Maybe for good measure I'll imagine a key-ring effigy of the same person hanging from my keys. Either way I'll see those things for real when I go to let myself in, and I'll remember to make the call.

The linking system can also be used to remember speeches. If you know you have a series of points to cover in a presentation or speech, link those points together. Make sure each point can be represented as an image, then find vivid and unusual interactive links between them. A big advantage of using this system for a speech is that you don't end up reading from a card. You are likely to be far more entertaining due to the fact that you are improvising around points, and will look terribly impressive and relaxed too.

I used the system to link the names of legal cases with the

important legal precedents that came from them. In the example given at the start of this chapter, *Pharmaceuticals Society of Great Britain* v. *Boots Cash Chemists* (1953), I made sure that I imagined a top businessman at the Boots pharmacy counter (the business suit told me he was an authority figure in Boots, and I imagined that to be a pharmaceuticals expert) trying to hand over a single crisp £50 note for an incorrectly priced basket of socks. The assistant was holding up three fingers to demand an extra £3, which I imagined as three pound coins in the smart customer's wallet. The socks told me it was the Pharmaceutical *Society* ('soc' was a popular student abbreviation for 'society'), and not *Company*, as I might have thought, and the clear image of the £53 reminded me it was 1953. As another aid, I had the assistant in 1950s attire. Since my university days, however, I have come to use a better system for numbers, which I will teach you a little later.

It may sound a little complicated to set it all out like this, but in practice it's rather easy. After all, once you start to imagine a scene like this, you have to put certain details into it: he has to be paying for something, so why not have the goods remind you of some other important fact?

Should you need to learn a script for a play, this system is also immensely useful. Link a key idea of the other character's previous line with the first words or idea of yours, so that as he reaches those key words, you are automatically reminded of what you must say next.

Making such linking images in your imagination is at the heart of many of the systems I will teach you. The rest of the chapter will be of no use to you until you are happy with the above, so please do make sure you understand and can actually use it effectively before getting involved in the following techniques.

THE LOCI SYSTEM

One drawback to the linking system, as you'll have been bright and attentive enough to realize, is that if you get stuck on one word, the whole chain breaks down. Surely, for the blossoming new student of all things retentive, this is simply not good enough. Allow me, then, to introduce to you with embarrassingly inappropriate enthusiasm a mnemonic that involves no such danger: the 'loci system'. At its best, this mnemonic contains a delectable sorcery and a saucy Lecter-quality that make it irresistible. Fans of the Thomas Harris novel *Hannibal* will be aware of Lecter's memory palace: this is the loci system taken to its delightful extreme.

The loci system, synonymous with the Greek art of memory, has its origins in a tale about a banquet that took place around 500 BC. Simonides of Ceos (I won't ask you to remember all of these names, but I do hope that you'll pay attention) was a poet, hired by the noble Scopas to offer a poem of praise to the latter at a huge party he was throwing. Simonides recited the poem as planned, but Scopas was jealous of the opening fawning remarks to the gods, which preceded those to himself, and paid the poet only half of his agreed fee as retaliation for this divided doxology. Simonides was then approached by a messenger and asked to step outside. Within those vital minutes of his being without, the angry gods destroyed the banquet hall, Scopas and the entire party. Bodies were so terribly mutilated that they could not be recognized. The ancient Greeks were not great with dental records, and there was no way of identifying the deceased. However, our poet hero knew the loci system and was able to identify each and every dinner guest as he had memorized his or her location around the banquet tables.

This story comes from Cicero's *De oratore*, and Simonides' methods were first explained in 85 BC by an unknown Roman author in a fascinating textbook on rhetoric called *Ad Herennium*. In the Middle Ages, interest in the system was given new life by St Thomas Aquinas, who strongly promoted its use as part of his rules for living a pious and ethical life, and it also became widely used by the Jesuits. Later, Matteo Ricci, a sixteenth-century Italian Jesuit priest who worked in China, wrote much about it in his *A Treatise on Mnemonics*. But it was the colourful character Giordano Bruno who really did his best to spread the word around that time.

Bruno was a Jesuit monk, an astronomer, an astrologer and a spy who was excommunicated and travelled around telling all with ears to hear about the systems. For him, mnemonics were magical devices, tied in with astrology and Hermetic occultism. He developed a system of imaginary memory wheels, showing the orbit of the heavens, and attached to them symbols for the arts, language and science. It was a kind of mnemonic orrery, and he believed that through this system the order of the cosmos could be understood. This level of esoterica soon had him branded a heretic, and he was burned at the stake in 1600. Meanwhile, the loci system was taught in many English schools until 1584, when Puritan reformers declared it unholy for encouraging bizarre and irreverent images. This beautiful and life-enhancing ability therefore lost its place among the proudest achievements of human consciousness because some religious zealots didn't like the level of imagination it provoked.

In its simplest form, the loci mnemonic works by attaching images to places along a familiar real-life route you know well. The images represent items to be remembered, and are placed in fixed locations you know you will always encounter on that route. For example, let us imagine that the route you choose is the path along your street to your home, and then into the house and each of the rooms in a natural and fixed sequence. If you decide on a starting point now, some way down your street, and begin to mentally walk towards your house, notice a few familiar points along the way. For example, there might be a shop or two you always pass, a zebra crossing you always use, or a post-box that stands out. These are your 'loci', or locations. Then, as you approach the door to your building, make the porch or entrance-way another location. If there is a hallway to an apartment door, you might find further loci to use: a lift, a letter-rack, and then the door to the apartment itself.

Now you need to mentally walk through your house. You can do this for real, but there is an advantage in simply doing it from memory, namely that you are less likely to overlook in the future those things that will occur to you now. Find a fixed object in the hallway to use as the next location. Then move into the first room, and choose something obvious there. If you are in your sitting room, you might want to use the television, your fish-tank, your DVD collection or your sofa. Then move into another room and choose another location. Continue this until all the rooms of the house have been used, and you know where your finishing point is.

Now re-cap that route in your mind and check that you anticipate and pay attention to each location. This will serve as your fixed route, and it is important that it is very familiar.

Now let's use it for memorizing. Let's imagine you have a list of things to remember for the day. Here is a suitably bland generic one:

1 : Buy stamps.
2 : Take suit to dry-cleaner.
3 : Tell X at work to call Y (think of actual people).
4 : Get mobile phone fixed.
5 : Feed the parrot.
6 : Phone Dave.
7 : Record *Trick of the Mind*.
8 : Buy rubbish on eBay.
9 : Double-check video-recorder.

Now begin your loci route. Your first task is to buy stamps, so mentally place an obvious 'stamps' image in front of your first location. You are not 'linking' here so much as simply placing a strong visual representation of each task where you can see it. If that first location is a shop, perhaps imagine a huge stamp stuck across the window. It must be something clearly visible. Then move on to your second location, and vividly attach to it the second item on the list, such as a sparkling suit or coat (use an item from your wardrobe) radiating dazzling light, to represent the dry-cleaning errand. Take a second or two to lock each of these into your mind. Continue with the list above, or substitute your own tasks, linking each to the next location on the journey. If 'phone Dave' links with, for example, the refrigerator in the kitchen, you might wish to walk in and see him stood by the open fridge, on your phone, drinking your milk. Obviously dispense with these random examples and use your own as they occur to you.

When you are done, you now have in your mind a familiar journey you can take, in your imagination, at any time you wish to review your tasks. As you embark upon it, take a look at each location along the way, and your tasks will present themselves to you. If any are hazy, take a moment to change the picture to something more memorable. Remember, the images must be *vivid* and *clear* (which means you need to take a moment to represent them as large, bright pictures to yourself), and *unusual* enough to stand out. You'll find there really is no effort required in seeing each item to remember, as long as you clearly placed them there.

The joy of this system is that if you do forget any one item on the list, you can continue your journey to the next one without trouble. As already noted, the linking system does not have that advantage. If you are making a speech, this method is perhaps preferable, as the process keeps moving you forward to the next point. With the linking version, you may have to backtrack to check what your previous point started out as, in order to know what comes next.

Memory Palaces

Once you have mastered this principle, you might like to take it to higher levels, where it really can become a thing of beauty. As it stands, the system as I have just shown it to you does have certain limitations. Firstly, you are limited by the number of loci on your journey, and cannot remember more than one list at a time. If you tried to start another list simultaneously at that shop with the giant stamp on the window, you'd get terribly confused.

So the first step is to expand the number of loci in, say, each room of your home. The kitchen offers not only a refrigerator, but also a cutlery drawer, an oven and any number of places where images can be attached. All that's important is that your room does not become cluttered, so that the images are clear and distinct. That is why it is a good idea, wherever possible, to have the action take place *inside* something: for example, Dave sat *in* the fridge allows you to have something happening *next* to the fridge as well, without Dave and that something else getting in the way of each other. It used to be considered important to place great distance between loci, though it does seem that this is not the case. However, *distinction* between loci does matter.

Once you do use multiple loci for each room, bear in mind you need always to go through them in a fixed order. Contrary to the Greek recommendation, I use a system of moving clockwise, so I always start with something on my immediate left and work my way around the room.

Another way of expanding your loci system is to allow for the use of permanently retained information. In other words, rather than just using it for information such as tasks and speeches which you can comfortably allow to fade from memory (the loci themselves remain fixed, but the objects placed in them will fade when not used), you can also designate other rooms, spaces or buildings to hold useful information you prefer to keep hold of. So once you are very familiar with your loci system at home, you may wish to expand the setting to form a more complex interconnection of buildings, which you can imagine as a sprawling palace. You can begin by adding an extra door to the imaginary representation of your house and have it open up into another familiar environment. In that new building you keep the information stored, and you wander around it occasionally to re-awaken and review what you have there.

When I first began using these techniques, I used my old school to expand my memory places. However, it quickly occurred to me that places which are dim in the memory, or which have associations that are both good and bad, are less than ideal: both serve to distance one from the picture and make it more of an effort to imagine oneself inside the place, looking out of one's own eyes, as it were. I re-read Thomas Harris's chapter, where we see that Lecter is able to lose himself inside a labyrinth of palace rooms and grand chambers, and I realized the pleasure of using far grander environments to store useful data.

This is more in keeping with the original use of the system set out by the author of *Ad Herennium*. Students were encouraged to find and use suitable places from life for the 'artificial memory', rather than relying on their homes. The loci inside each building were expected to be of moderate size, clearly lit (but not too bright), and placed about thirty feet from each other. Anyone unsure about finding sufficiently good loci is told that he should have no problem, 'for thought can embrace any region whatsoever and in it and at will construct the setting of some locus'. This suggestion of using fictitious places to complement real-life ones does allow for the construction of some wonderful imaginary dwellings, extending in all directions and with countless different rooms for different purposes.

Whether you use fictitious or real places to add to your expanding palace, this improvement relies on you being very familiar with them. Personally I would not recommend the use of invented spaces, as you must first concentrate on remembering *them,* which seems pointless. If I find myself in a suitable and aesthetically appropriate place that I wish to add to my own palace, I make a point of memorizing it, perhaps even photographing it for good measure, and then returning to it a few times to really fix it in the memory. If you do choose to employ this system, I can recommend, as does the Roman author, that you spend your time memorizing the real space when it is as free from crowds as possible. In this way I have 'taken' floors from museums (ignoring all but the exhibits which tend to stick most in the mind), as well as London parks, parts of my school and university, favourite theatres I have visited or performed in, stately residences and the homes of friends. Many of these I link together with grand stairwells and marble hallways, inspired by the chapter in *Hannibal*.

If, for example, you wished to remember a list of the works of Shakespeare in the order that they were written, you might ideally take a trip to the Globe, or the Swan in Stratford, and walk a fixed route through it a few times, choosing enough loci that stick so firmly in the mind that they are no effort to remember. You might begin with the entrance to the theatre, then the foyer, the box-office, the bar and so on, placing at each point a clear representation of what you wish to remember. However, they must be firmly imprinted on the memory, as it is important that you never struggle to recall the loci themselves, no more than you would struggle to remember the rooms in your own house. Once you are very happy that you can take that journey in your mind and recall everything, you can then walk back through and place an image for each play in each locus.

I mention this example because once, during a theatre run in glittering London's busy West End, I used the interior of the Cambridge Theatre to commit to memory the Bard's plays in order. This theatre forms part of my own memory palace, always holding that information. The process took about ten minutes and has stayed well in my mind. By taking you through the sequence as it still remains in my head, you will see how a loci journey might work. I have mixed the strict loci method, which normally consists of fixed, isolated images, and involved characters which move and interact with me to aid the mnemonics. I've also used the peg system, which I will explain later, to include some numbers.

Coming in through the stage door, I see two rather grand gentlemen in the little office to my right (*Two Gentlemen of Verona*). They offer me a mug (*'mug', in the peg system that follows, is a code for 39, so this tells me there are thirty-nine plays*). I say hello, and move towards the lift, which necessitates climbing a few stairs ahead of me. In doing so, I find a schoolboy coming the other way with homework that has been much corrected by a teacher in red pen, and we find ourselves unable to pass each other: we amusingly step to the same side, then again, and again, laughing at our repeated mistake (*Comedy of Errors*). As I open the lift door, out steps the imposing figure of *King John*, splendid in his regal attire but bearing the face of John Major, so that I am never confused as to which king it is. I step in, and the lift begins to rise. On the first floor I am joined by Prince Harry with bees buzzing around his head (*Henry VI Part One: the 'bees' represent 6 from the peg system, which will be explained later*). He is followed by Anthony Hopkins in character as *Titus Andronicus*, but Titus does not make it into the lift. I pass floors two and three (*Parts 2 and 3*) with Harry, and then the lift stops and he and his buzzing irritants step out. As they leave, I hear Harry's wife shouting gracelessly at him (*The Taming of the Shrew*).

I get out of the lift on the top floor, where my dressing room was situated. As I leave the cabin, I feel the unpleasant sensation of stepping into a sticky brown stool (*Richard III*), left by the company dog, and I see next to it a disappointed note from the cleaner saying that all the affection she puts into keeping the place clean has been wasted (*Love's Labour's Lost*). I walk to my dressing room, but first see that the side of the corridor has been made into a balcony overlooking a painted scene (*Romeo and Juliet*). Walking closer to it, I see that the balcony is decorated with carvings of fairies, and in the middle is a man with a donkey's head (*Midsummer Night's Dream*).

I cross now to my dressing room, and see that there is not one but two good-luck cards pinned to the door from my good friend Richard (*Richard II*). Before I can open the door, it opens for me, and the writer/comedian Stephen Merchant comes out and walks past me (*Merchant of Venice*). We greet each other, and I enter. Inside, there is immediately to my left a statue of Harry again, but this time shown with a whore (*Henry IV Part One: the 'whore' relates to 4 in the peg system*). Moving always left to right, next to it is the fridge, and I open it to see a group of tiny women laughing about their husbands (*Merry Wives of Windsor*). In the further corner, by the entrance to the make-up and changing area, I see a second statue of Harry and the whore (*Part 2*), and then I look on my sofa. Sat there is a nervous old lady in a terrible state about nothing in particular (*Much Ado About Nothing*), and next to her on the little table is a smaller statue of Harry, but this time with a beehive for his bees (*Henry V: again, the peg system will give us 5 from this image*). Now I step into the make-up area, to see that the cleaner has taped a note to the mirror, telling me proudly that she has left the room *As You Like It*, and I am grateful. When I look to my right in this room, I see that the white shower curtain has a blood-stained rip in it, and I am reminded of *Julius Caesar*.

I leave my dressing room and decide to take the stairs down to the stage. As I approach them, I see that there is a child's wind-up toy spinning at the top, and I am reminded that the century has now turned. We now continue with the plays written from 1600 onwards. Stepping down onto the first step, I see that the first few have a layer of cress growing on them (*Troilus and Cressida*). Halfway down the stairs, in the corner as I turn, there is another statue, this time of an unhappy pig, *Hamlet*, and etched into the wall just past him I see that an equally unhappy actor from a previous production has scratched marks on the wall like a prisoner to count the nights of his performances: I see twelve (*Twelfth Night*). However, at the end of the marks he has carved a 'smiley' into the plaster, and I guess that he was happy enough to be done at the end (*All's Well That Ends Well*). As I come to the bottom of the stairs, I see a racist slogan scrawled on the wall (*Othello*) and I use the side of a ruler that hangs at the base of the stairs (*Measure for Measure*) to try to scrape it off.

I enter through the door into the backstage area, and see that the stage is set for a Greek play. I see the Acropolis and a friend from school stood before it – Timothy (*Timon of Athens*). I walk across the stage and step down into the auditorium. Sat in the front row is an old man with two rather fawning daughters at his side (*King Lear*), and a little further back a bloodstained king (*Macbeth*). My feet strike what I think at first is a pipe across the aisle, but I see it is a periscope from a submarine (*Pericles*). I pick it up, and a small piece of coral (*Coriolanus*) falls off it, presumably snagged during some nautical voyage. At the door at the back of the stalls I find Anthony (*Antony and Cleopatra*), one of the executive producers of my TV programmes, who would sometimes come to see the show. I walk through into the lobby and find Michael, my manager, loudly playing the cymbals (*Cymbeline*). I pass him and look out on to the street: it is covered in thick snow (*A Winter's Tale*). Needing the fresh air, and continuing on my journey, I decide to brave the weather and step out anyway, but as I do I am knocked over by a sudden and terrible *Tempest*, and it is only through the ministrations of two helpful twins (*Two Noble Kinsmen*) that I am brought back to my feet. Ahead of me, walking down Monmouth Street towards Seven Dials, I see the great old magician Cardini, who, drunk as ever, seems rather lost (*Cardenio, the play lost to us in written form*). Finally, I turn and look back at the theatre. In place of the large picture of me that had graced the façade of the building, I see a huge painting of Henry VIII, in familiar garb.

Such is my journey through the theatre in which I performed.

Your home can link to a place like this through an extra doorway or a favourite garden, which also stores a wealth of information you have wished to keep. That way you can begin to enjoy the pleasure of wandering around in these private locales during occasional quiet moments, unlocking their secrets for your own edification. The auto-hypnotic quality of such excursions really makes the whole process quite delightful, and it is important to re-awaken these from time to time to make sure that items don't fade. After a while, each journey happens quickly and easily, and you are propelled forward quite automatically.

One final thought. The Greeks suggested that you add a marker every five loci on your journey. For example, a hand with the fingers splayed as the fifth loci would remind you that this was number five on the list. That way if you needed to recall, for example, the twelfth item on your list, you could walk straight to the 'ten' marker and then continue on two more. It's a rather neat addition, and echoes the 'turning of the century' marker I placed at the top of the Cambridge stairs.

THE PEG SYSTEM

Both the linking and the loci systems allow you to memorize anything that can be represented as, or reduced to, a list. Unlike those two, the peg system allows you to work with digits, so you can use it to remember reference numbers, hotel rooms, phone numbers and PIN numbers. It still is generally used in tandem with the linking system, and provides you with a way of connecting digits to each other or to words, names or other information. And, unlike the use of the markers in the loci mnemonic, it allows for a much more organic way of linking items on a list to their position on it.

For now, let us put aside the imaginary journeys of the loci system and return to our original thoughts about the simple use of linking to make one given piece of information effortlessly yield a second which we wish to know. We can incorporate the peg system into our palaces and travels later.

Here's the premise: numbers are not words, and therefore cannot be visually linked. However, if each number could be represented by a word, you would be able to link away quite happily. Here, then, is one very simple way of turning the numbers 1 to 10 into words, by choosing words that rhyme with the numbers:

1 – Bun	6 – Sticks
2 – Shoe	7 – Heaven
3 – Tree	8 – Gate
4 – Door	9 – Line
5 – Hive	10 – Hen

Easy. So, if you wanted to remember the first ten words on our list from before so that if asked you could call out the word that comes at a given number, you would now link each word to its number rather than to the next word on the list. The first word on the list was *telephone*, so this would link to *bun*: an image, perhaps, of an iced bun being used as a phone, with currants arranged to look like a keypad on the front. And so on. If someone asked you for the word at position number one, you would think *bun* and immediately see a telephone.

This is a simple method, but it has real limitations. Rhyming gets more difficult, for example, once you get into the teens. A way of getting around this, if you like this system, is to repeat the same objects in each group of ten (so 2, 12, 22, 32, 42 etc. are all shoes), but let each group of ten dramatically affect the object in some distinct way. For example, all the objects when repeated as numbers 11 to 20 are to be seen as on fire; 21 to 30 are all freezing cold; 31 to 40 are all bright blue; and so on.

Personally I am not a fan of this system, because of such complications and other limitations. I shall teach you instead my preferred system. It requires a little more groundwork but will prove ultimately much more useful. It allows you to remember longer strings of numbers (such as, say, a phone number), which the previous peg system would be hard pushed to do.

We are going to begin by turning the digits from 0 to 9 into common consonants. The choice of letters will be dictated only by which consonant we can connect most easily with that number. And occasionally we give ourselves a useful alternative. The following is the list I use, and I shall explain each one:

0 – z/s : ('z' is in 'zero', and the 's' sound is most similar to 'z')

1 – l : (they look similar)

2 – n : (two downward strokes on a small 'n')

3 – m : (three downward strokes)

4 – r : (fou'r')

5 – f/v : ('f'i'v'e: again, they are similar sounds)

6 – b/p : ('b' looks similar to 6,

		and 'p' and 'b' sound and look most similar)	8 – ch/ sh/j	:	(because of the 'gh' in 'eight', and then 'j' is the nearest to these sounds)
7 – T	:	(7 and capital 'T' kind of look similar, especially the way I write my 'T's)	9 – g	:	(again, a written 'g' can resemble a 9)

Read through that list a few times and check that it makes sense for you. Then cover the page and see if you can remember them all. Once you have them, please carry on.

Now, let's imagine you have to remember a new PIN number: 1743. (If that is indeed your PIN number, please don't hesitate to be hugely impressed and immediately call the news.) You can represent those digits as LTRM. Now, you need only turn those four letters into a word or phrase to remember the number. Essentially you add vowel sounds to see what you get. I would think of 'Light Room', or 'Le Tram'. As soon as you have one, link it to the idea of getting money out of the cash machine, and you're done. For example, for 'Light Room', you might imagine a cash machine in a room with white walls and lots of lights, or for 'Le Tram', getting out of a tram in France to grab some euros. Now you have that image, you don't need to worry about remembering the number. Just let the image of the cash machine trigger the picture of the tram and decode it. When adding letters to make a memorable word or words, just be careful not to use any other letters that are already used in the system. It's best to stick to vowels, 'h's and 'y's.

Recently I went through the process of changing banks and had to remember several new PIN numbers for the new bank. First I turned each number into a word or two, as above. To continue with the 1743 example, for my business current account I would have imagined myself wearing a very nice business suit as I stepped off that French tram. The picture for my personal current account, on the other hand, would have involved me in my normal clothes.

By now you'll have realized that if any of this sounds ridiculous, that really is the point. By spending a few seconds fixing these odd images in your head you are working in tandem with the way our brains make connections, as opposed to the supposedly more 'sensible' (and less effective) ways in which we are normally expected to try to remember information.

Here's another example. While filming in Las Vegas a while back for *Messiah*, we stayed in one of the emphatically grotesque hotels that line the strip. On the first night of our arrival, while saying our exhausted goodnights after a long and vile journey, we arranged to meet in the morning at the quite unholy hour of six. As I left I realized that before I made that meeting in the morning, I would first need to collect something from Coops (my PA), who was in one room, and take it to Sarah-Jane's room, where she was to endure the harrowing and sickening process of applying my make-up for the show. Of course, the hotel in question had some thirty floors, and three thousand or so rooms, so the two room numbers that were shouted at me by Coops and Sarah-Jane as I headed for the lift were each four digits long. I had neither pen nor paper, and I really had to remember what they were. I couldn't risk walking around the floors of that place at half past five with no sense of a destination. Those of you familiar with these hotels will know how nightmarish they are: not only are the corridors labyrinthine and simply endless, but any attempt to return to the hotel reception requires a fifteen-minute walk through the blaring, screaming slot-machines and gaudy découpage of the ground floor. As it turned out, I returned to my room that night to find that I didn't have my key. Barely able to see or walk, I have never hated the world more than when I took the lift twenty-seven floors back down and made my way back through the sensory assault that is the Flamingo casino to the front desk, let alone when I was then told that I needed my passport to be issued a new key (my passport was already locked safely in my room). I don't know what happened after that. I may have slept in the lobby; I may have killed a woman.

But I am straying from the point. Two room numbers were shouted at me, I had no writing tools, and I was seemingly in no state to remember what I was hearing. So I turned the numbers into letters, and the letters into words, and then attached that to the person whose room it was. Coops was 2037 (I can still remember it) – NSMT. I remembered 'Nose Mat', and imagined Coops welcoming me into his room with a tiny bristly doormat under his nose, to catch any detritus from his nostrils. Sarah-Jane's was 1530 – LVMS, or 'Live Mouse'. I imagined her applying my make-up with a squeaking rodent. I could then go to sleep for the few remaining hours left to me in the knowledge that I would easily conjure up these pictures in the morning as I headed for the lift. They stick very easily in the mind, precisely because they are vivid and unusual. You might want to prove this to yourself by running again through those twenty words you have in your head from when you learned the linking system. See if you can still do it. Remember that at no point have you even tried to learn these words, apart from the very first time, when you were not supposed to succeed.

There is another way of looking at the peg system. Let us return to our list and imagine we wish to learn which word comes at each number. That way, instead of just reciting the list, you could have your by now quite fascinated friend call out any number and you would be able to tell him the corresponding word. Similarly, you might need to attach numbers, dates or scores to names or places – the same system applies. Well, we're now able to use the peg letters 's', 'l', 'n', 'm' and so on to form word-images for the numbers in a way that will allow us to move into double digits with ease. Let's take our letters for 0 to 9 and add a few vowels or soft consonants to turn them into words. These are the words I use:

0 – z/s	: zoo	5 – f/v	: hive
1 – l	: ale	6 – b/p	: bee
2 – n	: hen	7 – T	: tea
3 – m	: ham	8 – ch/sh/j	: shoe
4 – r	: whore	9 – g	: goo

Now, as we get into double digits, we combine the letters in the way you already know, and form more words. Here is my list from 10 to 52, which means I can show you how to use the system in conjunction with a deck of cards. Notice that 18, 'ledge', has turned the 'ch' into a 'j' sound because it's the most similar. I could have used the word 'latch', but a ledge is rather easier to visualize than a latch, and simpler to use in conjunction with other images.

10 – l, z/s	: lice	20 – n, z/s	: nose
11 – l, l	: lily	21 – n, l	: nail
12 – l, n	: line	22 – n, n	: nanny
13 – l, m	: lime	23 – n, m	: gnome
14 – l, r	: lorry	24 – n, r	: Nero
15 – l, f/v	: laugh	25 – n, f/v	: knife
16 – l, b/p	: lip	26 – n, b/p	: nob
17 – l, t	: light	27 – n, t	: knight
18 – l, ch/sh/j	: ledge	28 – n, ch/sh/j	: notch
19 – l, g	: leg	29 – n, g	: nag

30 – m, z/s : moss
31 – m, l : mail
32 – m, n : money
33 – m, m : mum
34 – m, r : merry
35 – m, f/v : muff
36 – m, b/p : map
37 – m, t : mat
38 – m, ch/sh/j : match
39 – m, g : mag
40 – r, z/s : rose
41 – r, l : rail
42 – r, n : rain
43 – r, m : ram
44 – r, r : roar
45 – r, f/v : rave
46 – r, b/p : rub
47 – r, t : root
48 – r, ch/sh/j : retch
49 – r, g : rag
50 – f/v, z/s : fuse
51 – f/v, l : fall
52 – f/v, n : fan

Obviously each group of ten will start with the same sound, which makes things a little quicker to learn: all of the twenties, for example, begin with the 'n' sound. You will find that one or two better alternatives suggest themselves to you in place of the ones I suggest here, in which case by all means change them. For example, my word for 44 is actually not 'roar', as I've given it here, but 'Rory', after the soundman in our film crew. So change them for whatever works for you, but be careful not to add 'fill-in' letters which stand for other numbers, otherwise you'll get into trouble. And do make sure that the pictures are easy to visualize.

So here is a new list of random words, and this time I'll ask you to link each with its number. Begin with the first ten, first working out what each number translates into. Feel free to refer back to the previous pages, but see how many you can work out or remember on your own. After you've done this with ten, try the next ten. For example, when you read '1', you think '1 = ale'; then connect 'ale' to the word in position number one, in this case, 'flower'. Here you can perhaps imagine a flower stuck in a pint of beer instead of a vase.

Take that mental snapshot, attach any appropriate feelings to the picture if you can, then move on.

1 : flower	11 : lavatory
2 : pants	12 : clipboard
3 : laptop	13 : thumb
4 : parrot	14 : buzzer
5 : whale	15 : shell
6 : nipple	16 : wallet
7 : stadium	17 : magnet
8 : Tony Blair	18 : thread
9 : tissue	19 : monitor
10 : wedding	20 : wheelchair

When you've done it, tell yourself a number, and let it all unravel. Turn the number into a peg word, then see what it connects with. Have a friend help you with this, calling out random numbers and ticking them off as you go, until you really get the hang of it. Pay attention to those you get wrong, as more often than not you'll notice that you didn't take that second to really cement a clear, vivid and unusual image in your head.

Remembering Long Numbers

The system is great for remembering telephone numbers or strings of digits, as I've mentioned, but it's best when mixed with other ways of finding links between numbers. For example, take the following random string: 876498474505773498724. It's fairly impossible to learn by rote, but quite fun to use with this system. I look at the number as a story, alternating as feels easiest between the peg system and other ways of grouping the digits. Here I would look at the numbers as follows:

I hear a countdown from eight, but the counter realizes she's missed five, and stops (8764). Fair enough, she's nearly a hundred years old (98) and even gets aeroplanes muddled up (474 instead of 747). The aeroplanes fly over her beehives . . . she had three beehives in a row but the middle one is missing (505), so she put a ToTeM (773) pole in its place. She did this for her 98th (498) birthday. I only gave her a TeNneR (724) as a gift.

You can then run through the story in your mind and unpack it to reproduce the correct numbers in sequence. Note that where there was a non sequitur, I introduced a link (the aeroplane flying over the beehives) to make sure I got taken on to the next part of the story. Again, on the strength of reading through my description, you should find that you can now recall the number. Try it, bearing in mind that it's far more potent when you use your own story.

As you have no doubt gathered, the peg system is a little more involved, but including numbers does allow for some extraordinary memory feats. I shall now outline a few for you to try, and I hope that the idea of performing such demonstrations inspires you to persevere with the system.

Memorizing a Deck of Cards

This is something I have used many times. Sometimes it can work as a stand-alone feat, at other times as a hidden technique for a kind of card trick. Bear in mind that sometimes in my performances I pretend to use memory skills but don't; and sometimes I use a lot of memory work but pretend it's something else. At other times I'm perfectly honest. Ultimately, it's the overall effect that interests me most, and I take my cue from that.

Let's imagine you have shuffled a deck of cards and wish to memorize them in the new order. If you want merely to rattle off all fifty-two cards in that order, then the linking system would work best for you. But if it is important to know the *position* of each card, then you need to attach each to its number, one through fifty-two. But how can you use either system with playing cards? The answer, perhaps not surprisingly by now, is to turn each card into a word-image. The process is as follows. Let us imagine that the first card of the deck as you look at the faces is the nine of hearts – 9H. Firstly, say it to yourself as 'Heart Nine: H9'. Now we make a word, beginning with H and using the peg letter for 9, which is . . . (can you remember?) . . . 'g'. So we make the word 'hag', for example. Could also be 'hug', but 'hag' might be easier to visualize in the long run. Then we connect 'hag' with our peg for its position (1 or 'l', which gives us 'ale') and we have an image of a hag, or a witch, drinking a pint of beer.

Card two, let's imagine, is the six of spades. Just follow the same procedure:

Reverse 6S = **S6**
Use peg to create a word: S6 = S+b/p = **sob**
Use peg to code the position: 2 (second card) = **hen**
Now link 'sob' (6S) with 'hen' (2): our image is of a **sobbing hen**.

So, at this point, if you needed to know what card comes in the first position, you would conjure up a picture of ale (1) and see where it took you (an old hag drinking it). The 'hag' would then be decoded as hearts/nine (it'll take you a few seconds at first), and you would know that the first card is the nine of hearts. Similarly, if you were asked what position the six of spades occupied in the deck, you would find the picture for this card (S6 = s+b/p = 'sob') and then you'd quickly see a hen sobbing. 'Hen' could then quickly be turned back into a 2, and that would give you the position.

I'm sure this seems impossibly complicated already to you. Feel free to skip this section if you don't feel it will ever be of any use. But hey, you wanted to know what goes on in my head.

In a moment I will show you the list of images I use for playing cards. There is a small issue with the jacks which I shall explain first. As 8 translates into 'ch/sh', we have already shown that a 'j' sound is close enough to use here too (such as 18 = 'ledge', which is better than 'latch' or 'lush'). However, we then have a problem: the jack of any suit could be confused with the eight of the same suit. For example, the eight of hearts translates as (H8 = H+ch/sh/j) 'hedge'. But if we followed the same procedure, the jack of hearts would want to do the same: HJ = Hedge. We'd have the same problem with the jacks of all the suits. One way around this would be not to use the 'j' option with the eights, and have 'hatch', say, instead of 'hedge'. But because I do use the 'j' sound in place of an '8' for the positions (e.g. 18 = 'ledge'), this would get too confusing. My solution is not to use the peg system for jacks and just go straight to an appropriate image. For example, because a jack is a boy, I see the jack of hearts as Cupid. I use this also with other picture cards: the king and queen of hearts, for example, I see as a bridegroom and bride. It's easier and quicker than coding and decoding them each time, and allows you to get round the difficulty of having to use the 'q' sound with queens. Others, like the ace of spades, which has a connection with death, I use in a similar way. Feel free to change them if they don't work for you. You should be careful, however, not to link cards to word-images that are already used for the numbered positions, otherwise that will also cause confusion.

Here, then, is the list of images I use for playing cards. I have italicized all the words that do not come from the peg code.

AS–*Grim Reaper*
2S–sun
3S–Sam (a friend; or 'sum')
4S–sore
5S–safe
6S–sob
7S–soot
8S–sash
9S–ciggy (cigarette)
10S–sissy
JS–*boy digging*
QS–*housekeeper*
KS–*gardener*

AC–*a big club*
2C–can
3C–cum (you would)
4C–car
5C–cough
6C–cob (corn on the . . .)
7C–cat
8C–cash
9C–cog
10C–kiss
JC–*young guy at a club*
QC–*brothel madam*
KC–*bouncer* or cock

AH–*a big love-heart*
2H–*lovers* (not 'hen')
3H–home (not 'ham')
4H - hair (not 'whore')
5H–hoof (not 'hive')
6H–hoop
7H–hat
8H–hedge
9H–hag
10H–horse
JH–*Cupid*
QH–*bride*
KH–*bridegroom*

AD–*a big sparkly diamond*
2D–*Dan* (my TV editor)
3D–Dom (my brother)
4D–door
5D–dove
6D–me (DB)
7D–dot
8D–dish
9D–dog
10D–dizzy
JD–*diamond thief*
QD–*the Queen*
KD–*an old jeweller*

These are the words I would then link to the positions the cards occupy in a shuffled or specially arranged deck. Now, when this is coupled with apparently shuffling the deck, the end result can be quite startling. In an early episode of *Mind Control*, I had a croupier call out any card in a shuffled deck and I was able to cut straight to it while the deck sat on the table. In reality, the deck was shuffled using a sequence that brought it back to the memorized order, so when she named any card I was able immediately to know its position. Then I had to estimate the correct place to cut to, in order to produce the card. While this might sound impossible in itself, it is perfectly achievable with practice. I also had some leeway in that there was the possibility of producing the card either from the underside of the pile I cut off or from the top of the pile that remained, if that makes sense. It allowed me to miss by one and still seemingly get it right.

Now, for the truly obsessed advanced student (and I have every faith that you are well on your way to becoming one), the following test might appeal. Firstly, you need to have the coded images for cards very clearly in your mind so that you can run through the deck and conjure up each one in turn without thinking much about it. We won't worry about the positions of the cards. Now, remove five cards at random from a genuinely shuffled deck and put them away, without seeing what they are. Then deal through the balance of the deck, and for each card conjure up the picture but then mutilate it in some way. For example, the ace of spades Grim Reaper is cut up into bits with his own scythe; the boy dancing at the club (jack of clubs) is shot. Each mutilation should clearly destroy the thing in question. Now, once you have done this, you can then mentally run through all the card images in your head, a suit at a time. Those you did not destroy will stand out very clearly to you, thus you'll be able to tell which cards have been removed. With practice, this can be a very impressive feat.

This technique is useful for card games involving a discard. Bridge players could, for example, memorize all the cards that have been played in this way. In blackjack it is very useful to know which cards have been dealt in order to know whether it is likely or not to be safe to bet on the next card. Poker does not lend itself as easily to this technique, although in seven card stud, in which cards are 'mucked' along the way, it would be useful to remember what those discards are.

Clearly this requires a bit of effort, but if you have an interest in playing cards at all, it is well worth the patience (pun intended but immediately regretted) required. For others of you, perhaps this next idea will appeal more.

Memorizing Football Scores

There now follows a list of the results of FA Cup Finals for the last twenty or so years. For real impact, it is worth stretching this to fifty years, but then it would take a little too long to take you through that here. I am not a keen football fan, and won't know any of these results before typing them. I will learn the list with you as I take you through it, and we'll both see how we do.

2005–06 Liverpool 3 Westham 3 (after extra time)
Winners – Liverpool after penalty shoot-out (3–1)
2004–05 Arsenal 0 Manchester United 0 (after extra time)
Winners – Arsenal after penalty shoot-out (5–4)
2003–04 Manchester United 3 Millwall 0
2002–03 Arsenal 1 Southampton 0
2001–02 Arsenal 2 Chelsea 0
2000–01 Liverpool 2 Arsenal 1
1999–2000 Chelsea 1 Aston Villa 0
1998–99 Manchester United 2 Newcastle United 0
1997–98 Arsenal 2 Newcastle United 0

1996–97	Chelsea 2 Middlesbrough 0
1995–96	Manchester United 1 Liverpool 0
1994–95	Everton 1 Manchester United 0
1993–94	Manchester United 4 Chelsea 0
1992–93	Arsenal 2 Sheffield Wednesday 1
1991–92	Liverpool 2 Sunderland 0
1990–91	Tottenham Hotspur 2 Nottingham Forest 1
1989–90	Manchester United 1 Crystal Palace 0
1988–89	Liverpool 3 Everton 2
1987–88	Wimbledon 1 Liverpool 0
1986–87	Coventry 3 Tottenham Hotspur 2
1985–86	Liverpool 3 Everton 1
1984–85	Manchester United 1 Everton 0
1983–84	Everton 2 Watford 0

To be impressive, we want to put the complete scores into our system, not just the winners. This means we need to link each date with each team and their individual scores. As I have hinted, there's no reason to stick to the system if a better aide-memoire suggests itself. All that matters is that the information gets remembered; exactly how is neither here nor there, so feel free to mix it up a bit.

Because the top of the list seems most complicated, let's work up from the oldest score at the bottom. First, for each one, let's just use the later of the two dates. So our first score is for '84; we'll forget about the '83. '84' translates as 'ch+r', which gives us *chair*. Now, if we abbreviate Everton as E and Watford as W, we have E2, W0. That codes as E+N, W+S. Now we need to code that. I would suggest that rather than making words, we see ENWS as an anti-clockwise route around the points of the compass, starting at East. East, North, West, South. So if we imagine a chair making that journey, we'll have combined all the necessary data into one memorable picture. The image of a man secured into a chair which he is sailing across the world like a boat, only *backwards* from china, gives me that information quite vividly. I see him with two oars out in the middle of the sea, facing the wrong way, and then I pull back to see his route on a map that has the points of the compass marked. I see his anti-clockwise journey depicted with a dotted line, starting at East.

Read the rest of these slowly, and work out the coding for the numbers for yourself as you go.

Next, '85, and it's M1, E0. That gives me *shave* (or *chav*) for the year, and ML, ES. Looks like the word *miles* or *moles* to me. I'll use the image of Myles, my accountant. If I picture myself shaving him, that links the two words. Unless you know a Myles or a Miles yourself, you might want to imagine someone shaving some moles.

'86: L3, E1. Or, *shop: lamb, eel.* I think of a shop that sells only lambs to eels. It's become fashionable in the eel world to carry around a small lamb as an accessory. I see an underwater shop that specializes in such things.

'87: Coventry 3, TH2. Because there are a few teams beginning with a C, let's substitute the image of a cathedral for 'Coventry'. We get *Shit: Cathedral 3, TH+2.* Here I find the easiest answer is to depart from the peg system and imagine that I can squeeze out three prize stools while sat in a cathedral, whereas my father and brother (both Spurs fans) can manage but two, as they sit in the stands with their football scarves on. It doesn't matter that the method is a little different: the word 'shit' will still take me to that image, and I can easily work it out from there. You might want to substitute the image of my family members for two cowboys with bright shiny spurs on their boots.

'88: Wimbledon 1, L0. So as not to confuse this 'W' with 'Watford', let's use the image of a *womble*. That gives us *church: womble 1, lazy.*

If we stick with the number '1' rather than decode it, it gives us the easy image of a womble with a big number '1' on his dungarees, who is notoriously lazy. He is always in church, sleeping all the time in the back pew, his bold red number '1' clearly visible, while Madame Cholet is back home cooking and could really do with his help.

'89: L3, E2. Shag: LM, EN. Let's go with a lamb shagging Edward Norton. Not an easy image to conjure up, but make sure you clearly picture it. I have soft lighting, silk sheets and Sinatra on the stereo. Admittedly, Norton doing it to the lamb would be easier to picture, but the lamb should be dominant, as it were, as that will help us arrive at the winning team first.

'90: M1, Crystal Palace 0. The image of a glittering crystal palace is better than worrying about confusing Cs with Chelsea or Coventry. So, *gas: M1, Crystal Palace 0.* A trail of gas, working its way up the M1, finally reaching a glittering crystal palace at the end of the motorway, and then dissipating into *nothing* (nil). To further cement the idea of nothingness, I would imagine the palace as merely a shell. Inside would be only empty space.

'91: TH2, Nottingham Forest 1. Again, the image of a forest is probably easier to work with. So, *gale: thin, forest 1.* There is a gale blowing, and this terribly thin guy is stood in the forest trying to urinate (a 'number one'). We see how thin he is, and how he can barely stand up in the wind.

'92: L2, Sun 0. With so many teams beginning with S, let's have the sun represent Sunderland. We have *gun: line, sun 0.* I take a gun and aim a straight line at the sun. I see that line coming out of the end of the gun right up into the sun. I shoot, and the sun disappears. Nothing is left.

'93: Arse 2, Wed 1. Game, or gum: arse 2, wedding 1. There is a prize of a stick of gum to either of the two arses who can get to the wedding by one p.m. We see the stick of gum in the church as the bell

strikes one during the wedding ceremony, and then immediately the door bursts open and these two backsides rush in on little legs.

'94: M4, Ch0. Gary: merry, chase. I imagine Gary (a boy I hated at primary school, but you can use Gary Lineker if you like) suddenly turning ever so cheery and then running off calling 'chase me' rather camply back at me, strikingly like the comedy homosexual character created by Duncan Norvelle in the eighties.

'95: E1, M0. Guff: eel, moss. A tiny fart – where did that come from? Ah, the rather red-faced moray curled up on the moss bank. Smells of shrimps, the dirty eel.

'96: M1, L0. Gob: M1, lazy. A giant mouth, being carried all the way up the M1 because it's too lazy to walk.

'97: Ch2, Mid 0. Gut: chin, Midas. I picture a huge gut, then follow it up to a huge chin. Ah, I see it is the legendary King Midas, turning anything to gold by touching it with his enormous gut or chin.

'98: Arse 2, N0. Gash: arse 2, nose. A terrible gash splits an arse clean in two, and then you delicately place your nose to the resulting mess to smell it. Lovely.

'99: M2, N0. Gag: money, nose. Although 'man' would work for 'M2', it's a little vague to picture. Instead I imagine myself gagging as money is forced down my throat while my nose is pinched. Rather like my relationship with Channel 4.

'00: Ch1, Villa 0. Sissy: chilly, villa 0. A sissy guy who feels cold as he heads for his Spanish villa, only to get there and find the 'villa' is an empty shell (nothing).

'01: L2, Arse 1. Ale: line, arsehole. A pint of beer is poured in a straight line down the cleft between the buttocks and straight into the Dot Cotton's mouth (or bottom hole). You might want to imagine a ruler placed there to make sure the line is straight, so that you don't forget that component.

'02: Arse 2, Ch0. Hen: arse 2, cheese. Oh dear. A mutant hen with two distinct arses, one of which produces cheese.

'03: Arse 1, South 0. Ham: arsehole, south 0. Well, if you take a piece of ham, run it down past the arsehole and go any further south, there's suddenly nothing. Next time you marvel at a memory expert on television, bear in mind that these sorts of things are going through his head.

'04: M3, Millwall 0. Whore: mum, wall 0. Let's convert 'Millwall' into 'wall' to separate it from other Ms. Who's that whore? Why, it's my own mother (God forgive me), stood against a wall, making nothing at all.

'05: Arse 5, M4 on penalties after 0–0 score. Hive: arse F, M, R. One final arse image: coming out of a beehive, this hopping bottom has just a FeMuR sticking out of it, and is trying to kick penalties. So far, nothing.

'06: L3, West Ham 3, 3–1 to L on penalties. Bee: Lamb and West Ham neck and neck. A bee buzzes down onto the neck of a lamb (Liverpool 3), which is restrained next to a west-country pig (round-vowelled hog wearing a farmer's outfit). Both are about to be slaughtered. They lie neck and neck, and the bee buzzes from one to another. The lamb kicks (penalties) his way free (wins) and hides in the mill (3–1). Or, if you like, the pig kicks the bucket and becomes a delicious MeaL.

Right, that was fairly revolting, and it has done nothing to improve my interest in football. But let's see if we can do it. No looking: what was the result in '86? See if you can do it before you read any further.

'86 . . . that codes to shop. The shop sold lambs to eels. So that's Liverpool 3 Everton 1. Check? Yes! Try another. What was the result for '90? '90 becomes gas. That goes up the M1 to a gleaming palace – Manchester United 1 Crystal Palace 0. Easy.

What were the FA Cup Final results for '87, '92, '84?

REMEMBERING NAMES

It is bizarre that we forget names as easily as we do. It is so useful to us as social creatures to identify the people we meet and so nice for us to have our names remembered that one imagines we would have developed a natural ability to do this. We're far better at remembering faces, but it's worth noting that this is a different type of remembering. 'Remembering' faces involves mere recognition, which is a far easier skill than recall, the necessary process for retrieving a person's name from the memory. Generally, when people say that they are good at remembering faces but poor at remembering names, they are in fact describing a natural part of being human. Also, I do think that the social ritual of being introduced can feel like such a formality that unless we are particularly attracted to or otherwise interested in the person we're meeting, and therefore have a motive to remember their name, we seem to just go through the motions of pleasure at meeting the person and pay very little attention to anything we are told.

So this is the first step: when you are introduced, *pay attention*. Decide that you are going to remember this person's name, or even the names of everyone at the party. See yourself as that one charming person who calls everyone by their name throughout, and is able to say goodbye to each person at the end using all the correct names again. Take some pride in it. It'll give you something to do at an event you're not enjoying, and in the same breath it can help make you seem enormously confident and socially impressive. When we talk to someone for a second time later at a party and they have remembered our name, it's enormously flattering, and unless they are particularly repellent we will bond rather well with them. Equally, at a meeting, it is a huge advantage to be able to address everyone correctly, or to refer across the table to third parties in the same way.

Now that you are committed to paying more attention, let us consider what to do next. The smiling person at the party says, 'Hi, I'm Mike.' The following process takes about a second, and is my preferred route:

1. Quickly bring to mind someone you know with the same name. This could be a friend, a relative or a famous person (I think immediately of a Mike from school who now works at the BBC).
2. Imagine that the person in front of you has been made up to look a bit like this other person and is impersonating him/her. (Mike had ginger hair and his mum was the junior school librarian. I quickly see the person before me wearing a ginger wig in the old junior library, and it's done.)

A second route, if either of the above eludes you, or if the person has some distinguishing features you can't help but notice, is as follows:

1. Connect the name with another image. 'Mike' becomes a microphone. 'Alice' becomes an Alice-band. 'Bill' (though I use an image of Clinton) becomes an invoice. And so on.
2. Find something memorable about this person's features, size or appearance. Something around the face is best, and quickest. You might want to use their clothing if something stands out, but bear in mind that this would mean that you would not have the ability to trigger the name if you meet them on a separate occasion when they are not wearing the same clothes. A beard, glasses, a large nose, a scar or mark, spiky hair – there will be something about Mike you can choose. Alternatively, perhaps his face reminds you of someone, or a particular animal. As a caricaturist, I have always been good at seeing faces

in a rather exaggerated way and therefore have no trouble picking out idiosyncratic features and using them to recall names. Anyone can, with a little practice, learn to pick up on subtle but memorable features.

3. Link the two together. Mike's large nose becomes a microphone stuck in the middle of his face. Imagine Bill putting on his thick-rimmed glasses to read the 'bill' after dinner. Alice's mouse-like features suggest a mouse wearing an Alice-band. And so on.

This can take a beat longer, so if necessary, cover the moment with 'Oh, have we met before?' or some such thing. This gives you a few extra seconds to make the appropriate link.

Once you have the connection, you must then make a point of using the person's name whenever you can. Within reason, people can't get enough of hearing their own names, and it gives you good practice. You'll find that after a couple of repetitions, during and at the end of your conversation, the name will be well and truly stuck.

If you are at a meeting of less than, say, ten people, and you're not sure if you're correctly remembering the name of one of them, you can always run through the others and you'll usually remind yourself of the final one, or at least confirm it in your mind. At that point, it's worth clarifying to yourself the mental image you have for that person so that you don't forget it again.

Once this feels comfortable and familiar, I do think it's also a good idea to include in your system a way of remembering what the person does for a living, or what interests they may have. This may be vitally important (knowing who does what at a business meeting, for example), or just another way of charming the pants off someone. You can do this first by creating your mental image that tells you their name, then by introducing extra details to the picture which show the person carrying out their work or enjoying their interest. Mike, for example, could be asking his librarian mother for help with his barrister's wig, if he were indeed a barrister; or I could relocate the library to the top of a mountain if he were a climber. Generally speaking, if you are going to use this sort of system to remember other details about a person, it's better to make each image as efficient as possible. Therefore the 'microphone as a nose' would be better than the whole 'library and mother' image for Mike, because the former would allow you to use the immediate location you place him in to represent some other important detail, rather than it being part of the reminder for the name. In other words, Mike with a mic for a nose could be stood in a law court (to represent his legal career), and you have immediately packed two pieces of information into the picture rather than just one (Mike in a library talking to his mum). However, as with all these things, your only goal is to remember what you wish to remember. There are really no right or wrong ways of doing it, as long as it's working.

You'll recognize we are again using the linking procedure, and it is worth doing so to include the names of people's spouses, partners and (especially) their kids. What is more impressive than bumping into someone months after meeting them briefly at a party and asking them how Johnny and Jeff are? This is far from difficult: we fix in our mind the person with cash (Johnny) in one hand and capes (Jeff, after the strongman Geoff Capes) draped over the other arm, and the image returns easily to us when we see him again. For the tiny amount of effort involved, which amounts to no more than remembering to use this brief process, I cannot recommend enough the advantages of putting this into practice.

If you have attended an important social event or meeting and wish to retain the names of each person and details of their spouses, kids and interests, you can use a new set of rooms in your memory palace to store the meeting. Presuming that you have first made a mnemonic image for each person that gives you the details, you can now arrange them along the route through this new memory building. You can use the building where you met the people if it is familiar, or some similarly appropriate place. Each image will probably be quite involved, so this will be a room worth reviewing every now and then to make sure that the images are still clear. If this seems like too much trouble, then I would certainly recommend that you get yourself a notebook or filing system and keep some record of these people and such details. It's an extremely worthwhile touch.

If you are unconvinced that you really can bump into a person months later and still remember these details about them, then I can only advise you to try it, and let it happen when it happens. After all, when you meet someone you have not seen for a long time and you cannot quite remember where you know him from, what is the first thing you do? You look at his face and try to let your mind connect it with something. We desperately search for *any* clue that will tell us who the person is. Here, we are merely giving the mind a helping hand: a very clear image as a starting point. An image that will come to us in the future when a familiar face triggers it, with all the oddness and vividness with which we remembered to imbue it when we first created it.

An admission: I do find I struggle sometimes to remember names of volunteers when performing live. I normally have so much going on in my head that I don't take the moment to lock the name into my memory. If you do want to improve your ability in this area, it's worth writing out a list of common names and some visual hook for each one. Not only will these help you when you come across those names in company, it also makes you practise finding those links quickly when you need them.

THE IMPORTANCE OF REVIEWING

One of the delightful aspects of a memory palace is that you can review the information and bring everything back to mind without the process seeming tiresome. Indeed, you are merely imagining wandering around a pleasant and familiar environment, looking at things you have placed along the way. You can visit a different area of the palace each time you visit it, and the process should always be interesting and worthwhile. Certainly to sit daydreaming in a taxi and bring to mind everything you ever wanted to remember on a particular subject, be it work, study, interest or socially related, is an immensely rewarding feeling. To be able to run through the names of family members of each member of your staff; to know all the cases or facts you could ever need for your examination; to go to a meeting having memorized all the information you've been given, or found on the net, on each attendee . . .

Whether you are wandering through the intricate, oddly assembled palace of your new memory or just running through a long list of items you have pieced together, the process of reviewing is essential. Once any mnemonic has been set, you must then run through it and make sure it all works. Repeating the review a few hours later, and then again a few days later, really ensures that the information sticks in the mind and doesn't just drop from the slippery grip of the short-term memory. The use of the palace to store permanent information like this also means that you don't forget to review certain rooms, as you'll come across them each time you explore it. It is analogous to using the name of a person a few times in conversation after you have remembered it. Verbalizing the name a few times makes it stick so much more solidly, until you find yourself barely needing to touch upon the mnemonic at all.

Ever since I suffered a broken PDA for some time, I have used the loci system to remember tasks. Along my mental map of the street to my house I place bizarre and comic images that remind me to do various things. I regularly review the journey. Almost as soon as I started doing this, I noticed that a strange thing happened: I was much more likely to get on and carry out the task than if I had simply entered it into a portable device or left a note on my desk. Notes, electronic or otherwise, are only there when you choose to look at them, and there is no particular incentive to check them or to carry out the tasks they contain. We might glance at a list of things to do, but somehow the thought of necessary action or annoying tasks makes us want to leave them for later. The images on the journey system, however, are so colourful and interesting that the weary response simply doesn't kick in. As we will see later, the way we represent an image to ourselves (in terms of such things as colour, size and placement) makes a huge difference in how we emotionally respond to it, and somehow the naturally amusing and rich images of the loci system make those tasks more immediate and appealing. Also, the mental journey unavoidably pops up at a moment's notice, and perhaps not wanting to find I've forgotten anything over time makes me not only conjure it up frequently, but also want to carry out the tasks symbolized rather than have them hanging around down the other end of the street where they might get left. It's very effective, as long as you keep those images dramatic and interesting.

It is a shame that mnemonics are not taught in schools. The Renaissance replaced the love of the imaginary with a love of reason, and the art of memory, which had become associated too often with magic, began to die out. Later, during the Victorian period, science and information became paramount, and education became about rote learning and unimaginative repetition. As important as these shifts were towards embracing reason over superstition, they have meant we now have to rediscover memory techniques for ourselves. There is also a notion held by many teachers that education should be about understanding and reasoning rather than memorization, and that the latter is a poor substitute for the former. While that may be true when viewed from some angles, it does not take into account the fact that for a student the ability to memorize information is of essential importance, and the majority of students seem to value it at least as importantly as what might be seen as the 'higher' faculties. Especially in the case of younger children, learning such systems can clearly be an enormous confidence-booster and can make preparation for tests much more enjoyable.

PART FOUR

Tricks of the Mind

HYPNOSIS And SUGGESTIBILITY

HYPNOSIS AND SUGGESTIBILITY

During the summer holidays after my first year at Bristol University, I bought a bottle of liquid latex from a stationer's in Croydon to take with me back to the halls of residence where I lived during the academic part of the year. The rubber solution was to be used as an aid for painting: I was a great fan of Scarfe and Steadman at the time, both of whom, I heard, sometimes used latex as a liquid masking device. (Paint latex on and allow to dry, spray ink over a larger section of the canvas, then peel the latex off. *Voilà* – a non-inked area whose shape, size and position corresponds exactly to the just-peeled-off latex.) The bottle of latex sat for some time in my cupboard, and slowly the desire to use it for creative artistic activities was overcome by a hankering to abuse it in a non-sexual way.

One morning I applied a little to the underside of my left eye, and was much pleased with the resulting effect of swollen skin once it had dried. I went thus down to the communal breakfast to see if I could provoke a reaction. A few people did ask what I had done to my eye. I explained that it was a bit sore, but that I had no idea why. I kept the latex on all day and attended lectures and tutorials. The odd and slightly concerned looks made the day more interesting, and I owned up to no-one.

The next morning, then, it was only natural to apply a little more, as if the infection had somehow got worse. Anticipating this development, I had bought some make-up the day before, and with this was able to simulate bruising quite successfully. The result now was quite a deformity, and out I went into the world again to provoke some alarm at my condition. Over the next couple of days I continued the act in this way. Friends and acquaintances were insistent that I seek medical attention, none more so than the chap upstairs whose name time and embarrassment have caused me to forget. As much as I perversely delighted in the attention, I also felt a little embarrassed at their concern, and realized that to own up to the deceit would understandably annoy them. So within a few days I was stuck with having to continue the charade.

After a little less than a week, even though I was removing the latex every night, the solution was beginning to irritate my eye. Struck by the irony of developing a real eye complaint through this nonsense, I decided to apply less latex and wear an eye-patch instead. I still remember the very mixed expression of the girl in Boots on Whiteladies Road as I went in with one quarter of my face horrendously deformed to ask if she stocked any eye-patches. I had also, by this point, developed a quite convincing twitch in the eye which quite added to the overall effect.*

One person to whom I had had to own up was Debbie, one of my dance partners at the time. We were, for reasons that now seem

*Not to be mistaken for the *other* twitching thing I was starting to develop, namely a tiny and rapid nod of the head. The latter came from getting used to creating a compliant state in people – i.e., nodding to get them to agree with me – which soon began to appear of its own accord during times of general nervous energy. Unfortunately, that means it pops up while I'm doing things like performing or doing interviews. I don't think I've ever sported *both* twitches at the same time, which would have been amusing (although possibly frightening to the young or impressionable).

foreign and obscure, top of the Cha-cha 'A' team in the university Ballroom Dancing Society, and we would proudly swing our booties to strict-tempo classics at student competitions across God's clean England. Clearly she had to know the truth behind my 'infection' as she had the unenviable task of spot turning, underarm turning and New Yorkering in very close proximity to what appeared to be a heavily diseased face. On one memorable night we were rehearsing our sexless and grotesque routine on the first floor of the Students' Union and a chap came over and asked if he could have a look under my eye-patch. Debbie was amused but good enough not to say anything. This prompted an exposing of the eye, followed by an offer of a lift from this guy to take me down to the eye hospital. I thanked him for his concern but said (as had become my story) that I didn't trust doctors. The chap replied that he was in fact an eye surgeon and insisted that I go with him immediately to have it seen to. Debbie, who was enjoying a mid-cha-cha-cha refreshment at the time, laughed involuntarily at this development and snorted soft drink from her dancer's nostrils. He spun round to look at her and said, with some anger, 'I don't know why you're laughing; this guy is probably going to need plastic surgery.' At this point, Debbie excused herself and ran to the toilet, crying tears a bystander might have mistaken for concern.

I owned up to the doctor, as there was no avoiding the matter. Doing so was fairly excruciating. By now fully ashamed of myself, I allowed the apparent infection to die out over the next few days, and a little while later told people that it had been a sham. The guy upstairs who had shown unusual concern for my welfare admitted that his reaction had been driven primarily by guilt: he had been brewing beer in the communal baths and had feared that the lingering fumes had done some damage.

I barely need the benefit of hindsight to see that this was a sustained, pathetic and childish play for attention, and while a secret part of me remains undeniably pleased that I did it, the outside part finds it quite torturous to think back on. I mention it only because transparently insecure ploys of this sort were clearly signs of a desire to perform, and they led organically into the equally diaphanous practice of getting myself known as a hypnotist around the student community. Please, don't for a moment imagine that there was anything cool about me at the time. I wore violently ill-coloured clothes that mismatched to a degree seen only in the quieter but equally unfathomable jacket/trouser combinations of professional academics. I was no stranger to purple and green boots and a floral shirt, bowtie *and* braces, oblivious to how objectionable I must have been. And to polish it all off, happy to talk to anyone about God.

From time to time I would have friends of friends come round to get hypnotized. I had borrowed whatever books I could from the library, and bought a few from one of those evil alternative bookshops my pastors had warned me about. I had an induction script that lasted about forty minutes, which I would use to lull my subjects into a trance as they slumped in the 1970s orange and brown comfy chair that was the focal point of my student room. Perhaps, on reflection, it was the feng-shui that brought it all together. I'm sure it wasn't my natural charisma. Once I felt they were suitably hypnotized, I would then tentatively suggest that perhaps an arm was feeling lighter or a foot was too heavy to lift. If such things seemed to work, I would be delighted, and then slowly awaken them. As my confidence grew, I learned to shorten the induction and try more interesting tests, and would finish the session by implanting the suggestion that if they came back on another occasion I would be able to place them back into a profound trance simply by clicking my fingers and telling them to 'sleep'.

A formative moment arose one evening when someone came for a session whom I believed I had hypnotized before and left with this suggestion. As it turned out he had visited before, but we'd only spoken about hypnosis, not tried it. However, thinking he was primed to respond to my cue, I sat him down and told him to 'Sleep!', clicking my fingers in front of his face. He immediately closed his eyes, lolled his head and drifted off into a trance. My realization, after the session, that this was the first time I had hypnotized him was very confusing: how could he have responded to the suggestion if I had not given it to him? I realized that day that hypnosis works not because of a carefully worded magical script from a self-help book, but because the subject *believes* the process is effective. Over time I have refined this understanding, but the revelation was an important one.

A BRIEF HISTORY

The first real hypnotist, Franz Anton Mesmer (from whom we of course get the modern word *Frank*), arrived in Paris in 1778. Mesmer believed there was a quasi-magnetic fluid that flowed through our bodies and indeed the whole universe, and that interrupting the flow of this energy caused the various ailments from which we suffer. We would do well to keep this man in mind when we listen to certain of our friends talking seriously about 'chi energy' or psychic healing. Firstly with magnets, and then with his hands, he would cure his patients by making magical passes over their bodies to realign this mystical force.

Mesmer's methods were fantastically theatrical. He is reported to have seated his patients around a tub of water and iron-filings, their knees pressed together to allow the magnetic 'fluid' to flow between them. Long rods would protrude from the bath, and these would be used to heal afflicted areas of the body. Music would play, while attractive assistants provided a highly tactile service that generally induced the ladies to suffer convulsions. Mesmer would only then appear in a purple robe carrying a huge magnetic staff; he would calm them by moving the end of the rod against their faces, stomachs and breasts. (That is what the modern NHS should be petitioned to fund, not nonsenses like homoeopathy. Prince Charles, take note.) These outrageous displays seemed to encourage what in modern terms would be seen as a psychosomatic release of suppressed sexual tension, and certainly Mesmer seemed to encourage noisy or violent responses to his strange passes. Eventually, two Royal Commissions discredited Mesmer's methods and attributed any strange phenomena to his patients' imaginations rather than an invisible cosmic fluid. Though they might just have been disappointed that they didn't get their breasts touched.

However, interest in Mesmer and his followers spread, and it was John Elliotson (1791–1868) who led the animal magnetism movement here in Britain, combining it with his interest in phrenology (the now discredited study of the bumps on the skull to determine character). Naturally, the medical profession was extremely set against it, although one John Esdaile, a surgeon stationed in East India in the 1840s, shortly before chemical anaesthetic was made widely available, reported that he had carried out some three hundred operations using the 'mesmeric sleep'. In 1819, a Portuguese priest, the Abbé José Custudio di Faria, was the first practitioner to separate the effects of mesmerism from the notion of magnetic influence. Di Faria asked his patients to close their eyes and enter a sleep state without the use of magnetism or Mesmer's histrionics, and noted that his influence was due to suggestion rather than magical control.

The term 'hypnotism', please bear with me, was first coined by James Braid, a Manchester surgeon, in 1841. He saw the trance state as one of nervous sleep and named it after 'Hypnos', the Greek god of pretending to have sex with a mop on stage. Braid had his patients fix their gaze on a bright light and was able to achieve results without any quasi-epileptic symptoms or even the paranormal side-effects that had begun to be claimed by the magnetists. Indeed, at this time the new wave of knowledge regarding such things as electricity and the human nervous system rendered old-fashioned magnetism laughable to serious scientists, and the respectable community lost interest in it.

Most influentially after Braid came the French neurologist Jean-Martin Charcot. He regarded hypnosis and 'hysteria' (epilepsy) as aspects of the same underlying neuropathological condition. His subjects were all female epileptics, and it has been suggested that this alignment of early hypnotic practice with the release of what we now see as epileptic symptoms, even from Mesmer's time, seems to be responsible for the persistence of many modern-day classic hypnotic phenomena. The classic 'tests' for suggestibility used in clinical research into hypnosis, which involve trance states and different forms of catalepsy, may be a perverse throwback to the days of epileptic 'demonstrations'. It's a chilling thought.

Charcot's rival was Hippolyte Bernheim (1837–1919) at the University of Nancy, who moved hypnosis away from set procedures with hysterics and promoted verbal suggestion and work with other ailments. Probably known unfairly at school as 'Hippo the Nancy Boy', his became the preferred approach, and Nancy became a popular therapeutic centre. However, by the turn of the twentieth century interest in hypnotism was dwindling in Europe, and that was followed by a decline in America and Britain. Hypnotherapists found patients harder to hypnotize, and other therapeutic methods became prevalent. A while later, Freud's works on psychoanalysis became popular and hypnosis was all but forgotten as a serious therapeutic tool. It was only with the later discovery of huge X-ray glasses that allowed the subject to see the audience in the nuddy that serious clinicians became interested again in the field.

Many claim that the American Milton H. Erickson (1901–80) is the father of modern hypnotherapy, and from the 1920s he worked to encourage a 'permissive' approach to therapy: the commanding 'you will' language of the hypnotist shifted to a new 'you can'. Perhaps as patients grew more educated than they were in hypnotism's heyday, the stern, flamboyant image of the hypnotist, still shaped by the figure of Mesmer, grew less appropriate. And perhaps the self-obsession of the modern American, let alone the modern Californian, where the industry was to eventually take off, necessitated a more patient- (or 'client'-) centred approach. Erickson suffered from polio throughout his life, but used auto-hypnosis, or self-hypnosis, to control the severe pain he had to endure. He was unorthodox, famous for his indirect methods and clever ways of handling resistance, and he felt there were no bad subjects, only inflexible hypnotists.

Anyone who develops an interest in modern hypnotic techniques soon sees that Erickson is revered with a sense of the magician in a way that Mesmer would have encouraged for himself. He certainly had the same penchant for purple clothes as his predecessor. Reading about Erickson and his miraculous successes through his principal devotees, one sees that the magical reputation survives primarily due to the telling and re-telling of remarkable anecdotes. The following is randomly taken from a website on Ericksonian therapy, and is an anecdote (as given on the site) regarding anecdotes (told by Erickson to the boy) which go back to an anecdote that would have been written by Erickson or told about him at some point. It gives a flavour both of Erickson's style and the respect he provokes from his followers.

> *Often, Erickson didn't use a formal trace* [sic] *induction. Instead he talk* [sic] *stories that has* [sic] *a deeper meaning. Sometimes that meaning was clear, most times it was not. At least not to the person's conscious mind. For example, a twelve-year-old boy was brought in to see Erickson about bedwetting. Erickson dismissed his parents and began talking to the boy about other topics, avoiding a direct discussion about bedwetting altogether. Upon learning that the boy played baseball and his brother football, Erickson elaborated on the fine muscle coordination it takes to play baseball, compared to the uncoordinated muscle skills used in football. The boy listened raptly as Erickson described in fine detail all the muscle adjustments his body automatically makes in order to position him underneath the ball and catch it: the glove has to be opened at just the right moment and clamped down again at just the right moment. When transferring the ball to another hand, the same kind of fine muscle control is needed. Then, when throwing the ball to the infield, if one lets go too soon, it doesn't go where one wants it to go. Likewise letting go too late leads to an undesired outcome and consequently to frustration. Erickson explained that letting go just at the right time gets it to go where one wants it to go, and that constitutes success in baseball. Therapy with this young man consisted of four sessions that included talks about other sports, boy scouts, and muscles.* But bedwetting was not discussed, and 'formal hypnosis' was not conducted. The boy's bedwetting disappeared soon thereafter.*

*Hmm.

It is an odd tale that vaguely makes me want to go to the toilet, and equally as fascinating as another I read of a boy with the same affliction treated by Erickson. This other boy, if I remember correctly, was approaching his tenth birthday and Erickson again made no attempt to 'correct' his behaviour. Instead, he told the parents to stop insisting their child wear a 'bedwetter' placard to school and to cease punishing their son. However, as he left, he turned to the family and said, 'Of course he wets the bed; he's just a baby nine-year-old. I'm sure a big grown-up ten-year-old wouldn't do that.' The result was that the child stopped wetting the bed on his tenth birthday, the idea being that he wanted to be seen as a grown-up. Another great story, and there are many hundreds like this to capture the imagination of one interested in the power of communication.

There is a dilemma here which typifies much post-Erickson hypnosis and its Frankenstein grandchild, neuro-linguistic programming, or NLP. The 'permissive' approach encourages the telling of anecdotes to the client which, though they may be fictitious, indirectly suggest a therapeutic change. Certainly this would seem to be a common-sense tool where one might wish a person to see a difficult situation in a more helpful light. However, the methods by which the techniques of Ericksonian hypnotherapy and NLP are actually taught to student practitioners tend to reflect the methods employed in the therapy itself. For example, one such method for teaching which is widely used is that of exactly this sort of anecdote-telling, and much of the evidence of the efficacy of Ericksonian hypnotic techniques (and NLP) comes from these anecdotes rather than from any actual testing or documented case histories. Many verbatim transcripts are given of 'sessions', but these tend to be far less juicy than the tales told of, and by, the people responsible. In fact, in NLP, the subject of testing is generally mocked (with the amused disregard for fact shared by true believers of any kind). So there is an interesting conundrum: anecdotes are told about the miraculous changes created by the founders of these schools with little importance paid to how accurate the facts are in order that they might inspire the student to approach his work with an attitude of creativity, of 'anything is possible', and to achieve the artistic level of competence of the people he hears unfounded stories about. The shining stars of the field are tagged with another buzzword, 'genius', and become the sum of their anecdotes.

In these approaches, which sprang from or were popularized by the sixties mentality of 'change your head, don't change the world', it does become hard to separate fact from fiction. It has also been shown that Erickson didn't always report his clinical work accurately, and some have questioned how effective some of his thinking seems to be. For example, Erickson's way of encouraging his daughter to 'get over' orthodontic treatment she underwent was to say to her, 'That mouthful of hardware that you've got in your mouth is miserably uncomfortable and it's going to be a deuce of a job to get used to it.' Displaying some doubt about Erickson's claims for himself, the scientist McCue wrote, 'The authors [Erickson and Rossi, 1980] contend that the first half of the sentence acknowledges the daughter's discomfort and the second half, beginning with "and", "is a suggestion that she will 'get used to it' and not let it bother her". To the present writer, however, the sentence implies that the recipient of the hardware will have considerable difficulty in getting used to it.'

Erickson was clearly a fascinating, charismatic and effective individual who richly impressed the people who wrote about him. Tales will always abound about such people. They are always fun or inspiring to read. Therapeutic approaches are very hard, though by no means impossible, to subject to any real testing, and it remains for the wave of Ericksonian practitioners to prove the worth of his ideas by recreating his magic. Sadly, most therapists tend to be strangers to charisma, so I suspect that, regardless of what magic touch Milton really had, his real legacy has been merely to facilitate a shift of attention among many therapists from 'hypnosis' per se into 'heightened communication' – something apotheosized by the world of neuro-linguistic programming, which we will look at a little later.

WHAT IS HYPNOSIS?

When a man who bills himself as a hypnotist makes grown men dance around or impersonate Elvis on stage, we call his subjects 'hypnotized'. When cult members are made to act against their best interests, even to the point of suicide, we might refer to them as 'hypnotized'. Yet paradoxically we are told that we cannot be hypnotized to do anything against our will. We could also use the same word to describe someone being talked into hallucinating, or undergoing surgery without anaesthetic. You might think a participant on my show who is acting unusually is under some sort of 'hypnosis'; certainly I am often described as a 'hypnotist' by journalists. Business seminars sometimes teach 'hypnotism' or 'hypnotic language patterns' to their delegates to improve their influential power, and internet seduction courses offer similar promises to lonely males (as far as I'm aware). Characters in films are induced by sinister characters to commit crimes – they are 'hypnotized'. In February 2005 the *Los Angeles Times* reported that on the streets Russian gypsy 'hypnotists' were making people hand over their belongings without question. We also refer to recordings of relaxing music mixed with empowering suggestions as 'hypnosis tapes', and we might talk of being 'hypnotized' by dreamy music or a candle-lit church service. Some people tell me they don't 'believe in' hypnosis; others seem to use the word to describe almost anything.

Is there one type of hypnosis that is real, and other cases where the word is just used metaphorically? How can listening to a relaxation tape and being made to commit a crime be the same thing? Does hypnosis require a 'trance' state? If someone is put into a special trance and told to unconsciously carry out something when they awake, can that be the same as suggestions given in a normal waking state?

There are currently two major clinical schools of thought with regard to what hypnosis is. The first promotes it as a 'special state'. Paramount to the logic of this school of thought is the idea that the hypnotized person is able to achieve things a non-hypnotized person cannot. If it can be shown that there is nothing special at all about hypnosis, then this line of thinking becomes redundant. Pitched against these 'state' theorists are the 'non-state' theorists who argue that in fact the various phenomena of hypnosis can be explained quite happily without thinking of 'trances' or 'hypnosis' as meaning anything special or peculiar or akin to a special state of mind. Their thesis would fall if the 'state' theorists could prove that something unique happens to the person who is hypnotized. Occasionally, one reads in the paper that hypnosis has been 'proved' to be such and such, or that a subject hooked up to an EEG machine shows this or that brain activity when in a trance, but these are largely press releases from the 'state' theorists who have an inherently more media-friendly view of the field. Such articles are invariably a little sensational and, despite them, the 'non-state' theory is becoming the received way of understanding what hypnosis is. And of course, we must remember that it is largely up to the 'state' theorists to prove their point, not the 'non-state' guys to try to prove a negative.

It may seem odd to think that all the bizarre phenomena we might associate with hypnosis can be explained in normal, non-hypnotic terms. Don't people suddenly give up smoking? Act like lunatics on stage? Enjoy eating onions for our entertainment? Even undergo surgical operations quite painlessly? The key to understanding how this might be is first to forget the idea that there is any one special thing called 'hypnosis'. I tend to see it like 'magic', in the sense of conjuring. We know magic isn't real: it just boils down to a diverse set of techniques expertly employed by a skilled and charming entertainer with a goatee. He may palm cards, use gaffs and duplicates, employ special cabinets and secret twins, or execute a cover-pass while tabling the deck and keep a break with the third phalange of his left pinkie. Methods might be fascinating, simple or stupid, but the effect is the thing. However, we use the term 'magic' to describe the end result. The 'magic' is the final effect when all those methods are combined to form a particular type of performance. The word is an easy way of describing the mixture of methods and techniques the performer employs ('he does magic'), and also gives the spectator a word to describe her own experience of the performance, which might range from puzzlement to utter transportation ('it was magic'). The word is useful because we understand by it that a certain thing has taken place which breaks down into different mundane components, but the end result is what matters.

I think it is rather the same with hypnosis. The hypnotist uses certain methods, or the subject shows certain behaviours, which when put together create an overall effect we can label as 'hypnosis'. We can comfortably call it that without needing a single definition of what is really going on. Also, in the same way that a magician might secretly apply 'magical' methods or trickery *outside* a performance environment to bring about some desired result we wouldn't really think of as magic (clever shoplifting brought about through misdirection, for example – we've all done it), so too, seemingly, hypnotic techniques can be employed covertly in a way that might also make us question whether there is a better word to describe them in that context. 'Suggestive techniques', for example, could be a better term for what might be used in a situation where 'hypnosis' is apparently happening but the obvious trappings of trance and so on are absent. Equally, in the same way that magic is easier to recognize or define when one has a clear interaction between a magician and spectators, so too hypnosis becomes easiest to label as such when there is a person or agency (sometimes a recorded voice) playing the part of the hypnotist and another person in the role of subject.

So what actually does go on then? What is the nature of that interaction if it is not strictly 'hypnotic' in the same way a trick is not strictly 'magical'? The fascination with this question is one that has occupied me from when I first began using relaxation techniques on my fellow students. Whatever it was clearly relied on the expectation of my subject rather than any special powers I might have developed, but how might that lead to some of the phenomena I was producing? I was able to convince some highly susceptible friends of mine that I was invisible, to the point where I would have them freaking out at floating objects in their bedrooms. Surely no amount of mere expectation could create such an event?

There are real problems with being able to tell what actually happens. To return to our 'magic' analogy, imagine we are a race of aliens trying to work out what the experience of magic is. (Before certain factions of my fan-base get too excited, let me clarify that I don't believe there are real aliens trying to work this out. For a start, they're too busy impersonating our world leaders.) What would we have to go on? We could watch some magic ourselves, but a) it might not really do anything for us, and b) it would tell us only what our own experience is. We could run tests where we interview people who have witnessed magic tricks and try to find out what it was like. Certainly people say 'it was magic' and 'he did some magic on me' in the same way they say, 'I was hypnotized' and 'he hypnotized me', so certainly this holds as an analogy. However, we would run into a few problems. Firstly, the range of responses to a trick might be enormous. Some people might believe it was real magic; others might not believe it was real 'magic' as such, but might believe that the magician possesses an extraordinary psychological or even psychic skill. Some might find it an irritating puzzle; others might have seen right through it but feel it would be rude to say so. What one might find quite commonly, though, would be the experience of people being happy to play along 'as if' it were magic, to the point where they are happy to use the word 'magic' in describing it. Certainly they wouldn't want to upset the magician by telling him they didn't think the trick was real: that would be spoiling the game. It would seem a very tricky thing to investigate (pun initially not intended then noticed on later reviewing and intentionally kept, but only after insertion of this parenthesized clarification).

Similarly with hypnosis, it is very hard to tell what a subject's experience consists of. On stage, a common finale is for the hypnotist to make himself invisible (as I've mentioned I did with my friends) and then articulate puppets to elicit strong reactions from the punters on stage. This is often termed a 'negative hallucination', where the subject is instructed *not* to see something that *is* there, instead of vice versa. It obviously does not entail really seeing *through* anything or anyone, but it is presumed that the subject might hallucinate what he knows is behind the 'invisible' object to fill in the blank he imagines. Generally this good-natured fun can provide a fascinating end to an enjoyable and intelligent show, and can be every bit as entertaining as the one where the woman kissed the vibrator thinking it was Brad Pitt.

I also used to finish with the invisibility suggestion, but as I would generally follow the performances with an informal chat about it all, I would always ask the subjects what they had actually experienced.

Out of the, say, ten or so subjects who were given the suggestion, the responses might break down in the following way. Two had obviously been able to see me and had been openly separated from the rest of the group. Two or three would swear that the puppet and chair were moving all on their own and that they could not see me, even though they may have guessed I was somehow remotely responsible for the chaos that ensued. The remaining five or six would generally say they were aware I was there moving the objects, but that something in them would keep trying to blank me out, and they could only act *as if* I were invisible.

This is a very interesting state of affairs. It begs the next question: is there a qualitative difference between what happened to the people who knew I was there but made themselves ignore me and those who said they really didn't see me? The former case sounds as if the subject was concerned with complying with my requests, albeit at a very immediate gut level, due perhaps to a certain pressure to conform. This 'compliance' explanation is an important one. It is not the same as consciously 'faked' behaviour, but neither is it a special product of a real trance. The case where I was apparently not seen at all seems to suggest a genuine negative hallucination. But how do we know that the latter group didn't see me? Only because they testified so. They were being given every chance to 'own up', but clearly we can read their answer as simply more compliance. If you are going to fully enter into an imaginative game where you really try to experience the hypnotist as invisible, and then later the hypnotist asks you what you experienced, is it not reasonable to expect that one of the following situations might then occur?

1. The subject is a little embarrassed at the idea of owning up to not having quite experienced what was being asked for, and prefers to insist that it was real.

2. The subject is prone to convincing herself of all sorts of things in everyday life as very suggestible people tend to do, and really did convince herself at the time that it was entirely real. This is preferable for her to the thought that she was freaking out on stage for no good reason.
3. The subject has entered into the hypnotic experience with enthusiasm and has enjoyed being a star of the show. Now she has a chance to outshine the others by demonstrating that she was indeed the most successful on stage: she *really* experienced it, while most of the others did not.

Now, the moment we talk about compliance, or less-than-honest testimonies, it sounds as if the subjects are merely faking. This does not have to be the case. There is a wide range of possible experiences that can explain the behaviour of the subject on stage (or in the laboratory) which may or may not involve simple faking:

1. Firstly, there is the case where the subject is indeed faking, and is being encouraged to fake by the hypnotist. In many commercial or cabaret shows, the hypnotist is interested only in putting on an entertaining evening. The professional will happily whisper to a participant to 'play along' rather than have the show fail. Paul McKenna tells the true (I hope) story about a successful hypnotist (you know who you are) who was having problems one night with his subjects. To remedy the situation, he whispered off-mic to the most extrovert guy on stage, 'Play along and I'll give you fifty quid after the show.' The subject decided to act the part for the cash, and soon became a spectacular fool on stage, accepting anything the hypnotist said and lifting the show immensely. At the end of the act, the hypnotist sent him back to his seat, then pretended to re-hypnotize him

as he sat back with his friends. He clicked his fingers and the stooge dutifully acted as if he had fallen asleep. 'When you wake up,' the entertainer declared into the stage mic, 'you will believe that I owe you fifty pounds. And the more your friends tell you I don't, the more annoyed and insistent you'll become that I do! Wakey wakey . . .' Just love that story.

2. The subject is faking, but only because he feels too embarrassed to call a halt to his performance. In a full theatrical show, or where the hypnotist is rather intimidating and deals unpleasantly with those who 'fail' to fall under his spell, it is very difficult to put your hand up and say, 'Actually, you know what? It's not working on me.' This is just the result of social pressure, and happens quite a lot.
3. The subject is really trying to experience the suggestions as real and is helping the process along by doing his best not to 'block' them and really 'going for it'. In effect he is still acting them out, and playing the part of the good subject, but he will be more confused as to whether he was hypnotized or not. More often than not he will imagine that he must have been under the hypnotist's power, as the show certainly swept him along. Classically, he will say that he 'could have stopped at any moment'. This third option is, I think, quite a common experience.
4. The subject is again very happy to help the process along by acting out the suggestions regardless of any strange compulsion to do so, but at the same time is the sort of person who can easily 'forget himself' and seize the permission granted by the hypnotic demonstration to act outrageously. Perhaps this is helped also by being the sort of person who is naturally effusive and who tends to accept unquestioningly what he is told by authority figures or people she has a strong rapport with. Afterwards, it is more comfortable for him to put his actions

> down to an amazing experience he can't explain, credit the hypnotist fully and believe he was in a special state. Most probably he will believe the hypnotist has his perceived ability anyway, so it's an easy step to take.

Whether or not this is all there is to hypnosis, it is certainly possible to explain what happens in ordinary terms without recourse to the idea of a 'special state'.

It is clearly remarkably difficult to defy the instructions of an authority figure. My favourites amongst you chose to watch *The Heist* and will have seen the re-enactment of Stanley Milgram's famous obedience experiment of the 1960s. In both the original and our version,* the subject comes to the laboratory and meets a scientist and a middle-aged confederate of the scientist who is posing as another subject. Each subject chooses his role as either 'teacher' or 'learner' in a rigged draw, and the confederate becomes the 'learner'. The unsuspecting teacher then watches the bogus learner get strapped to electrodes designed to give electric shocks. The learner, according to plan, informs the scientist that he has some heart trouble. The teacher is then taken into another room and sat in front of a terrifying machine that can apparently deliver shocks to the learner from a harmless 15 volts to a deadly 450 volts in 15-volt increments. Labels underneath the voltages describe the shocks as ranging from 'Slight Shock' to 'Danger: Severe Shock', and then to a sinister 'XXX'. The teacher then asks memory questions to the learner through a microphone and has to shock the learner each time he gives a wrong answer. The shock is to increase by 15 volts with each incorrect response.

In reality, of course, the learner-confederate receives no shocks

*Ours was kept very similar to the original as seen in the 1963 footage. Even the electrocution machine we used was a replica of Milgram's, and now sits in my office near all my awards.

at all. However, in some versions of the test, taped screams and refusals to carry on are played from the other room in response to the supposed punishments. That is, until the learner suddenly becomes silent, and the highest shocks are then delivered to a horrible unresponsiveness from the other room.

Milgram's test, familiar to any psychology A level student, was designed to see how many people would continue administering electrical doses to the point where they were clearly lethal *just because the scientist was insisting that they continue*. Psychologists were asked to predict the results, and they guessed that one-tenth of 1 per cent of subjects would continue with the experiment to this point. The extraordinary result, which has been sustained through re-creations of the test, is that around 60 per cent of people will go as far as to deliver the lethal shock. Not, that is, without much sweating or trembling and frequent complaints to the scientist, but still they carry on.*

*The experiment quickly came under attack from armchair moralizers and the psychology profession who were proved wrong in their predictions. Most people who know a bit about the Milgram experiment believe that the subjects suffered terrible trauma as a result of the experiment and that some even killed themselves. This is utterly untrue. There were follow-up questionnaires sent out to the participants after the experiment – some sent out as long as a year afterwards. Only about 1 per cent expressed remorse at taking part. The overwhelming response to taking part was one of fascination with the experiment, and many subjects expressed a readiness to take part in it again, posing as either teacher or learner. So, while the experiment raised interesting questions about experimental ethics, the terrible reputation it now seems to have is really unwarranted. And anyone who watches the footage will see how sensitively the participants are dealt with.

Very often I get criticized for seeming recklessness with subjects on my shows. In fact it's very important to me that they enjoy themselves immensely and finish with a very positive experience of the process. That level of attention is not always shown in the show itself, as it can detract from the drama or pacing of the show. In the *Zombie* sequence, for example, I made sure the guy involved would be fine with the process through an elaborate set-up that didn't compromise his status as a naïve subject but which did make sure he'd be more than strong enough to deal with what was in store for him. On reflection, I think it would have been worthwhile including that in the show to illustrate the lengths we went to.

On the other hand, I have known participants involved in very popular 'reality' shows who have suffered breakdowns as a result of their experiences. A friend of mine who took part in one was told by a cameraman that the contest he was involved in was rigged from the start, and later found out from a friend at BT that the production company had bought a block of 80,000 votes to rig the viewers' final phone vote. Combined with how disgustingly he felt that he and others were treated on the show, which involved being told how they should behave to conform to a 'type' the show wished to cast them as, this 'reality' experience left him in tears for a week.

That I find disgusting.

For an authoritative entertainer or clinician to have people carry out harmless activities just by telling them to seems pretty straightforward in comparison.

SEEMINGLY UNIQUE HYPNOTIC PHENOMENA

Coming to understand the hypnotic experience on and off the stage in terms of quite ordinary 'task motivators' such as focused attention, role-playing, imagination, response expectancy, social conformity, compliance, belief in the hypnotist, response to charisma, relaxation, rapport, suggestion and the whispered promise of cash rewards helps enormously in learning how to understand the subject without needing to talk about bogus trances and so on. But perhaps you are unsure how, if hypnosis isn't a special altered state, people can undergo painless operations, or magically give up smoking, or hysterically eat onions thinking they're apples.

Clinicians are able to answer these questions by setting up tests where successfully hypnotized people are compared to non-hypnotized but otherwise motivated people, to see if there is a difference in their ability to achieve the same phenomena. If the non-hypnotized group are still able to achieve the same feats, then clearly those feats are not uniquely hypnotic, and are no evidence for hypnosis being some special state. This comparison of hypnosis with other task motivators (such as when the subjects are told that they can easily achieve a phenomenon if they really make an effort) tends to yield the result that both hypnotized and merely motivated people are equally successful.

A memorable example for me of this occurred during one of our rehearsals for *The Heist*, when my writing partner Andy Nyman and I were having this very discussion, and the subject of eating onions on stage came up. If you are not entirely familiar with this stunt, the 'hypnotized' subject is given an onion and told that upon awakening he will believe it to be a delicious apple and start eating it enthusiastically. It's a revolting sight, and seems to be proof of the power of hypnosis, at least on stage. Andy rightly said, 'I bet I can just eat one,' and went and grabbed a decent-sized onion from my fridge. (Larger onions tend to be used by stage performers for this stunt, and as many of you will know, they tend to be milder than the smaller ones.) He brought it back to my living room and took a few huge bites out of it without any complaints. Aside from improving his breath considerably, this amusing moment was seeming proof (presuming that Andy does not have an insensitivity to onion) that the stunt can be easily achieved without hypnosis. All it took was a 'task motivator', namely the desire to prove a point, for it to be perfectly achievable.

One of our foremost experts on hypnosis, Graham Wagstaff, has extensively reviewed research into hypnosis and conducted much himself, convincingly concluding that it is unnecessary to think of hypnosis as a special state responsible for any of these phenomena. His important book *Hypnosis: Compliance and Belief* seems finally to answer the centuries of sensationalism surrounding the field in a sensible and far more interesting way. He examined the nature of compliance both during the hypnotic session and afterwards, when subjects describe their experiences, and also the nature of some subjects' genuine belief that they had indeed been hypnotized.

But what of those feats that seem really hard to explain without seeing hypnosis as 'special'? I shall very briefly touch upon a couple of areas you might think don't sit comfortably with this behavioural approach to understanding the field. The result of this understanding, I think, is to realize some fascinating aspects of being human.

Painless Surgery

Hypnotic analgesia – the control of pain through hypnosis – can offer perhaps the most visceral and dramatic demonstration of the seeming power of the hypnotist. A subject pushes a needle through the back of his hand; a woman gives birth without drugs or, apparently, stress; an operation is carried out on a wide-awake patient who is able to watch the surgery taking place. Such things seem not only hugely impressive but also important enough that we wonder why, for example, hypnosis is not used more often in surgery. The immediate answer to the last point is, of course, that it can only be used on people who are hypnotically responsive enough to have any use for it, so probably it will only be appropriate for a few people. Also, this small number of people may be the same small proportion of the population who have a very good capacity to control pain anyway.

As Wagstaff points out in his book, the effects of hypnotic analgesia cannot be separated from the simple effects of relaxation, belief and distraction on pain. By simply relaxing comfortably (sometimes through familiarity with the situation), believing that a process won't be painful, or being distracted in the right way, we notice only a small percentage of the pain we would experience if we were dreading, expecting or paying attention to it. Pain is famously exaggerated by worry and drastically reduced by the placebo effect, a fascinating area I will inflict upon you in a later chapter. So while these techniques are undoubtedly effective without calling upon compliance as an explanation, they are not uniquely hypnotic either.

When considering the case of surgery under hypnosis, there is an important point to be appreciated. The skin is the most sensitive area of the body, whereas the internal organs and tissues tend to be insensitive to pain. While we may be sensitive to the pulling and stretching of our insides, we can be cut almost anywhere inside and feel little or nothing. So again, operations may be rendered painless through no more than the quite normal effects of relaxation and suggestion to minimize the pain of skin incision. Wagstaff refers to a 1974 medical paper which stated that modern surgeons usually administer a general anaesthetic over a local anaesthetic only to alleviate fear and anxiety rather than because it is necessary. A surprising fact, and when this understanding is coupled with the fact that very often such 'hypnotic' operations do actually still use anaesthetic on the skin, the whole notion of a 'special state' controlling pain, let alone the entire practice of 'hypnotic surgery', starts to seem a little redundant.

Hallucinations

One of the most memorable sequences from the hypnotism show I saw as a student involved the participants hallucinating an enormous elephant walking into the room and up onto the stage. Once they had all stroked it and described it, they were told to lean against it. At the hypnotist's command, the animal 'disappeared', and several of the subjects tumbled to the floor.

I tried a similar thing one afternoon, when I was talking to the two entertainment managers at one of the halls of residence in Bristol. One of them, Gavin, did seem rather a responsive type, so I offered to try a couple of things with them both to see if we'd have any success. As I thought, this one chap was very susceptible, and after a few preliminary routines to amplify his responsiveness, I told him that he would take us back to his room and find a rhinoceros in there when he opened the door. He awoke. We chatted for a while, then he suggested adjourning to his room for a cup of tea. The three of us (I'm not embarrassed to say that two of us were smirking like schoolchildren) headed through fire doors, along beige hallways and past noticeboards and pay-phones and eventually reached his door. He found his key, and politely ushered us in first. 'No no, after *you*,' I insisted, and he turned to step inside.

Gavin half entered the room, froze for two beats, then quickly stepped back out and closed the door without letting us see inside. He looked at both of us, then asked me if I'd mind if he had a quick chat with his colleague. I stepped aside and he whispered some worried words into the other chap's ear. The latter managed to disguise a laugh as a sort of sympathetic exclamation of disbelief – an incongruent display of guffawing, frowning and nodding seriously with no eye contact made. Gavin was clearly asking him for advice as to what to do, and after a little of this mumbled exchange his colleague turned and explained. 'Gavin has a rhino in his room,' he said; and now facing away from his friend, he broke into a grin with clear relief. Gavin looked a little embarrassed and opened the door to show me. The two of us peeked into the room. It yielded, of course, the regulation thin bed, orange curtains, orange chair covered in clothes, open wardrobe, ashtray, four books, film poster, kettle and juggling balls (very popular at the time), but definitely no rhinoceros. I can't say I wasn't a tiny bit relieved for a fleeting second.

'We have to get it out,' I heard from behind me. 'It'll break through my floor. Fucking shit.' Presumably Gavin was thinking ahead to his chances of election to president of the Students' Union, and he wasn't going to let a massive horned herbivore stand in his way. Getting the rhino out hadn't occurred to me, but it certainly sounded like fun. In fact, we encouraged him.

I suspect that if anyone had walked past as we all mucked in to squeeze the luckily rather docile mammal through the small doorway, we would have looked rather odd. Gavin's colleague was pushing at the enormous rump end, and Gavin was himself pulling and guiding it from the front. I helped from the side, laughing with the guy at the back, patting its imaginary thick skin and offering sarcastic words of encouragement, such as 'up your end, Gavin', 'it's coming' and 'the rhino is certainly making its way through the door'. Illogically, given the size of the doorway, it did eventually find its way through into the corridor, though Gavin was worried about the splintering of parts of the doorframe, which he seemed to perceive. We headed for the exit that would take us out of the building, Gavin paranoid that we would pass someone who would freak out or call security.

I'm unsure if we made our way down any stairs, but certainly we ended up in the car park. We did now pass a few people, who saw of course nothing but the three of us walking slowly with Gavin a little way ahead of the two of us. Memorably, Gavin was offering calming advice to anyone who looked over, such as, 'Don't ask! It's fine,' or 'No need to panic, it's all taken care of.' Sometimes he offered just a simple placatory 'I know, I know' with a roll of the eyes. This still constitutes one of the more vivid memories of my student days.

We took the rhinoceros over to the wheelie-bins area which, surrounded by high walls, sensibly offered partial concealment. I felt that we had probably had enough fun at this guy's expense, especially seeing as my main motive in demonstrating my skills was to secure a booking at the hall for my show. So I offered to deal safely with the animal by making it disappear. Gavin seemed incredulous, but I assured him it would work. After securing his agreement and assuring him that no harm would be done and all damage caused would be immediately reversed, I had him watch the animal while I threw out my arms in its direction, palms forward, and cried, 'Rhino, be gone!' The exhausted student watched as the animal turned to space-dust and disappeared – or however he imagined it. Gavin went over to inspect the empty air he now could see in its place. He was impressed.

There is no way of knowing what Gavin was *really* experiencing.

Was it all for real? Did he see a solid rhino as clearly as I can now see the computer screen or my (well deserved) *Arena* Man of the Year (Entertainment) award in front of me? Presumably he wasn't just straightforwardly play-acting, as one would have to search hard to find a motive for fakery. He was going to decide whether or not to book me for his students, so he would have had a vested interest in *not* pretending it was working if in fact it wasn't. The trouble is, it's extremely hard to tell. One could argue that he might have felt at some level he *should* play along, given that I was supposed to be the 'accomplished performer', but this would seem to be stretching things a little. On the one hand he did seem to really believe there was something there; on the other, his reactions were not always quite the authentic ones one might expect in such a situation. But who's to say? Was his comical readiness to take it outside into the car park, rather than just to call the hall offices in a panic, a sign that he was in part 'playing along with the scenario', even if he was doing so with full emotional and imaginative involvement? Probably the most effective way of finding out what he'd really experienced would have been to re-hypnotize him and have him go back through the experience, giving him full permission to describe honestly what he saw, as opposed to what he was communicating with his words and behaviour. Even this is not necessarily a sure-fire method, though.

On one occasion, after having played around with invisibility scenarios on stage, I found that a friend, Pete, picked up well on a suggestion not to see *himself*. It was just the two of us when we tried this; there was no pressure to play along as one might feel on stage. He could apparently look down and not see his own body, and reported that it was like viewing the room through a camera. He was intrigued by the experience, but again I suspect that although there was no obvious need for him to pretend it was working or in some way to impress me, he would not have wanted to see me waste my time and may indeed have been playing no more than an imaginative game to help provide some results. I think that if I had genuinely been unable to see myself and appeared to be viewing the world through such a camera lens, I would have found the experience absolutely extraordinary and made more of a fuss. Again, it's very hard to tell, and I could not trust his memory of the event now if I asked him.

While this suggests just imaginative role-playing, I think of a contrasting example with another friend, Dave (I limit my core group of friends to people with the dullest Anglo-Saxon names), who was very responsive to hypnosis and in particular to me making myself invisible. I met up with him after being out of the country for a year or so, and he told me that he had been walking through the centre of Bristol one day and a carrot had hit him on the side of the face. Presumably the airborne vegetable had been hurled surreally from a window, but interestingly he was convinced for a while that it had been done by the invisible me, as he had grown accustomed to my occasional gremlin activity. He thought I must be back in the country, that I had hypnotized him not to see me, and was mucking about. This incident seems to play against the imaginative compliance theory, and would suggest that his previous experiences with the invisibility suggestion had been convincing enough for him later to align this 'real' scenario with one of them. Again, though, it's ever so hard to tell. How serious was he really being when he said that he was convinced it was me?

With either positive or negative hallucinations, the central question is a semantic one: when the hypnotic subject says he 'sees' the target image, does he mean that he can imagine it vividly or that he really sees it as something indistinguishable from a real, solid object? I have no doubt that you can, with a bit of relaxed concentration, vividly picture Jonathan Ross stood in the room before you.

With a bit of imaginative 'entering into' the situation, I'm sure you could get up and walk around him, or even have him talk to you. However, unless you are a lunatic, there'd be no problem distinguishing him from the *real* Jonathan Ross, should the shiny-suited star suddenly walk into your reading space and stand next to your pretend version. Piss-easy. If you're not clear on this, try it. Imagine the *real* Jonathan Ross next to the first one, and you'll soon see what I mean.

More thorough research than the above-suggested 'Ross' experiment has taken place to investigate the nature of such hallucinations, and Wagstaff reviewed the results in his 1981 book. He summarized, 'the evidence that subjects can genuinely experience suggested hallucinations is sparse, but even if a few can, hypnotic induction seems unnecessary. Motivating waking instructions seem equally effective by themselves.' It's a little unclear from the text as to what motivating instructions might cause a genuine experience of a hallucination. However, we've all had the experience of looking for a pen that is right in front of us, unseen, yet in full view (akin to a negative hallucination) or seeing something 'wrongly', such as recognizing a friend in the street before realizing it's a stranger. So the idea of everyday minor 'hallucinations' need not seem so foreign.

How do you test to see what the limits of these hallucinations are? To test negative hallucinations, one scientist used optical illusions familiar to us now, where superimposed lines over a shape seemed to distort the shape underneath: for example, a square looked wider at the top or one line looked longer than the other, though in fact the square was perfect and the two lines measured the same. Good hypnotic subjects were told to negatively hallucinate the superimposed lines, the argument being that if they genuinely did not see them, the square would not appear to be distorted and the lines would be seen as identical in length. It's certainly a good premise and, interestingly, the subjects still perceived the square and lines as unequal, even though they claimed not to be able to see the lines. Experiments for 'positive' hallucinations created a situation where the phenomenon of after-images was employed. Normally, if we look at, for example, an area of bright red colour for twenty seconds or so and then at a white surface, we will see a green after-image. Other colours give rise to different after-images in this way. If you've never come across this, you should go and try it. Would hypnotically hallucinated colours also give rise to after-images? Well, various tests have showed that people would report the after-image they *expected* to see – if they were told that red creates a blue after-image, then they would see blue – and when the subjects have no knowledge of the after-effect, they don't report it at all. Another test for positive hallucination was devised in 1970, where the successful hallucination of a green filter would have allowed a pale-green number to become visible on a red background. None of the subjects could see the number by hallucinating the filter, but all could when the real filter was used.

These experiments are typical of research in this area. However, I can't help feeling that they just make the same point again and again, and seem a little misplaced after a while. I am not surprised that a subject does not naturally see an after-image from a hallucinated colour, in the same way a subject can't be hypnotized into having real X-ray vision. We have three types of colour receptors (cones) in our retinas which are responsive to blue, green or red. When we stare at a colour for a long time the appropriate cones start to fatigue. When the colour is removed, the information from the different receptors is not well balanced, and we see these after-images. In other words, this is a physiological response to *really* having those colours placed for a length of time before the eyes. I think there's a common-sense difference between this and just vividly hallucinating the colour, even as solidly as if produced by a hallucinogenic drug. I would also imagine, albeit not as a clinician and with no knowledge of psychedelics, that the first situation would produce an after-image and the second would not.

While it is important to know that these hallucinations do not produce those kinds of real-world after-effects, these and many other similar experiments do not answer the more interesting and subtle question of how real the images are *to the subject*. Aside from the issue of compliance, it certainly does seem that some people will allow their imaginations to 'run away with them' for a while to the point where the experience is more convincing for them than it would be if they were merely playing along to somehow humour or even fool the hypnotist. I also think of cases where subjects have told me they have exhibited 'fake' behaviour on one occasion and 'real' on another. For example, a girl I knew in my first year at university was very responsive to hypnosis from me, but after performing brilliantly on stage for another hypnotist she told me she was faking for him. She enjoyed it when it was done informally but found the stage setting silly and too distracting. On the other hand, an actor chap I knew seemed an excellent subject in a room with his friends but afterwards told me he had faked it; then on another occasion I had the same chap up on stage and he told me afterwards with surprise and delight that he hadn't been faking. If he was being honest about his experience, then somehow the stage environment and audience had allowed him to 'get into' it more and it had felt very different.

It is also suggested by Wagstaff that the phenomenon of people forgetting certain things after being told to do so under hypnosis is probably another example of compliance. It is, after all, quite easy to stop yourself from remembering what you were doing at a certain time as long as you don't try too hard to remember. Wagstaff felt it was likely that this was what was happening in clinical experiments when subjects successfully 'forgot' a piece of information. While it may be the case that this is just another misleading phenomenon,

I am reminded of a subject to whom I suggested post-hypnotic amnesia for the hypnotic session we had had. In other words, she would not remember that she had been hypnotized. This sort of suggestion I had imagined would 'wear off' after a few hours or so. I was therefore surprised when I spoke to her a couple of weeks later that she had suddenly and spontaneously had the memory 'pop' back into her head one morning as long as a week after the session, and had responded with some surprise. That seems a quite different scenario than just acting 'as if' you've forgotten when people ask you if you can remember.

However, as with all these anecdotal cases, they cannot be taken as firm evidence of anything; they are just interesting scenarios to add to the discussion. And it should be remembered that the 'compliance' explanation need not be synonymous with 'playing along', but instead can be compared to the combination of pressure, willingness to succeed and certain expectations held by the participant. Perhaps this, combined with a 'suggestible' personality, is enough to create seemingly hypnotic behaviour and for the occasional subject to convince herself that she acted as some form of automaton. It's very hard to be sure. I'll never know if Gavin really saw the rhino, but maybe it doesn't matter.

HOW TO HYPNOTIZE

Let's put aside our questions as to exactly what it is and look at how to actually do it.

The Dangers

I learned hypnosis using clinical and self-help books, all of which warned against the dangers of stage hypnosis. Probably few of you will be interested in using hypnosis as a performance piece, but it is worth looking at the issues involved so that you can understand how best to use it responsibly if you decide to use it at all.

The Campaign Against Stage Hypnotism was founded after a young girl died from an epileptic seizure some hours after she participated in a hypnotism show. While the process of hypnotism does not cause fatal epileptic attacks, it was argued that a suggestion given to the girl to experience a huge electric shock on stage set off a phobic reaction she had to electricity, resulting in the epileptic fit later that evening. The hypnotist was not held responsible in court as hypnosis was viewed accordingly to the behavioural definition we have considered above and no direct causality could be inferred. Perhaps understandably, the girl's family felt that the case was not treated with the appropriate seriousness and they still campaign against what they see as a potentially dangerous form of entertainment.

A common argument against the culpability of the hypnotist runs as follows. If you went to see a ventriloquist and then crashed your car on the way home or complained of headaches, you would not blame the ventriloquist. If you died in the crash, your distraught family would not seek to put an end to ventriloquism. Stage hypnotists, and many clinical hypnotists, argue that because hypnosis is merely tapping into people's potential for role playing and compliance, it cannot be held responsible for untoward events that happen following a show.

Speaking from my own experience, I am reminded of an incident when I performed a hypnotic show at a Freshers' Ball in Bristol many years ago. It was my local Students' Union, and I had performed there several times. When I invited participants onto the stage that night I noticed that one girl who had come up was clearly very drunk. As people in such a condition make poor subjects, I asked her to return to her seat before I continued with the demonstration. A couple of hours after the show I was meandering around what is apparently the largest (and ugliest) Students' Union in Europe making the most of my VIP pass when I heard an announcement over the Tannoy system: 'Will the hypnotist please come down to the foyer immediately.' I duly left Kajagoogoo's dance-floor and hurried down to the reception area. A crowd had already gathered, and I was ushered by a St John Ambulance official to the centre of the throng. There on the floor was the girl I had sent back to her seat, apparently unconscious. 'I'm told she was on stage with you,' one of the medical crew said to me, and I answered that indeed she had been, although she hadn't been hypnotized. Still, they thought I should have a go at bringing her out of what might be a hypnotic trance. I offered to have a go, although I knew it had nothing to do with me. So in front of a hundred or so students I tried to talk her out of a trance as if she was in one, and obviously failed. By that time an ambulance had arrived, and she was taken away.

I found out some weeks later that she had passed out due to severe alcohol poisoning and had had her stomach pumped at the hospital. Apparently she nearly died. I immediately began to wonder what would have happened if she *had* died. As awful as that would have been, I also knew that her parents would have been told that I had hypnotized her and hadn't been able to bring her out of it. I was young, and there are no qualifications for being a stage hypnotist; that certainly would have been the end of my career. Just because she'd drunk too much. As it was, I was never hired there again, not even to do magic tricks.

Every stage hypnotist has to deal with this sort of thing, and whether the fatality that sparked the campaign was really connected with the hypnotism to the extent that the hypnotist should be blamed is something that will never be ascertained. However, I do think that the question of responsibility is an important one. Stage hypnotists are understandably very eager to defend themselves by saying that it's all fun and make-believe and that no damage can be caused. I don't think that is quite right, even though I largely agree with the behavioural approach to understanding these performances.

The problem stems from the nature of the shows. Sadly, it is not difficult to perform stage hypnosis, and many people are attracted to it who clearly have no sense of taste or responsibility. While it may be hysterical to see your friends stripping to music blaring from a ghetto-blaster in the corner of a pub, or grown men crying like babies because they think they've 'just watched the saddest film in the world', this unfortunate focus on embarrassment and low-level humour brings with it certain issues. Primarily, the hypnotist is unlikely, even if he knew how in the first place, to be at all sensitive to any discomfort shown by his participants. At the end of the show he will probably want to lose them quickly from the stage without taking care to make sure they are completely happy and feeling fine. If a subject has been humiliated on stage or has any reason to resent the hypnotist or to find the show upsetting in retrospect, it is quite understandable that she might complain of after-effects such as depression or paranoia. If, perhaps after a few drinks and trying to keep up with rapid repeated 'sleep' and 'wake' instructions, she feels like a confused and disorientated human yo-yo, she might develop headaches or keep falling asleep after the show is over. Equally, it may be that one of the instructions given on stage and dutifully carried out by the subject with strong emotional involvement in front of a baying audience has left the subject feeling disturbed. During a television investigation for and against stage hypnotism, one woman told of how she had been instructed on stage to look everywhere for her breast, which she could not find. She searched in a state of urgency and worry, imaginatively acting out the instruction and really getting into her role. She spoke afterwards of the traumatic scenario of trying to communicate her panic at the time to her husband, only to find that he just laughed along with everyone else and didn't help her. She was seemingly left with a haunting fear that she might have to have a mastectomy one day, and that her husband would find the whole thing hysterical.

The irony is that a hugely entertaining hypnotic demonstration can be carried out without recourse to embarrassment or crudity. In fact, from my experience, a vicarious sense of embarrassment felt by the audience only weakens the show, though of course this depends on your audiences. Personally I find it excruciating to be sat in an audience that is screaming with laughter at the plight of some poor chap on stage who is clearly upset at some suggested event. As this subjective question of taste is too closely related to the question of avoiding dangerous scenarios, I find it difficult to consider objectively what the best approach to regulating stage hypnosis should be. But certainly it seems wrong that the argument of 'hypnosis isn't real' should absolve the hypnotist of all responsibility towards the welfare of his participants. If a hypnotist were able to say to the audience, 'If you come up, please just play along with everything,' it might be argued that the subjects should then be responsible themselves. However, given that he is going to manipulate, bully or cajole rather vulnerable people into anything from playing along to really living out what he suggests, and in a way that might be very confusing or unsettling for them, there is a sense in which one should not just immediately decide that he can walk away from any duty of care.

Now perhaps one might argue that according to that logic, a magician should then be held responsible if a participant in a card trick takes the magic way too seriously and loses so much sleep following the performance that he develops an illness. However, this would be a very unusual case, and clearly a reasonable person would not be expected to react in that way. In our hypnotism scenario, though, it is more understandable that a participant might leave the show troubled if handled unprofessionally.

Understanding the issue in terms of the common-sense, sensitive handling of volunteers, rather than debating whether hypnotism itself is to blame, does allow the conscientious performer to steer a safe course. If you do decide to look seriously into learning hypnotism, I advise you to fully take on board the following:

1. *Do not try to hypnotize anyone who is clearly disturbed or has epilepsy.* If in any doubt, just don't. Avoid anyone with any history of mental illness.
2. *Do not get involved in therapeutic change unless you are suitably qualified.* Plenty who are qualified probably shouldn't be doing it, so don't you get involved.
3. *Treat hypnosis as a gentle tool, not as anything dramatic or showy.* Leave the theatrics until you know how to make people feel comfortable with you, and you really know what you're doing.
4. *Everything you do contributes to the hypnosis.* Imagine that the person is hypersensitive to his surroundings. If you or other people present appear flustered in the face of an unexpected response, such as the subject not waking up when he's supposed to, your subject might well start panicking himself and not feel he can wake up.
5. *Always make sure at the end that the person is completely free from any belief that they might still be hypnotized.* His belief is everything. There is only his belief. If he leaves thinking he

is still 'half under', he will be. Take your time to bring people thoroughly out of the 'trance'.

6. *Take it slowly, and only try it in a controlled environment.*
7. *Treat it first as a relaxation tool, and slowly move into administering behavioural suggestions.*

Language

PACING AND LEADING

Hypnosis is based primarily on the understanding of *pacing* or feeding back the subject's experience to him and then *leading* him to the new desired behaviour. Consider, for example, the difference in your reaction to the following statements. Read each slowly a couple of times and note your response to them:

1. You want to scratch.
2. As you sit there, and as you, despite your environment, really focus on these words, and as you carry on reading this page, and the more you try not to think about it, the more you'll notice the increasing feeling of wanting to scratch.

The first example is an outright command to scratch, and you may or may not decide to scratch on the basis of it. In the second, however, the desired action (scratch) is now connected to things you are already doing: *sitting there, reading these words, trying not to scratch*. It just gets under your skin more, doesn't it? And as you sit there feeling all the itches starting to tickle in different places on your body, you'll notice that this sort of language has a much more seductive quality to it.

The simplest form of pacing and leading (I'm still scratching) is this 'as you X, so you Y'. The first piece of behaviour, X, is something that is known to be true. It might refer to how the subject is seated, what he is looking at, or what you know he will be experiencing in his head. The desired behaviour, Y, is connected with it as if the two are somehow interdependent. Sometimes a hypnotist will include several pieces of pacing (X) before sneaking in a lead (Y):

> As you sit there and listen to my words, with your eyes closed, feeling your hands there on the arm of the chair, allowing my words to relax you as your breathing becomes regular and peaceful, I'd like you to let yourself begin to drift away into a kind of sleep.

There are two examples of leading statements hidden in the above. The most obvious one is the 'I'd like you to let yourself begin to drift away into a kind of sleep', but the other is 'allowing my words to relax you'. Everything up to the word 'chair' is simply feeding back to the subject what the hypnotist is observing. Then, the idea of his words relaxing the subject is snuck in along with those items of pure feedback so that it is accepted as something equally self-evident. Consider the following as you imagine dangling a watch in front of a subject's face:

> And as you listen to my voice and look up at the watch, watching it as you relax in the chair, you'll notice that your eyes start to grow heavy as you listen to me. That's right – and as you notice them blinking, so too you can keep listening to me as you relax and as you allow them to grow heavier. As the rest of you relaxes in the chair, so your eyes get heavier and you blink more and more and just allow them to close so that you can drift off into a sleep . . .

Here, the only fact that you know is that if the subject looks up at any dangling object, the muscles in his eyes will grow a little tired, or his eyes will smart, and he'll want to blink. That's all. However, all the 'as you's' that link the idea of blinking with the action of looking at the watch and eventually drifting off make it very easy for the subject to think 'It's working . . . my eyes *are* getting heavier . . . I must be drifting off . . .' and to follow along with the statements being made. Despite the fact that to an onlooker it looks as if you have just made someone go to sleep through some sort of hypnotic power, you can start to realize that in fact you are only guiding your subjects down an easy path to what you want them to experience. You are not *making* them do anything. Think of it like a seduction.

Pacing and leading are used in many forms of persuasion. Good teachers and communicators know how to respond to a bad suggestion from a classroom or boardroom with something like, 'Yes, that's a great idea, and I think where that really works is xxxxx [picking out a positive aspect of the bad idea]. I think *also* that xxxxx [now shifting across to a better idea, as if it had grown out of the bad suggestion] . . .' Here the person does not feel disregarded, even though his idea really had no value. He has been paced, and then led into a better idea which he might even think he came up with. A common technique used by effective teachers (particularly good English teachers) upon being given a wrong answer in class is to act as if the child has spotted something at some deeper level than that at which the subject was being discussed. The teacher can then lead around to the desired answer without making the child feel stupid.

A hypnotic session will be typically led by this process throughout, and the hypnotist will often minimize the effect of any unexpected noises or disturbances by referring to them (pacing) and then suggesting that they will enhance the trance state (leading).

'The sound of the telephone relaxing you more'; 'And as the sound of those sirens help you drift away . . .', etc.

PRESUPPOSITION

Here we hide the instruction we'd like the subject to pick up on by presupposing it to be the case. Consider, for example, the case of the clever parent who wants her child to go to bed by eight-thirty. She might offer the double-bind, 'You've been really good today, so you can decide whether to go to bed at eight or eight-thirty.' The child, of course, chooses the latter happily, whereas the words 'You have to go to bed at eight-thirty today' would probably not have been met with the same compliance.

Presupposition also tends to be a fault of leading questions that can interfere with the fairness of such things as market research and the reliability of eyewitness reports in police interviews. In a classic demonstration, students are asked to watch a film involving a car accident. They are then asked, 'How fast do you think the car was going when it passed the barn?' or 'How fast was the white sports car travelling when it hit the bus?' In fact there was no barn, and the car was not white. In formulating their answers, many of the students will report afterwards remembering a white sports car or a barn featuring in the film.

In hypnosis, a sentence such as 'you'll notice that your eyes start to grow heavy as you listen to me' is also a useful presupposition. It presupposes that the eyes are growing heavy, and only questions when the subject will happen to notice it. It's a little like the old Kellogg's Cornflakes slogan 'Have you forgotten how good they taste?', or 'Do you still have sex with your dog?' Both presuppose what the speaker wants to communicate by questioning something peripheral to the real message. This technique can allow the hypnotist to suggest an action without eliciting a negative response. Saying, for example (in Ericksonian style), 'You can wonder how deeply you are going into trance' nicely presupposes that they *are* going into trance (whatever that is) and it may have the effect on the listener of relaxing him even more by having him believe that he is sinking deeper into some special state. 'As you sit there I want you to notice that your body is growing heavier' nicely combines pacing, leading and a presupposition (that the body is indeed getting heavy), and would seem to be more effective than the command 'your body is getting heavy'. Outside Hammer horror movies, such direct language is rarely used nowadays.

TONE OF VOICE

Practise talking with a gentle, relaxed tone, which will enhance the 'trance'. If you sound harsh, you won't be as effective. Find phrases that trip mellifluously off the tongue, such as 'enhance the trance', and let them provide texture and a sense of dreaminess to the experience. Repeat yourself, and allow yourself to fully relax as you talk, so that the subject naturally relaxes with you.

USE OF IMAGERY

Appeal to all the senses of your subject by referring to things you'd like them to see, hear, feel, smell or even taste in their hypnotic 'state'. If you have your subject imagine a garden, have him see it vividly, but also refer to the feel of the grass under his feet; the sound of the birds in the trees; even the smell of the flowers. Only when these things are multi-sensory will they seem potent and real. Be sure to allow the subject to fill in the gaps as he wishes, but be careful not to contradict something about a picture you might have suggested. His image of the garden may be quite different from yours. You might refer to a brook which you imagine to be in the garden, but he might have decided to lose himself in a real garden from his childhood which contains no such brook. Such errors will usually cause confusion and probably bring him out of the trance* a little.

Structure

Think of practising hypnosis as learning how to induce a profound state of relaxation in a person, brought about by suggestion. Once that state is induced, people will show varying degrees of suggestibility, which seems to tie in with how responsive they are in everyday life. Think of the following stages as a framework:

1. Prepare subject and induce light stages of trance. This may involve the suggestion of eye closure.
2. Deepen the trance through a metaphor such as going down stairs.
3. Carry out your hypnotic work.
4. Fully awaken the subject.

What number 3 consists of will depend on what you are doing. For one hypnotist it will be suggestions of being able to re-create the trance in the future and creating a mental space where the subject can go to profoundly relax. Another might use it to help the subject find ways of stopping smoking. A stage hypnotist might use it to suggest ludicrous behaviours that the subject will exhibit when he wakes up. This latter case is known as *post-hypnotic suggestion*, and for that we would have to add a fifth stage to the list:

*I'll continue to use the word 'trance' as if it were a real thing. The word is, however, just a shorthand term for whatever that half acted-out state of compliance is that the subject enters when he follows the hypnotist's suggestions.

5. At the end of the session, make sure that the subject is free of any suggestion, and assured that he is no longer hypnotically responsive.

Here's what I suggest you do if you wish to learn this. Read this chapter and then record an induction to try with yourself. Find out what works well for you and what doesn't, as the chances are those same things will work or not work for other people too. Not wanting to be responsible for every schoolboy who buys this book and tries to hypnotize his classmates, I shall not give a verbatim script for you to use, but rather pointers that you can put together and try out. With this in mind, and now that you also understand the basic approach to language and instruction, let's go back through those stages in more detail.

PREPARE YOUR SUBJECT

'Prepare' means to have your subject sitting comfortably, ready to relax. While there is no need for soft music or a dark room, it's best to avoid bright lights or noisy surroundings. Where possible, take the phone off the hook, switch off mobiles, and make sure that you won't be disturbed for half an hour or so. Your subject should ideally be open to whatever will happen (they don't need to 'believe' in hypnosis), not too nervous but not bouncily over-enthusiastic either. Bear in mind that you are not really inducing a special state, although you will talk as if you are. Instead, you are utilizing the subject's expectations and beliefs. So if you appear unconvinced at the start that he will be a good subject, the chances are that he won't respond well. You must be confident, unflustered, and act as if you've done it a hundred times before, even if you haven't.

INDUCE LIGHT STAGES OF TRANCE

METHOD ONE: TENSION/RELEASE.

This is a simple, direct way of kicking off a hypnotic session. It works well with groups, where one-on-one suggestions would take too long, as would waiting for each person to drift off. Have the subject close his eyes and tense up every muscle in his body. Tell him to make sure that he keeps breathing normally, but to tense the muscles in his feet, legs, stomach, chest, shoulders, arms and fists. Have him hold it like that, then tell him to relax. As he relaxes, there will be a certain response you know he will experience. You can pace the fact that his body will grow heavier in the chair, then lead this into behaviours you want at this stage. For example, 'And as your body grows heavier and your breathing becomes relaxed and regular, so too you can listen to me as you sink down in the chair and let yourself start to drift off comfortably.'

METHOD TWO: EYE CLOSURE.

Alternatively, have your seated subject look up at a point near the top of the wall in front of him. This is to make sure that his eyes are looking upwards, but not uncomfortably. Instruct him to relax as he looks at that point. This is a classic clinical induction used by many therapists, who sometimes like to use an odd or flamboyant object to induce the trance in this way, rather than just a spot on the wall.

Pace the fact that he is sitting there, listening to you, looking at that object, and lead into the desired behaviour. This is like the watch example earlier. Use the same sort of language. You know that eventually his eyes will grow a bit tired and want to blink, so don't be frightened to predict that behaviour, but instead make it sound like the onset of a trance in your seamless flow of layered suggestions. *As* he listens to you and looks at the wall, *so* too he can allow that relaxation to spread over his body and allow his eyes to grow comfortably heavy *as* he continues to sit there, and *as* he feels his arms on the chair he can feel his eyelids wanting to close, and *as* they blink he can allow himself to relax more into a nice trance . . .

DEEPEN THE TRANCE

Remember, there is no real trance to deepen. However, the idea of going deeper into a special state is easy for the subject to visualize, and engages his imagination in the right way. So, once you can see that the subject is a little slumped, has his eyes closed and has clearly relaxed, you need to amplify that relaxation.

The easiest way is to have him imagine himself at the top of a staircase. Tell him that each step down will relax him more and take him deeper into the sleep. This is a good point to allow for any future confusion the subject might experience. He is not going to become a zombie, and he will remain aware of what you're saying throughout. If he expects actually to fall asleep, or to experience something extraordinary, he will be disappointed, and might decide that it isn't working. Again, we see that the importance lies in working with the subject's belief, for he must be *convinced* that he is indeed going into a trance and that everything is proceeding as planned. So it's a good idea to tell the subject that as he finds himself going deeper into the trance, he will still hear and understand everything you say, and will be *aware of himself going into the trance*. This phrase nicely utilizes the fact that he will remain aware of what's happening and focuses that awareness on a useful aspect of the proceedings.

Tell him you will count from one to ten as he walks down the stairs, and that when you reach 'ten' he will be at the bottom of the stairs and in a profound state of relaxation. Have him walk down, and pace everything that is happening (*as* I count, *as* you take each step, *as* you breathe, *as* you listen to me, *so* each step, each number, each word can take you deeper).

CARRY OUT YOUR HYPNOTIC WORK

For now, let's use this staircase to create a useful place for our subject to return to whenever he likes. This will also allow you to practise well without worrying about failure.

At the bottom of the stairs, tell him to see a door in front of him. Explain that this door leads out to a beautiful garden; a perfect, idyllic setting that will be his very own to return to whenever he wants. Tell him to take hold of the door handle and get ready to open it. Now instruct him to go through, and immediately begin to describe a multi-sensory experience, while allowing him to find details for himself. Don't talk about paths or specific components of the garden, or, if you do, clarify that you want him to place those things in there. Remember to include the things he can feel, hear and smell. Tell him to feel the warmth of the sun on his face, and the gentle breeze that keeps the temperature at a perfect level. Emphasize that he should make this garden as delightful as possible, so that he can relish coming back here whenever he wants.

INTRODUCING PHYSICAL SUGGESTIONS

One good way of testing the responsiveness of your subject is to now suggest some physical behaviours that will provide you with feedback and help you deepen the trance even more. Suggest that there is a nice chair in the garden in just the perfect spot, and that he should go and sit in it. Have him then notice that his right arm is very heavy, so heavy that he can imagine it stuck to the arm of the chair. Have him imagine a force binding his arm to the arm of the chair, and then have him try to lift it in a way that *presupposes* failure on his part. For example, the words 'try as hard as you can to un*stick* your arm' create a powerful suggestion: now he is putting effort into *trying*, which presupposes that he won't be able to do it, and the words 'stick your arm' will effectively echo in his mind.

He may at this point a) lift the arm in the air, b) struggle to lift it but fail, or c) sit motionless as if he is putting no effort into it at all. Option b) suggests the best type of subject, and is the clearest and most useful pointer to you that he is responsive. Where he does not move at all, you can presume that he is so relaxed that he has taken the suggestion to mean that he simply can't summon up the effort even to try. If he just lifts his arm, he will hopefully at least find it heavy. In which case, treat it like a success, and say, 'Excellent – and as you notice how oddly heavy that arm has become, let it take you down now even deeper into the state as you bring it back down and just let go and relax . . .' See what you did? You're even acknowledging his confusion or tension which might have resulted from it not working, and offering him the chance to 'let go' and relax by going deeper into the trance. He should accept this with relief and go with it, even if you find that he's not a terrific subject.

If this suggestion has proved successful and you want to take things further, now tell him that his other arm is getting lighter. Have him imagine a helium balloon tied to his left wrist and all the natural heaviness draining out of his arm – *as* he starts to *notice* how light it is becoming. Presuppose the increasing weightlessness, talk about it becoming 'lighter and lighter', and have him wait for it to start moving up in the air all on its own. When the instructions to allow the hand to rise slowly into the air are mixed with plenty of pacing, this can be a very effective suggestion. Because you are working against the natural heaviness of the hand following all the relaxation that has taken place, this might take a while to get going. However, it is important to be constantly encouraging, so remember to pick up on every movement that happens and build on it, incorporating it into the pacing. Pace the feeling of the hand coming away from the arm of the chair. Pace and lead and presuppose that hand into the air. If the hand twitches its way upwards, tell him to wait for the next twitch that will send it rising. Let him feel that it's really working and it will.

When the hand has risen as high as you feel it will go, you can then have the subject allow it to come down, and in doing so suggest that he will sink deeper into the trance. The relief that the subject feels as the arm levitation concludes is enough to make this 'deepening' technique very effective. When you find that you can make this work well, you can use it as a way of starting the induction from a waking state. I would generally use this 'arm levitation' at the start of the session, as it can be very convincing for the subject and a nice way for me to tell how responsive he is. I have the subject keep his eyes open as his hand comes up to his face, and then have him close his eyes and drift into a sleep as it comes back down again. When the hand first moves he will often laugh or express surprise, but by the time it has picked up speed and come up to the face, he should appear dazed and dreamy; my levitation instructions are accompanied by a flow of suggestions that the subject 'need not drift off into a profound and comfortable trance until that hand touches you on the face and your eyes can finally close properly' (a massive and layered presupposition that the trance will occur and that the eyes will meanwhile grow heavier and heavier and close as a final expression of relief). What works to make the arm move, seemingly of its own accord, is the fascinating phenomenon of 'ideomotor movement', which we discussed earlier.

As we are using this session and the imaginary garden to offer our subject a useful technique to use himself whenever he likes, we must also explain to him now that he can re-create the trance for himself. Have him lie on the grass in the garden, and re-create all the wonderful feelings and sensations that accompany it. Then tell him that by finding a quiet time when he will be undisturbed, he can close his eyes and imagine the staircase once again. Explain that by imagining himself going down the stairs and through the door he will be able to return to the garden and enjoy the benefits of the relaxation it offers. He can use this to 're-charge', to clear his head or to help him get to sleep. He can use it while revising for an exam, as it may help to be able to review his revised material in such a relaxed state. Talk him back through the procedure and also assure him that when he uses this on his own he will be able to open his eyes and wake up whenever he wants.

Finally, emphasize the importance of his using this regularly at first, in order to lock it in the mind. If he neglects it, it will be difficult to bring back.

FULLY AWAKEN THE SUBJECT

The final stage is to bring the subject fully out of the state and make sure that he is fully refreshed. I would have him imagine walking through the door and back up the stairs as I count back from ten to zero, as this will further cement in his mind the idea that he can go back down at a later date to return to the garden. Explain that as he walks up the stairs he will feel all the drowsiness and heaviness leave him, but that he need not open his eyes until he reaches 'zero', which will be at the top. Then slowly take him back up the stairs and allow your voice to become more natural and chatty as you reach the very top. Instruct him to open his eyes and be fully wide awake.

Use this time to get further feedback from the subject. Was the garden real for him? What did it feel like? Ask him how long he felt it took: a good subject will tend to think it took far less time than it did. It's not uncommon for an hour-long session to feel like ten minutes. Reiterate the importance of using the self-hypnotic technique regularly until he can slip into it easily, and you're done.

Trying a Post-hypnotic Suggestion

Once all this is second nature, you may wish to experiment with a post-hypnotic suggestion. To do this, you will first need to find a good, responsive subject and have him primed to go quickly back into trance. This is because you'll only be putting him 'to sleep' in order to give him the suggestion, and then you will wish to awaken him so that he will carry it out.

A much smaller percentage of subjects are responsive enough to carry out bizarre post-hypnotic suggestions than those who will demonstrate arm levitation and so on during the trance. Do not think of administering post-hypnotic suggestions as a mini-stage show. Your subject will likely be fully aware of the fact that he is carrying them out, so treat it with a sense of exploration and sensitivity. Some suggestions will work better than others. An energetic type might happily carry out suggestions that involve movement, but you are unlikely to have people jumping around thinking chairs are boiling hot unless you are in front of an audience and appealing to the subjects' extrovert nature.

Firstly, the subject needs to understand that he will go back into the sleep when you tell him to. You can give this as a post-hypnotic suggestion: 'When I click my fingers and tell you to "sleep", you will go straight back down into the trance.' Each time he then does this he builds up a stronger responsive pattern to your instructions, which allows for more demanding suggestions to be given. Equally, you can tell him that he can come out of the trance easily *and fully refreshed* when you count backwards to zero each time. Make sure that he is indeed quite awake every time that you do this.

I would suggest you try out the following post-hypnotic suggestion, to have the subject forget his own name, but only when the procedure to this point has become second nature. Note how the instructions are worded: the pacing and leading, the repetition of the central suggestion, the reference to how the subject will react at the moment when he is asked, and the relating of it to ordinary life experiences which help it to take root. The words are not magical and can of course be changed, but this is a good example of making them persuasive. I would also suggest that you try this when there are a few people present, as the pressure to comply is greater in a group.

> When you wake up, you won't be able to remember your name. The more you try to remember it, the more you will forget. Just like all of those things that you try to remember but find impossible; all of those things that are right on the tip of your tongue but just get further and further away the more you try to remember them. In the same way that you forget a tune or a name, you will have no recollection of your name when you awake. When I ask you what it is, you won't be able to remember, will you? The more you try, the more you'll forget. All memory of your name will be gone the moment you open your eyes.

Then awaken him from the state by counting backwards to zero. Ask him his name, but frown and use a tone of voice to suggest that he can't recall it. Look puzzled yourself. Shake your head as you ask him to try to remember, thereby cueing him to fail. Remain in control. If it doesn't work, don't worry. Try with different people on different occasions and see how they respond.

Where post-hypnotic suggestions have been given, they can be cleared simply by having the subject believe that they are cleared. As they don't exist outside his belief and responsiveness to the ideas you give him, they're much easier to take away than to give. However, it is always a good idea to re-hypnotize the person at the end and tell him that upon wakening he will no longer be hypnotized, will remember his name and be free from suggestion.

This is necessarily a very brief guide to the basics of hypnosis. Please use it tentatively and with sensitivity, and with time you will come to grasp its nature. Personally, I have dispensed with formal hypnosis and come to utilize the communication techniques I feel lie behind its effectiveness. I use people's capacity for compliance and imaginative engagement to achieve certain aims when I perform. Equally, I can use it quite dramatically and instantaneously. I think, though, that these things are best discovered over time by a person with serious interest who is prepared to pursue a certain amount of study.

One final word of warning: I'd be wary of the large number of so-called 'hypnotic courses' sold in downloadable format on the net. Some of the individuals who sell these are utterly reprehensible, especially those who use my name to peddle their wares, of course. At the moment there are any number of e-books and so on supposedly teaching my techniques. They don't, regardless of what they claim. Don't waste your money.

NEURO-LINGUISTIC PROGRAMMING

Anybody with a third of an interest in hypnosis will be hard pushed not to have heard of NLP. When I began reading about and practising hypnosis as a student I became quite enthused about NLP, mainly due to the narrative style and astonishing content of the books written by or about its founders, Richard Bandler and John Grinder. They are quite addictive reading, especially to one without scepticism, and I started to incorporate NLP into my hypnosis shows and any low-level therapeutic help I might offer someone, such as giving up smoking.

After about six years of familiarity with the techniques and attitude of NLP, and in a moment of unpleasant madness, I thought I might become a hypnotherapist full-time, and it seemed proper that I obtain some relevant qualifications. To do so, I attended an NLP course, given by Bandler and others, and achieved the relevant 'Practitioner' qualification. The course, perversely, put me off that career rather than cementing my ambition. I now have a lot of NLPers analysing my TV work in their own terms, as well as people who say that I myself unfairly claim to be using NLP whenever I perform (the truth is I have never mentioned it). To confuse things even further, it has recently made a home for itself as a fashionable conjuring technique of dubious efficacy.

'What is it?' I literally hear you, the frightened novice, ask. Well, you clever sausage, that is a show-off question and no-one's going to give you a straightforward answer. 'What is it?' indeed. Honestly. This isn't America. The words 'neuro-linguistic programming' suggest that it has something to do with language and the brain programming each other. However, it has been said that Bandler may have made the term up when a traffic policeman asked for his profession, so perhaps we shouldn't worry too much about the complicated title. If you're after a complicated definition instead, here is NLP as defined by Bandler on his website at the time of writing: 'Neuro-Linguistic Programming™ (NLP™) is defined as the study of the structure of subjective experience and what can be calculated from that and is predicated upon the belief that all behaviour has structure.'

It is fair to say that NLP is a large training programme dealing with communication and personal change. It is taught in courses and seminars, and can apply to businesses as well as being offered as a therapeutic tool. It stands as one of many similar enterprises, though it seems to be one of the most successful, along with the larger-than-life self-help guru Anthony Robbins, who credits NLP with changing his own life and starting him down a path of powerful personal change. At the heart of it lies the metaphor of NLP as 'software for the brain', or as a user-manual for experiencing the world in the most beneficial way. Another much-used phrase is 'the map is not the territory': in other words, our experience of the world reflects only how we represent it to ourselves, and this is not the same as the real thing. Undoubtedly this is a critical principle to remember when considering our beliefs.

Grinder (a linguist) and Bandler (a mathematician) started NLP in the mid-seventies by paying attention to how very successful therapists, such as Erickson, achieved their results. They 'elicited the strategies' of these top professionals, and later on others in different fields, so that the same strategies could be taught to others who wanted to achieve the same success. Over time they developed a model of how language is processed by the brain, and claimed that both affect each other all the time. Some of what we do in our brains (essentially, how we are representing the world to ourselves) is expressed in the language we use, and by paying particular attention to the language we use, we can have a powerful effect on the unconscious neurological processes of the listener.

Although the authors studied the work of many top professionals, they notably did not look at the work of neuro-scientists in formulating these ideas. Indeed, their approach was more pragmatic: to start with observed phenomena that seemed reliable, and then to set out teachable ideas based on what was *useful* or *seemed to work best*, rather than trying to understand why or how something might work. The pragmatic approach of the originators has now been swamped in a huge industry of daft theories and hyperbole, evangelical mind-sets and endless self-perpetuating courses, to the point where it resembles something of a pyramid scheme, with Bandler sat cheerily at the top. (Grinder, it seems, has a more careful view of what constitutes good NLP and is a little cynical of what it has become.)

I have seen Bandler at work and he undoubtedly appears quite extraordinary, in the way any good showman can appear. He is infectious and at once both charismatic and unpleasant. You love his world and adore his attitude while at the same time not quite believing him. It's not hard to take people from a group of suggestible, enthusiastic believers and have them experience what appears to be powerful change in front of the audience. That comes down to understanding charisma and performance. He certainly excels in those areas, which makes it hard to tell whether he's hugely effective or a great, brilliant, captivating con.

One aspect of NLP that will always make it hugely appealing is that it makes wild and dazzling claims, such as being able to make a genius out of anyone through a process called 'modelling'. Though Bandler himself might baulk at some of the exaggerated claims made by practitioners (most of them his disciples), he makes plenty of very strong statements himself about what can be achieved, and is now only one voice in a massive industry. (As nothing in NLP is set in stone, and as Bandler is an intriguing but slippery fish when it comes to pinning anything down on him, it seems fair to criticize some of these claims where they are made, in the absence of clear alternatives or even a clear central body to defer to.) To 'model', we must first elicit the unconscious strategies of the person we wish to emulate by asking certain key questions that will have them setting out every stage of their inner processes. Normally these are things the person does not think about and will discover for himself as the questions guide him. Then we try those processes out for ourselves, and through an imaginative process have ourselves think and feel as the person we wish to learn from. We are taking on their skills as our own.

Perhaps it sounds a little complicated, but you'd probably agree that being curious about people whose behaviour we respect, and bothering to find out if and how we might learn from their example, is a positive and worthwhile thing. It would make sense to believe so, although it may not occur to some of us to think of behaviours in that way. We tend to think we're stuck with our personalities and problems and that's that: there's certainly a lot to be learned from the self-help world which would have us learn how to put liberating new behaviours into practice. However, the problem for NLP arises when this is treated as something of a magical process. In one study, a group 'modelled' a sharp-shooter while another group were taught by traditional methods. Both were given the same amount of learning time, and both ended up with the same skills on the firing range. Modelling didn't prove a magical tool when it came to such measurable, specific skills. Personally, I remember the delight I felt watching an NLP disciple I knew demonstrate the results of his session of 'modelling' a juggler. It was clear, as he hunted for the twelfth time under his sofa for a coloured ball, that he was not learning any more quickly than if he had been taught in a more traditional way.

Now, modelling skills might possibly be of more use with learning low-level, less 'teachable' (and less measurable) skills such as charisma, or how effectively to approach challenges, but this is a much more pedestrian image of modelling than that which NLP uses to appeal to people. The image is given that little old you can become a Pavarotti or an Einstein through some magical and brief brain-programming process. While this undoubtedly may not have been quite the original intention of the technique, it is certainly the misleading concept peddled nowadays. Such exaggerated claims as these, unchecked and unaccountable in a sprawling industry that affects personal lives and big business, are perhaps a little concerning.

Another issue suggests itself here. Can I not choose to learn from other people in this way without calling it NLP? Don't we model ourselves on people or emulate mentors all the time? Of course, the answer is 'yes'. Because NLP has its roots not only in Bandler and Grinder's work but also in aspects of Freud, Jung and Chomsky, as well as all the therapists the originators were inspired by, and because it aims to take as its starting point what already works, there is little in its roots that is unique. One of the many irritating habits of NLPers is to claim anything remotely concerned with looking consciously at one's inner processes as NLP.

There have been attempts to study whether or not some of the more quantifiable claims of NLP do actually stand up. One such set of claims revolves around the notion of 'primary representational systems' and 'eye accessing cues'.

The Eyes Have It (some of the time)

According to NLP, we represent the world to ourselves in a visual, auditory or feeling-based (kinaesthetic) way. These are 'representational systems'. When we think about something, we will make a picture of it in our mind, hear something in our heads, connect with a feeling, or combine the above possibilities. For example, imagine you are asked if you want to attend a lecture about Smurfs at the Royal Albert Hall. In the second it might take you to answer 'yes', you might a) picture Smurfs, b) picture the Royal Albert Hall, c) hear a vague excerpt from what you imagine the lecture might be, or hear yourself asking that delicate question about Smurfette that has always concerned you, and then d) check your feelings on the above and note that the feelings are pretty good.

It is said by many NLPers that people tend to be predisposed to one or another representation system. In other words, one person will tend to make pictures in her head rather than hear voices, and another will prefer immediately to connect with her feelings. A composer, for example, might be expected to have a primary representational system that is auditory, because it is the sensory world of sound he is most used to. Other people in the NLP world would note that this can be misleading, that it is more accurate to say that people move between different PRSs all the time: so our composer may be 'auditory' when he is thinking about his music, but perhaps 'visual' when out buying clothes. This mixed PRS scenario seems more likely, though it renders the concept of a *primary* (and therefore usefully predictable) representational system redundant.

Why does a PRS matter? Well, NLP says that if we can know how people are representing their world to themselves at a certain time, it allows us to have greater rapport with them, and with rapport comes influence. For example, imagine you want to buy a new hi-fi. Your old one looks tatty and you'd like something more up-to-date. You have a certain image of the sort of thing you want. So you go into a shop and ask to see some new hi-fis. You are told, 'We don't have any: this is a health-food shop.' You go into a hi-fi shop instead and ask the assistant, 'I'm looking for a new hi-fi. Can I see some? There are some nice-looking ones in the window.' The assistant knows which hi-fi has had the best write-up in the magazines, which one performs better than all the others. So he tells you the name of the model. You ask him what it's like, and he says it sounds amazing. He talks about cones and speaker types, gold connectors and hi-fi specifications. You ask to look at it, and he takes you over. He talks more about the sound quality, but somehow you just aren't getting excited. On another shelf you spot a great-looking system, and become animated. What about that one? He tells you that the sound isn't anywhere near as good: the speakers aren't of the same spec, and the quality of the amp is inferior. You're confused, you don't know what you want. You leave and say you'll think about it.

A sales assistant who knew about PRSs would have handled this very differently. In the story above, the assistant's PRS as regards hi-fis is understandably auditory: he has worked in the business too long to be bothered about what the machines look like. He can easily hear the difference between a good and a great system and wants to pass on his enthusiasm. You, though, are primarily motivated to find something which will *look* great. The way you expressed your opening question to the assistant should have told him that. You're using a lot of visual words. You're *looking* for a new hi-fi. You want to *see* some. You like the nice-*looking* ones in the window. But because the assistant is stuck in his own PRS, the sale doesn't get made. You're confused, and feel disappointed. He should have listened to you, and then taken you to some great-looking hi-fis he felt were good *enough* sound-wise for you, and you'd have left happy.

I am very interested in sales techniques, and I do believe that often the customer will tell you exactly how you should sell him the product. Salesmen often make the mistake of having a set approach, and as a rule are nowhere near flexible enough to let the customer dictate the easiest path to a closure. Interestingly, the same miscommunication can happen in relationships. After all, this is all about the presence or absence of good rapport. For example, a wife complains that her husband doesn't tell her he loves her often enough. The husband can't understand this because he comes home with flowers or buys gifts more than any husband he knows.

One way of looking at this paradox is to point out that the parties seem to use a different PRS when it comes to what they feel is important in expressing affection. The wife might need to *hear* nice things more than *see* presents or flowers, whereas the husband, more 'visual' in this instance, thinks that 'seeing evidence' of affection is more important. It might be a big help if both could appreciate this, so that one or both could change their behaviour without feeling they were being treated unfairly. And is this not a common fault? How many of us take the trouble to work out *how* those we love feel loved? We tend to act in a way *we* would appreciate, but this may be way off the mark.*

So far so good. As with the above example, we can see that the words we use might give some clue as to which RS (let's leave out the P) we might be using. In fact, NLP does claim that the predicates we use directly connect with the RS we are experiencing. In effect, the person who says 'I see what you mean' is being literal: he is describing the fact that he is able to make a clear picture of what you are talking about. People using the auditory RS would say instead something like 'Sounds good to me', and a person thinking kinaesthetically might use the phrase 'That feels right'. Therefore in order to gain better rapport with a person, you are advised to use the same type of predicates to match their RS. You are literally 'talking their language', according to this thinking.

While this might seem acceptable to a point, it sounds like the sort of thing one would have to view in perspective. We are beginning to cross the line into NLP magic, where faith, or credulity, might gently beckon. The NLPers also tell us that you can identify

*An important point. Find out from those you are close to how they feel appreciated, and then put that into practice. Or ask them how they'd like to be remembered when they're gone. They'll give you a wonderful insight into how they want to be understood, and you'll win their hearts when, months later, you come out with exactly the right choice of words to express your admiration of them. There's no reason why this should be insincere, it's just a way of making sure that your sincerity has a real effect.

these PRSs by the eye movements of the person. Ask someone a question that necessitates them searching in their mind for an answer, and you will often see a movement of the eyes. That might be a dart off to the side before re-connecting with your gaze, or it might be a lingering rest high in the air as a person enjoys some brief reverie. The direction will apparently tell you what is going on in their heads. Here is the chart as taught by NLP:

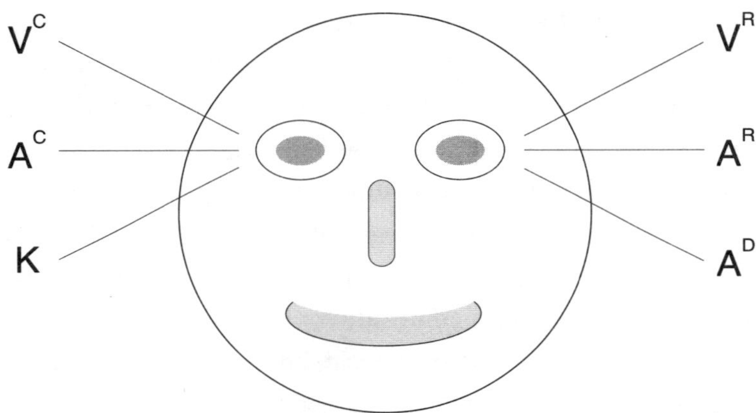

The chart points out the meaning of eye movements as seen when looking at a person opposite you. Even the most rampant NLPers admit that the chart does not apply to everyone; rather, it represents a rule of thumb. However, they would argue that whatever a person's pattern is, they will stick to it. The abbreviations signify the following:

V^C – VISUAL constructed images
A^C – AUDITORY constructed sounds
K – KINAESTHETIC/feelings
V^R – VISUAL remembered images
A^R – AUDITORY remembered sounds
A^D – AUDITORY digital (interior dialogue)

Looking straight forward, in this model, is a second cue that 'visual constructed' processing is happening. 'Constructed' means just that the sound or image is made up rather than something from the memory. So, if you try accurately to remember the interior of your bedroom as a child (pause from reading this for a moment and put the book down) you should find that your eyes wander up and to the side. Probably to your left, according to the model (visual remembered). Then, if you imagine what your current front room would look like with completely different decor, and really think about what that would look like, you should, according to this model, notice that your eyes shift across to facilitate the image (visual constructed). Similarly, if you listen out now for the softest noise you can hear outside, you should find your eyes move to the side on a level with your ears, rather than up and to the side as with the visual representations. This seems to tie in with a natural tendency to move your head to one side to hear better.

While this may seem a little esoteric, I do think it's fair to say that it seems to be reflected in what we glean during many interpersonal exchanges. If you ask someone if she fancies meeting your parents and she looks down for a moment before saying 'yes', you know that she had a moment of feeling unsure, weighed up some uncertain feelings or asked herself if that's what she really wanted. You might even want to say, if you're as nice as I am, 'Don't come if you don't fancy it', having picked up on a flash of uncertainty from her. If, on the other hand, she looks up for a second before agreeing, it seems more as if she gave it a split-second's thought but didn't have any conflicting feelings. So while I do find that the general thrust of the above picture is borne out in real life some of the time, I'm unsure about how reliable or useful it really is. Much, in other words, may rely on the initiated observer looking for signals that match his expectations.

This eye movement hypothesis has been tested many times by scientists, and routinely it is shown not to hold up. However, it is difficult to know whether this is because the claims are not true or the tests were not conducted fairly; NLPers naturally blame the experiments. The tests normally go as follows. The subject is not told what is being looked for, and is asked a series of questions the scientist believes will elicit a clear visual, auditory or kinaesthetic process. For example, he might ask for a kinaesthetic response – 'What would it feel like to swim in noodles?' – and note where the subject's eyes then move. Problematically, a question like this could of course elicit a visual response first (the subject pictures himself in noodles) or even an auditory one (the subject repeats the question to himself or runs through an answer), which would theoretically cause a different eye movement before the expected 'kinaesthetic' one. Although the 'correct' movement then might follow, this may not be noted in the results. Without examining the exact protocol of the experiments, it's very hard to tell how effective they are at testing these claims. Equally, though, if they are this difficult to test by observers who are trying to take as objective a stance as possible, one could argue that they can hardly be called reliable by biased NLPers who are making no such attempt. My suspicion is that if eye movement was really as reliable as NLPers say, there would be far more positive results in tests.

However, undoubtedly some people do seem to conform to eye movement patterns with notable reliability, so an awareness of the chart is perhaps worth having in the back of your mind. Fans of *The Heist* should watch again the sequence where the interviewed participants are remembering the list of memorized words they learned at the seminar. I had taught them the linking system, which means that each jump to the next word relied upon a bizarre mental image. Every time, you can see them remembering each image pretty much according to the NLP model. It's almost a textbook demonstration.

Similarly, tests have been carried out to see whether or not we really do feel more comfortable with people who match our representational systems. Again, they have failed to show that such a matching increases levels of rapport, trustworthiness or effectiveness. Indeed, one researcher found that therapists who matched their clients' language were in fact seen as *less* trustworthy and effective. But again, it is difficult, without knowing exactly how the tests were carried out, to know how effectively any number of other factors which could have contributed to these results were eliminated. The same difficulty crops up with pretty much any research into these rather subtle interpersonal issues.

We must be careful, though, not to think that this means the claims of NLP should not be properly investigated – with, presumably, the collaboration of NLPers and scientists who can arrive at an experimental procedure with which everyone is happy. NLP is a big business and worth taking seriously for that reason alone, although it was never the 'paradigm shift' Bandler and Grinder perceived it as. The course I attended was large (four hundred people) and highly evangelical in its tone. It reminded me a lot of the Pentecostal churches I had attended a few years earlier. Although I enjoyed much of the course and certainly got into the swing of it, the parallel with the church made me rather uncomfortable at times. One manipulative technique I found in both was the 'we can laugh at ourselves' mentality. NLP gurus or the happy-clappy leaders of a charismatic church will sometimes stand on stage and encourage their congregations to have a good old giggle as they themselves parody the nuttier excesses of their respective scenes; and as everyone laughs in response, any quiet reserve of intelligent scepticism in the room dissolves into nothing, and the scene is made safer and free from dissent. Now, other NLP courses may eschew the hype and theatricalities, but tend to make the opposite mistake of getting bogged down in technique. Both Bandler and Anthony Robbins package their goods primarily as an attitude, and clearly use the evangelical hype to render us as emotional and suggestible as possible in order to make sure that a) the message hits home and b) we want to purchase future courses.

In the fifth century BC, the Sophists travelled throughout Greece earning their living by imparting advice that would lead to political success. They gave lectures and took on pupils, charging huge fees. They taught young politicians how to persuade crowds to believe what they wanted them to believe. The Sophists bragged of their ability to convince a person that black was white, and to give satisfactory answers to questions one knew nothing about. They used clever word artistry and baroque metaphors to confuse and quieten their opponents, and were not interested in seeking truth. They responded to the public's desire to succeed without expending any effort or gaining any knowledge, merely by emulating success and cleverness. It's a very old business.

At the end of my course, which lasted only four days, I was given my Practitioner certificate. I didn't have to pass any tests or in any sense 'earn' my qualification. In many ways the course was about installing a 'go for it' attitude towards changing oneself or others for the good, so somehow, any sort of formal test would have seemed disappointingly pedestrian. So the four hundred or so delegates, some of whom were clearly either unbalanced or self-delusory, were set free after a highly evangelical four-day rally to potentially set themselves up as therapists and deal with broken people under the banner of NLP. We were told that after a year we should contact the organization and tell them why we should have our licence renewed. If we had been using our NLP creatively, they would send another certificate for a second year of practice. Because spending those few days in the company of hundreds of would-be NLPers had put me off ever practising it as a profession, I didn't think to contact the organizers again. But after a year or so I got a letter reminding me to call them to talk about sorting out a new certificate. I ignored it, but a short while later received another communication saying that they would be happy to send me one anyway if I would get back in touch. The ease with which they were happy to dish out their certificates struck me as suspect, and again I ignored their request. Not long after that, a nice new unsolicited certificate dropped through my letterbox, qualifying me for another year of practice.

TOOLS FOR PERSONAL CHANGE

TARGETED RAPPORT

Now, I have avoided making this book a 'self-help' book, which was the preferred option suggested to me by the first publisher who expressed an interest. My heart sank at the idea. Not that some of them aren't enjoyable reading, but, well, honestly. Can you imagine? A self-help book. The very idea. No. Shut your mouth-hole.

However, in this section I will discuss some approaches or techniques that may possibly be of use to you. Some have a very 'NLP' flavour. As I have suggested, if we remove from the NLP equation the grinning, flaccid course-junkies, delusional flower-fairies and ridiculous tactile businessmen, and some of the taken-as-read wild claims made by NLPers at all levels, there are some sensible enough tools and techniques from that world which are worth knowing about, as long as you don't become a True Believer. I remember an interview in the *Observer* in the nineties with a hypnotist where the interviewer started to feel something odd was taking place. He soon realized that the interviewee was copying all his body movements. The rest of the article was concerned with how strange and unnatural the interviewer found his subject, and how he kept testing the hypnotist by crossing and uncrossing his legs, moving his hands and so on, to see him immediately follow suit. What I loved about the article was that the technique the hypnotist was employing (the mirroring of body posture) is classic NLP, and like so much of classic NLP it failed because it had been turned into a 'technique'.

Most people, when they are getting on well, will be in a state of unconscious 'rapport'. They will tend to mirror each other's body language and so on without realizing it. Hence the common sight of couples sat opposite each other at tables in restaurants in mirroring positions. You will know the power of this phenomenon if you have ever sat up late talking to a friend, and then one of you moves from a chair to the floor. It's only a short while before the other person joins him on the carpet, such is the desire to keep the rapport going. For the same reason, there is the odd sensation we have all experienced (though we never think to mention it) of knowing when the other person is about to get up and leave. Suddenly there's something in the air, a moment or a shift, and then you know the other person is about to say they should 'make a move'. And if they don't, you have that feeling that they are outstaying their welcome. Here, you have established rapport for so long that the other person is following similar thought patterns and rhythms, and senses the natural end as you do. Or if he has privately decided that it's approaching time to go, he'll naturally interrupt that rapport, introduce a few unconscious shifts in body language to suggest a break, and the conversation will feel like it's ending.

Studies carried out on rapport show a fascinating array of mirrored behaviours that are far more subtle than body position. People in rapport tend to breathe at the same rate, adopt each other's facial expressions, blink at the same rate and use each other's language. Rapport may create those things, but the question is, do those things automatically create rapport? With its delight in modelling, NLP takes these by-products of rapport and teaches the student to consciously put them into practice. Breakout groups practise 'calibrating' each other's breathing and body posture, and matching representational language. I too have 'broken out' and taken part in such exercises, and I can report only an exaggerated version of what the *Observer* interviewer felt. Somebody copying my every move does not put me at my ease, though he certainly might appear fawning or retarded. Even if the mirroring is done a little more subtly, the idea that by then employing these 'rapport' techniques in a social situation you are guaranteed to come across as likeable and trustworthy is clearly daft. Many people learn these skills, like magic tricks, as a substitute for actual charisma. Clearly we can see that something gets lost in translation. In the *Observer* was a man who *taught* these very skills using them and achieving the exact opposite effect he was expecting. He was coming across as unnatural and weird.

Interestingly, an NLPer would probably want to scoff at that example and say that the hypnotist was making the mistake of using it dogmatically as a cold technique rather than absorbing it as an attitude. This is often brought up as an objection to accusations that NLP turns everything into a magical 'technique' which then of course doesn't quite deliver the goods. Some (admittedly more enlightened) practitioners argue that the skills must be absorbed into a general approach, and not thought of as dogma or special discrete methods. That might be true, but where, then, does that leave the idea of learnable rapport skills? If what was missing was the NLP 'attitude', isn't that just the same as saying 'he should have just naturally got into rapport', leaving the concept of learning modelled skills redundant?

If you have wit enough to strike the balance naturally, I think there is something to be said for understanding the power of mirroring. For example, imagine you are sat at a table and wish to have someone near you, or at an adjoining table, take an interest in you. This works best when people are seated and therefore in fixed positions; it's of less use in gatherings where people are mingling. As someone who tends to eat out frequently on his own, I used to play with this technique in restaurants, or occasionally at dinner parties if there was someone of interest sat where he or she could see me but we were not able to talk. I would also use this during law lectures where I found the speaker a little dull, as a way of having him or her take an interest in me and keep me engaged.

The game is to mirror the person subtly, constantly and peripherally, so that she (we'll use the feminine pronoun, but it need not be part of a seduction) finds herself feeling a connection with you and not knowing why. You are not talking to her or even looking at her; you can only watch her out of the corner of your eye. This allows you to be quite bold at times. If at a party, take a sip of your drink every time she drinks from her glass. Mirror her position as much as you can: lean back in your chair when she does, place your hands on the back of your head when she does, shift when she shifts. Sometimes an exact copy might be too obvious, as the *Observer* interviewer sensed; so if, for example, you see her drumming her fingers, you might swing your hand instead in a natural gesture. Do whatever you can get away with. You might be involved in a conversation with a third party at the time (this poor person really won't feel much of a connection with you at all). Just let your body move and react in the same rhythm as her. See it as a dance.

Then, after a while, you can test to see if the rapport is working. You can take the lead, and see if she follows. Take a drink, and see if she copies you. It's not magical and not difficult; you are just sending out signals of sameness in a situation where people are grateful for that kind of thing. It can make you oddly attractive, but it is by no means some grotesque 'instant seduction' tool. Such things are over-inflated and come from an unpleasant place. This is no different from building a rapport in order to connect with an important business associate at a meeting, picking up pens and shifting in the chair when he or she does. There's just more room for fun during a mixed social occasion, and you are doing it without being face to face, which hides things rather well. Above all, do it with a feeling of warmth and naturalness. If you are tense and uneasy you will destroy much of the rapport you are creating, unless she is tense and uneasy too.

Most likely, if you have done this fluidly and pitched it at just the right level, you will find the person in question comes over to make conversation with you later, and feels you're 'their sort of person'. It also encourages you to pay close attention to the non-verbal language communicated by another person, which is a worthwhile skill if you are then able to react sensitively to it.

Playing with Pictures

Do this for me. Think of an experience that makes you feel great, or terrible. Something that annoys or excites you. Do this now. Anything you feel strongly about. Good or bad – but please, nothing traumatic.

When you've settled on something, and felt the flutter of response, review what it was you saw in your mind. A short film or mental picture would undoubtedly have appeared, triggering that emotion. One of the more sensible tenets of NLP is that the way you represent this picture or film will affect the way you emotionally respond to it. To test this, try two things: first, enlarge the picture and make it brighter and more colourful. Turn up the sound and turn it into a sharp, high-definition image. Zoom in on it. Changing the picture in this way is very likely to increase your emotional response. Now try the opposite. Make the image smaller, and let the colour run out of it. Make it rather fuzzy and darker. If this is something you were witness to, shift the 'camera' to a third-person perspective: see yourself *in* the picture rather than viewing it out of your own eyes. Pull the black and white picture away from you until it feels far away. Doing this can cause your emotional response to dwindle away almost to nothing at all.

Here you are consciously controlling variables that your mind naturally finds for itself. You really can't feel strongly about anything unless you represent it vividly to yourself, which normally means large, close-up images seen through the first-person perspective. Equally, it's hard to get excited about something you think of in a far-off, fuzzy way. Compare what appears in your head when you think of a great time you recently had with a person – pause; do that now and note what comes to mind – with imagining going out and buying some jam with a work colleague who doesn't particularly interest you (now do that). At a guess, I'd say you saw the first image from your own perspective, right slap in front of you, clear and sharp and detailed. The second image of preserve shopping probably included you in it (i.e., was seen from a third-person perspective), was vague and difficult to pin down, maybe greyer, smaller, somehow further away, somehow not right in front of you like the first one.

By changing those variables – the size, shape, colour, brightness and position of the image – you can play a lot with how you naturally react to the content of it. One very useful idea if, say, you want to feel more motivated about a task is to look at how you picture something that *does* motivate you, then shift the problem task so it looks and feels the same as the one that naturally gets you all worked up. In fact, if you trick yourself into representing it in exactly the same way, you really can't *not* feel that buzz of motivation. It's a fascinating exercise. It can become a quick way of making yourself feel better about anything. If something is bothering you, shrink it down, desaturate the colour, move it away and shift to that third-person perspective; if you want to feel more excitement, make the picture big and buzzy and colourful, bring it in close and make sure you see the scene through your own eyes.

If you do find that making these shifts doesn't quite do the trick of changing the feelings, the chances are you haven't made the changes correctly. For example, take your image of the activity that motivates you and makes you feel good. Pinpoint something where you feel *very* motivated and focused. You wish to use this as a template to make your internal representation of a 'boring' activity more exciting. If you have difficulty succeeding in this, break the process down into the following steps:

1. Bring up the 'motivated' picture. You should have no problems thinking about it. If you do, change to another one. Hold the image in your head, or, if it plays like a film, loop it around a few times while you ask yourself these sorts of questions about the picture:

    i. Is it a movie or a still picture?
    ii. Is it in strong colour? Desaturated? Black and white?
    iii. Is it close to you? At arm's length?
    iv. How large is the image?
    v. Do you feel inside it, as if it were wrap-around?
    vi. Is any movement fast or slow?
    vii. Is the picture in front of you? Are you looking up or down at it? Notice its position.
    viii. Are you in the image, or looking out of your own eyes?

2. Now look at the 'unmotivated' picture of the task you wish to feel differently about. Ask yourself the same questions and see what's different or the same about the two pictures.

3. Now place the 'unmotivated' or 'boring' activity into the position occupied by the 'motivated' picture and make it look and feel like the latter. Change all of those variables and let it fall into place. Don't hold back, just let it feel like the motivated picture.

4. For good measure, put a bit of 'sizzle' into this new picture. Intensify it a bit more; give it more of what you've given it already. Sometimes it can be fun to imagine a theme tune in your head which captures the spirit, and play that as you have the new image burst with vitality. It might help to imagine a pressure sensation against your back, pushing you into the image. Play around with these things and you'll soon get the idea.

All well and good, but you now need to make this re-formating happen naturally. Because we tend to do what's familiar, the key now is to tell the brain to represent the picture in this more exciting new way rather than the boring first way. This you can do by repeating the action of moving the image from the old place into the new place, and bringing in all those changes. Literally start with it in the old, boring position with all its tedious qualities, then shove it into the new 'motivated' position, with all its colour and vibrancy. What's important here is that you only make the move one way: you're telling your brain 'Not this . . . *this*!', and you don't want it confused as to which way to make the change. So do the change quickly and forcefully five times or so in a row, 'clearing the screen' between each change so that you can begin each time with the picture in its start position.

Then test it. How do you feel about the old task? Unless there are other major issues that need to be looked at, you should notice an immediate improvement in your reaction to the task, in a way that feels quite natural and organic.

What appeals to me about these techniques is that they are just re-creating what you would naturally do anyway if you came to feel the new way about the task. As we don't have to insist on NLP or any other particular approach, we can safely assert that what becomes important is not a special technique but an attitude, of being able to shift your mind into a more positive gear through thinking in terms of *process* without always getting bogged down in the logistics or *content* of the problems at hand.

There is an intriguing physical correlative of this process: changing your physiology can make a marked difference in your emotional response to a troublesome thought. Find something else that makes you feel bad inside when you think about it. Something you know wouldn't be a problem if you were able to feel more confident in the face of it. Let your mind run with it a while, and you'll probably notice that it affects how you sit: you start slumping, or your head drops a little. Now do this. Stand up, put your shoulders back, straighten your back and look forwards and upwards. Try to feel bad about the same thing. You can't really, can you? Making physiological shifts like this are often a quick, easy way of getting your emotions to follow suit. If you need to do an extra set of particular exercises in the gym, or to walk into a room of people when you're feeling anti-social, or if you find yourself mulling over a problem and making yourself feel bad, try these sorts of shifts. Act as if you're in a more resourceful state, adopting the relevant posture and very often you'll soon find that your emotions follow suit.

Phobia Cure

Sat up late one night with my flatmate in Bristol, we thought it would be mature and responsible to start a local tarantula scare. I had long since graduated and had little to do other than the occasional magic gig and pay in my housing benefit cheques, and Simon, a philosophy student, understandably didn't have very much to do at all. So a couple of nights later we walked casually through the dark and deserted streets of Clifton Village, giggling and smirking, pinning our posters on trees and posts.

WARNING they screamed in large black print above a photocopied picture of an orange-kneed tarantula. The poster explained that several of these spiders had been lost in transit to the zoo and were believed to have settled in the Clifton area. They would be mainly active at night, and would seek warm places during the day. They 'should not be dangerous to adult humans if left undisturbed', but any found should be reported as many of them were 'believed to be carrying eggs'. At the bottom of the poster was the 'Tarantalert' (oh yes) number to call if you were to find one. The number had been picked from the *Yellow Pages*, and was in fact an insurance company in Cardiff. We posted a few through key newsagents' doors with instructions for them to display the poster for customers. We covered the sleeping square mile of Clifton Village with our rather nicely made posters and snuck back to the flat, still giggling like schoolboys.

The next couple of days brought an excellent response. People were talking about it in the street, and Simon and I reported to each other anything we heard. We wrote a letter and posted it one night in our local favourite greengrocer's, the still unparalleled Reg the Veg. This was a long and detailed letter, supposedly from the zoo, maintaining that grocers' shops were 'Class A' risk establishments along with florists and 'child day-care centres'. It outlined precautionary steps they must take against the escaped spiders. For example, they must check each individual piece of fruit every morning to see if a spider was clinging to its underside. Other recommended actions included stopping using fluorescent lighting and placing open jars of Marmite on the floor as the yeast fumes would render the spiders drowsy and more amenable to capture. To their credit, the staff probably realized the joke, but were good enough to display the letter on their wall, which only added to the general uneasy discussion in the village.

One morning the local paper ran the story SPIDER SCARE – A HOAX along with a condemnation from the zoo authorities and bewildered statements from an insurance company in Cardiff, which was suspected of being behind the stunt. Teletext, it was reported, had been duped and had run a big warning about 'giant spiders'. Determined to have the last word, we thought we'd fabricate a spider and place it somewhere visible but inaccessible in the village. We decided that it would have to be made out of pipe-cleaners, as a simple fake spider bought from a toy-shop wouldn't be funny enough. So eventually we made Boris, and late at night we attached him using one of Simon's guitar plectra to the inside of the archway next to the Clifton Arcade (and Reg the Veg), then covered him in cobweb spray.

The next morning we went to start a crowd. We waited for a group of people to walk under the arch, then we ourselves contrived to walk past them beneath it; only as we did so, one of us looked up and noticed our dodgy arachnid. After a while and a few false starts, we managed to get a crowd gathered in the archway, looking at our ridiculous pipe-cleaner assembly crouching in the corner. People stayed and moved on, which meant that after a few regenerations of the crowd we were no longer known to have started the interest. Some people knew that the story had been

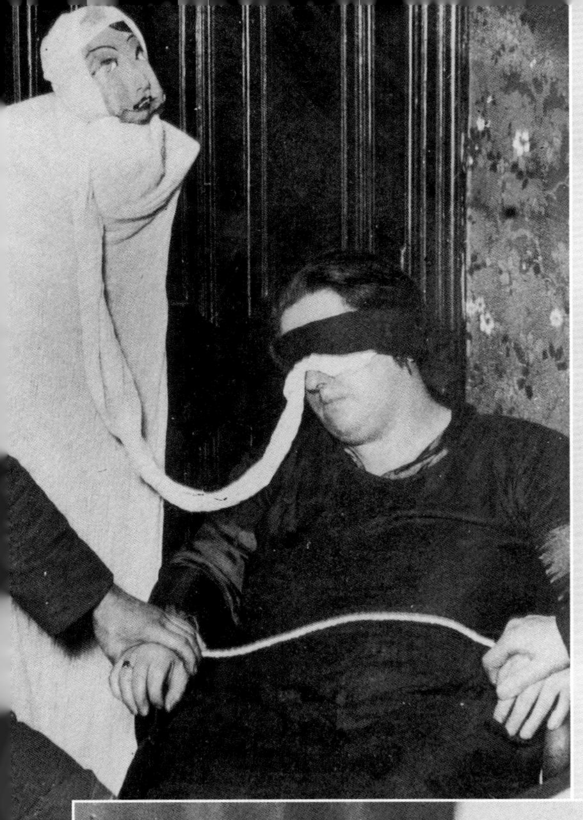

LEFT: *A photograph of medium Helen Duncan producing an ectoplasmic figure in a séance. Duncan was eventually imprisoned following accusations of fraud, which has made her a heroine of modern spiritualists who are determined to clear her name.*

BELOW: A *further example of ectoplasm being produced by a medium. Sitters were not allowed to touch the supernatural emission, presumably for fear that they might notice its close resemblance to muslin brushed with luminous paint.*

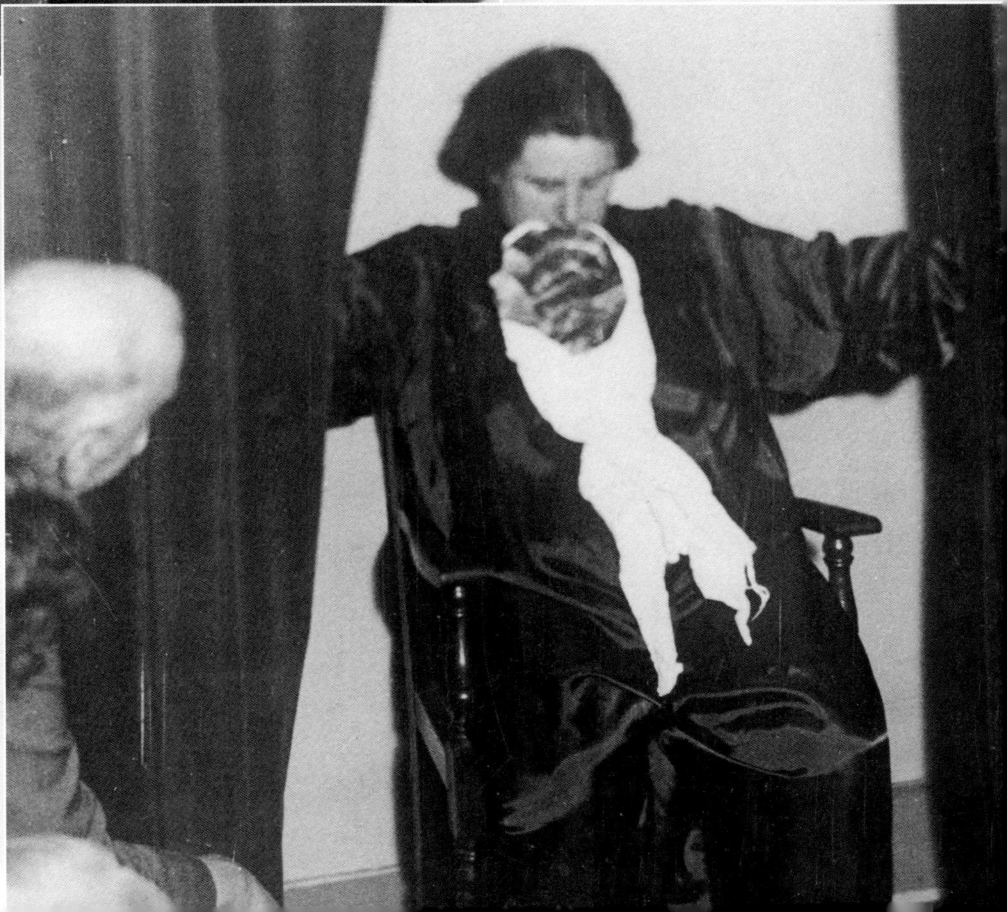

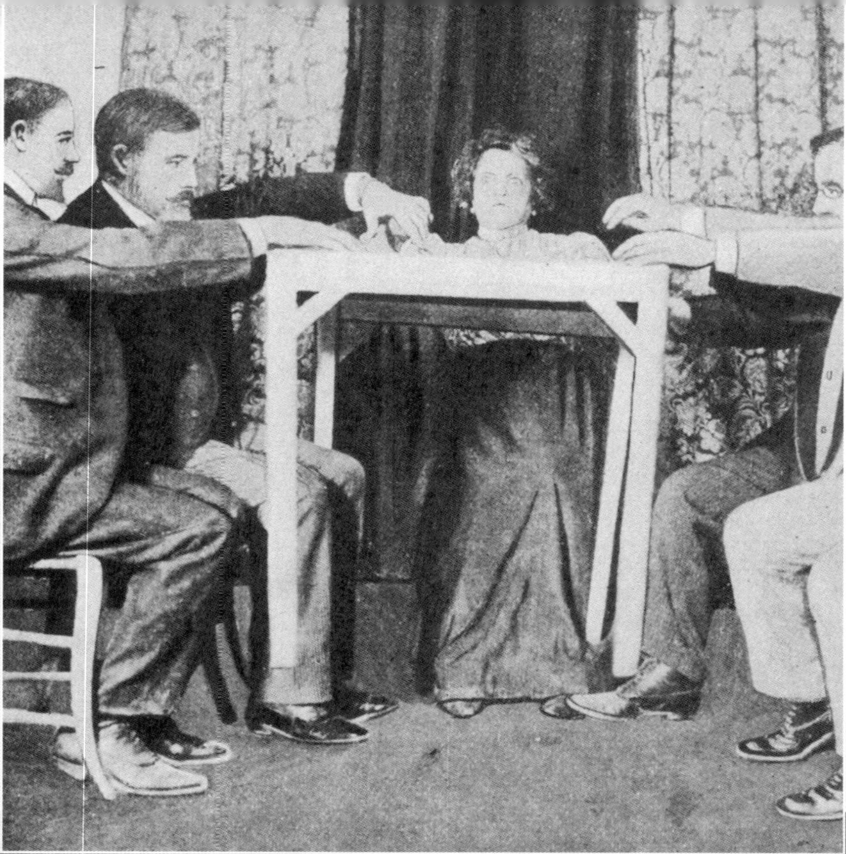

LEFT (ABOVE): *A classic and lovely illusion of the séance medium. Various methods are employed to allow mediums or accomplices to secretly attach themselves to and lift the table.*

LEFT (BELOW): *Wonderfully creepy picture of medium Ethel Post-Parrish in 1953, producing her Indian guide 'Silver Belle'. Post-Parrish still has a church in Florida today.*

RIGHT (ABOVE): *Milton H. Erickson, the father of Ericksonian hypnotherapy and guru to many in the field. His work largely inspired the founding of NLP, though I suspect he's rolling in his grave.*

RIGHT (BELOW): *The Fox Sisters (from left to right: Margaret, Kate and Leah). In 1848, Kate (12) and Margaret (15) were at the centre of strange spirit rappings from the walls of their house. Soon they toured the US and abroad, starting a craze which turned into the Spiritualist movement. By the time they owned up to the fraud (they were able to click their toe-joints together loudly to create the raps), it was too late to stop the religion they had started.*

A Modern Table Levitation. Demonstrating a table-rise at home for scientist Dr Robert Smith (senior fellow at University College, London). He sat quietly for a few moments afterwards and then said, 'Fuck me, I have no idea.'

LEFT: *A makeshift Ouija board: a familiar and creepy illustration of ideomotor movement at work. The sitters move the planchette themselves without being aware of it.*

LEFT (BELOW): *My portrait of Bertrand Russell, the most prominent British philosopher of the last century, and hugely influential in the areas of epistemology and logic. Ethically and politically outspoken, he was imprisoned twice. Russell's robust and blasphemous collection of essays* Why I Am Not a Christian *is an absolute joy.*

RIGHT (BELOW): *My portrait of Richard Dawkins, evolutionary biologist and a prominent voice of modern atheism. Post 9/11, the problem of religion needs to be addressed, and we have yet to see whether the rallying cry of Dawkins and others will have the desired effect.*

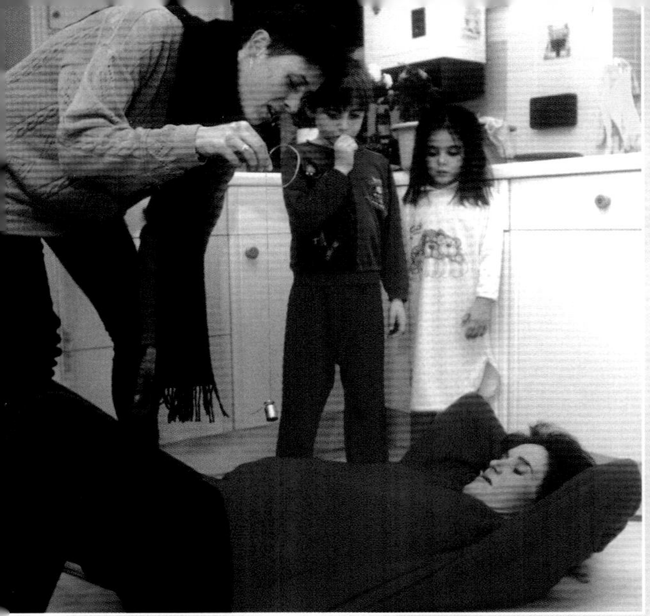

LEFT: *A woman 'predicting' the sex of an unborn baby with a pendulum. Notice how she is cheating: she can claim that the pendulum has identified a male foetus by the way that it swings, but is also secretly allowing her scarf to come up with the opposite result, to cover both options.*

ABOVE: *Your author with co-writer Andy Nyman After winning the Olivier Award for Best Entertainment 2006, following the run of* Something Wicked This Way Comes *at the Cambridge Theatre, London, directed by Andy. The Olivier Award is the most spectacularly prestigious for anything in the world.*

ABOVE: Russian Roulette (2003): *I try to secure myself a place in the Christmas 2003 Top TV Moments show. At the time, so-called 'reality programmes' had exploded on our TV sets like bad rubbish, and I was intrigued to know how far that voyeuristic urge could be stretched.*

BELOW: Messiah (2005): *The first of many trips to the USA where I could utilise my anonymity. The idea was to see how readily influential figures in paranormal belief systems would accept a con as real.*

reported as a hoax, but others weren't sure. Of course we helpfully interjected our own stories of having known people who had actually seen the spiders. It also took only a few suggestions from us for the crowd to create the story, and believe it, that Boris had actually crawled across the wall at some point during the morning's events. That was particularly rewarding. Someone suggested calling the local news, and of course we encouraged them.

A cameraman came, and he asked in Reg the Veg if they had one of the spider posters to include in the shot. They helpfully gave him one of them, and he filmed the tarantula cowering several feet above it. Sadly he didn't interview any of us, but he was accompanied by a well-dressed but very tense lady who spoke to him all the time from behind a clipboard with which she covered her mouth. I heard later she was from the zoo, which I hope was the case, though I suspect she was a news reporter.

After several hours of standing about and re-telling and exaggerating the story to each fresh crowd member, one guy suggested that the spider looked fake. We reminded him that it had crawled across the wall earlier on, but he was having none of it. Unable to protest, we had to watch as he climbed up the same wall we had used and poked at it with a rolled-up magazine. Its predictable lack of response brought relief from the crowd, and eventually he removed it from the wall with his stupid hands.*

*During our years as flatmates, Simon and I busied ourselves with other enjoyable ruses, such as a letter I sent to a complaining and noisy man who was in front of me in the housing benefit queue after I noted his name and address, which came up on the receptionist's computer screen. The letter contained a supposed quality report on his house and points he would have to address before his benefit could be raised. These included criticisms of the 'outmoded' decor in the hallway, a cracked and dirty salad drawer in his fridge, ketchup rings in cupboards and auxiliary hairs in the plughole of the bath. He was to bring photographic evidence that such areas had been addressed into the benefit office, and I really hope he did. The spider scare, though, felt rather good, and for any of my Bristol readers who may be interested, I believe the plectrum is still stuck under the arch. If it is, and you know where I mean, please be good enough to leave it there.

Now I am not phobic about spiders, but I do find them rather unpleasant. I would not, for example, want to be locked in a small cupboard with a torch and a thousand house spiders crawling all over my face and eyes and getting inside my mouth and nostrils. But the following technique, credited to Bandler, may be of real value to those of you who suffer from a phobia you know can be traced back to an incident when you were young. The results of this process should feel natural and casual, apart from the fact that the fear won't be there any more. I used this on a friend who had a terrible fear of spiders, and it was six months until he saw a spider to test if it had worked. He called me to say that he had just got a spider out of the flat through the textbook glass-and-postcard method and it had suddenly struck him that this was the first time he had been able to go anywhere near one without freaking out. This is what this phobia 'cure' aims to create: a natural and easy removal of the irrational, paralysing fear, leaving you with a normal, balanced, healthy reaction. After all, if you have a fear of dogs, you don't want to replace it with an equally compulsive love of them; you want the presence of mind still to spot the occasional vicious one and leave it alone.

The following technique may read a little oddly, so let me explain what it is based on. Perhaps I have a phobia of fingers (I don't) because when I was young my mother locked me in a box full of fingers (she didn't) and I freaked out (I didn't). Now, whenever I see fingers, I lose it (I don't). This is because the trigger of fingers sends me back into that emotional state (it doesn't) and I 're-associate' (I do NOT) with the early memory (I don't have one). See? My gut reactions, always there to help me, are just overcompensating (they aren't). In the case of a phobia of dogs (no), spawned from being bitten as a child, you can imagine that the gut fear is there as an overcompensating protection mechanism. Your instinctive reactions are always trying to work for you, but sometimes they go overboard. Once they get the message that you're better off without the overcompensating mechanism, they are generally happy to stay away and not come back. So the following process works by making it very hard to re-associate with the old memory, by making you feel distant from it at that 'reactionary' or unconscious level.

If you don't really have a phobia, use it to get rid of any limiting or unhelpful negative response you have to a bad memory. It won't erase the memory, but you'll be left with a more healthy relationship with it. You might want to get someone to talk you through this by reading the instructions out to you with the appropriate gaps, or learn the sequence first before going for it. Finally, best not to use this if your phobia trigger involves cinemas or anything involved in the process described. One chap I met had a phobia of dreaming, and the visualization involved made trying this uncomfortable and ultimately ineffective. Otherwise, give yourself some quiet space to go through this properly and genuinely, and I hope you find it as effective as it certainly can be. Before you start, I'd just remind yourself that the phobia was real by imagining the phobia trigger and feeling the bad feelings that come. In a few minutes you'll find those feelings have vanished, but it will feel so natural that you might doubt that the old trigger ever really bothered you in the first place.

1. Close your eyes and get comfortable. Imagine that you are sat right at the back of a cinema. You can picture a real cinema that you know well.
2. In a little while you are going to watch a movie of the memory that led to the phobic response you have. However, the movie won't be projected normally. It's actually a very old black-and-white movie in which you star, playing yourself. The movie will

be projected in a small rectangle in the middle of the big old screen, right over there at the front of the cinema. You'll be able to see it all, but it will be small. The picture quality will also be a bit fuzzy and washed out, as if the film is really old. There won't be any sound, but instead there will be a musical soundtrack. The music will be comical, so please choose something from a favourite TV show which sounds inherently funny. *Benny Hill*, *The Muppets*, *Monty Python* and so on tend to work very well for this. Bonzo Dog Doo-Dah fans may wish to use 'Jollity Farm'. Remember too that you'll be seeing yourself in the film, so this will be a new way of viewing the events.

3. Before we start the film, think of some situation where you know you are solid, strong and excellent. This can be anything from making sensational lasagne to being an expert on a pop star to being shit-hot at any weird thing you can think of. Let yourself feel that rather comfortable, smug feeling of power, and get it to spread into every niche of your body. Really exaggerate it and notice how it feels, letting your body remember it. You'll let this be your state while you watch the film.
4. On 'Go', you're going to play the film. But not quite yet. Up above you is the little projection room. If at any point you need to get more distance from the film, you can leave your body and float up here, where you can look down on yourself watching the movie from the back of the cinema. The film will play from beginning to end and tell the whole story of the memory in vintage fuzzy black and white. At the end it will freeze-frame, and if someone is reading these instructions out to you, you should let that very helpful someone know that you've got to the end by telling them. But keep your eyes closed. Ready? Start the music . . . Go.
5. Finished? Good. Now, keep it frozen on that last frame. Float

up from your seat and down into the picture on the screen. Meet your younger self. Congratulate your younger self for being so brave, and for having survived an unpleasant experience, or whatever is appropriate. Now move into the body of the younger you, so you look out of his or her eyes.

6. Although you are right at the end of the movie, make the picture now all colour, as you look out of the eyes of the younger you. In a moment, you are going to run the whole film backwards, at top speed, *with you inside it, viewing everything from that first-person perspective*. The same music will play backwards at top speed, but the fast rewinding will be over fairly quickly. When you get back to the start, you can open your eyes. That will complete the process. Ready? Full colour now, played backwards to the start and seen from inside. Go!
7. Good. Eyes open? Great. Now, check that it's worked. Think of that old trigger again. What's different now? Are you finding that the old response has gone? Can it be that easy?

Now what do you do? The next phase is to root your new, 'mature' or 'helpful' response in reality and memory by searching out the old trigger and noticing that you can be comfortable and happy in its presence. If you had a phobia of dogs, and you now feel OK about them, go find some dogs and get used to not being scared. This is quite an important phase: you need to become familiar with your new reaction (or lack of it), so that this new reaction starts to feel like you – if still rather new, delightful and exciting.

If you tried the above and nothing happened, check to see whether you really gave it your full involvement. If you tried it alone, do get someone to read it through for you as this really helps you focus. I've really seen it work wonders, but this may be due only to the fact that phobias are surprisingly easy things to lose. It would be good to see this 'cure' tested against a pure placebo cure, to see what makes this tick. I hope it works for you.

Self-confidence and the Image We Project

When I am not showing off with my tricks for money, I paint. Some of you who take an unhealthy interest in my life may know this. Having delighted in cartooning teachers at school, I now like to paint portraits that have anything from a whiff to a really quite unpleasant stench of caricature about them. It's a very peaceful and relaxing way of spending my time, and gives me a chance to catch up on the very latest advertisements on Classic FM.

One thing I sometimes hear from charming people who might like one of my paintings is that I have somehow 'captured' a character through exaggerating the features. The assumption, which I do find rather interesting, is that the features betray the character. Now, this may be no more than a confusing of the words 'caricature' and 'character': the former is commonly misspelt due to imagining some etymological connection between the two. Of course there is no connection: 'caricature' comes from the Italian *cari-* (to 'give someone') and *care* ('an enormous nose'), and has nothing to do with character at all. More likely the phenomenon of the character being expressed through the exaggeration of the features is due just to the right sort of smile or frown being captured, but either way I love the fact that we are prepared to see so much depth in surfaces.

Oscar Wilde spoke of the 'mask behind the man', the sense that the most profound thing about us is the appearance we show to the world; our affectations and obvious idiosyncrasies are often the things that count most and say the most about us. From this we can agree that my own sense of the inner 'me', by comparison, is likely to be speculative nonsense, and certainly tends to bear no relation to how I am actually connecting with the world at any real level.

It is an enormously refreshing and liberating concept, and in its way has been taken up by many a motivational self-help book, encouraging you to shift behaviours on the surface to stir up deeper waters below.

A person I know has a tendency to express herself quite aggressively and nastily in emails. Because I had received several of these and the lady in question was a friend of a friend, I spoke with her to discuss the problem. To my surprise, she insisted that she really held no anger, and blamed her 'bad writing skills' for the unpleasant communications. She said that she was not a nasty person; in her mind she was in fact utterly reasonable, and obviously I should not read the emails as evidence that she was a bad piece of work.

I thought this an interesting situation. We *all* think we are reasonable people. In fact we measure how reasonable other people are by comparing them to ourselves. A friend of mine who occasionally steals bits and pieces from supermarkets has it all justified in his head: *he's* not doing anything wrong; it's not really stealing. We are all likely to believe we possess the right levels of honesty, charm, intelligence and taste; and even if we think of ourselves as terribly shy or uninteresting, we'll make up for it by knowing that we're really decent, or honest, or – and this is the best one – *really interesting when you get to know us*. However modestly we talk about ourselves, we *think* we've got it all right, and are justified in our behaviour.

Right. We can see the foibles and annoying traits in other people, but don't they also think they're all sorted out and well balanced? So are they wrong and we're right? Or perhaps we can see it this way. I'm sure, delightful as you are, that you talk about people behind their backs from time to time. If you and friend X both know another friend Y, the chances are that you and X pick up on Y's frustrating habits, and sometimes sit and discuss them. It's therapy;

generally harmless and not meant nastily. But you do it. Now, *your friends will do the same about you.* This is because you have your own irritating habits that you don't even know about. Not only do you and X talk about Y, but also you and Y will get together a week later and talk about X in the same way; so too will X and Y talk about you. You're just another person with probably transparent insecurities that your amateur psychoanalyst friends will probably enjoy speculating about.

Another friend of mine has a skin complaint (please don't think I keep company only with thieves and freaks), and he once said to me that it's an embarrassing thing to have. I asked him why. He answered that people can spot it, and they find it revolting. The fact was that although he clearly does have eczema, there's nothing revolting about it at all. One might think 'Oh, he has eczema' and then forget about it, or in my case vaguely wonder how to spell it. So I told him that his opinion (that it was revolting) was so negligible compared to the millions of opinions of people who meet him (that it isn't) that perhaps he should decide that he's just wrong. Simple mistake: plain wrong. The experts on the subject of whether or not his skin is revolting populate the *rest* of the world; he's the one person whose opinion has *no* validity at all. We'll tell him if it's embarrassing or not. I think he understood.

I am in the situation where people who recognize me and meet me briefly will decide for the rest of their lives what sort of a person I am based on that momentary interaction. People who are really famous must find this paralysing. I try so hard always to be extra-friendly with people, to avoid the awful thought that they may have been left with a poor impression of me. Knowing what famous people are 'really like' is an understandable source of fascination: we are all interested to know, regardless of whether or not we have a small amount of fame ourselves. Once, at the start of my career, I hurried into a café in Bristol to look for someone I was due to meet but thought I had missed. As I went through the door, I was looking over the heads of everyone to spot my friend's ginger hair (I have no problem with that lot) and in my rather flustered state I didn't notice that a couple, on their way out, had opened the door for me. Unwittingly I had just rushed right past them with my nose in the air. I was only aware when it was too late. I heard a mumbling of my name and a 'Did you see that? Unbelievable' as they walked away. That was their experience of meeting Derren Brown, and they went away thinking I was a cunt. And I'm sure they still delight in telling other people when my name comes up, 'Derren Brown? Yes, met him once. An absolute *cunt*. Famous for it.' And I might as well have been. It still makes me cringe. I'm sorry. I hope they read this. The café was the Primrose Café in Bristol. Please read this.

On the same subject, though I am digressing a little, a similar thing happened to me while I was in a friend's flat in London during the making of the *Russian Roulette* special. The flat was on the top floor, and there were many flights of stairs to descend to reach the front door of the house. One morning I was being picked up to be taken off for some typically glamorous filming, and I quickly jogged down the stairs with the natural pace of one who has four floors to work his way down and no desire to spend more time than necessary doing it. I had no idea at the time that my flies were undone. A neglectful resetting of my lower garmenture after a last-minute wee-wee had left the trouserly copula less than interdigitate, but I was manifestly unaware of my manifest underwear. Worse, I was around the time experimenting with the uncanny freedom provided by the manly boxer-short, and Fortune's hand had that morning blearily fumbled in the smalls drawer of Providence and decided that such swaddling would serve as the day's netherwear of choice. So I was hurriedly bouncing down the many stairs with not only trouser boldly undone, but also private shorts jostling ajar. As I alighted from the bottom stair a key sounded in the lock of the front door, and I passed a couple coming in as I left. I wished them a bright and cheerful 'Good morning!' as I was aware that they might possibly recognize me. I was being more careful than usual to be charming. It was only when I stepped outside into the bracing September air and felt almost immediately an algid breeze in a most surprising area that I realized I had left the house with my cock hanging out. A moment's reflection told me that I had passed the couple at the door in the same state. I have no idea if they noticed, and with time I have learned to cling to the possibility that they might have brushed past me and not seen, but again the fear: 'Derren Brown? Yes, we met him once. His cock hangs out.' Putting a gun to my head came quite naturally after that.

The point is, what you *mean* to be is not what you *are*. What you *mean* to communicate about yourself is not the point: it is actually *what* you communicate that is the important fact. The woman who sent the nasty emails was being a horrendous bitch because she expressed herself like one. End of story, regardless of whether or not she thinks that's 'really her'. People never think it's 'really them'. The word 'bitch', for example, refers to how you communicate and deal with people, not some truth about your soul. Left on your own on a desert island, you can't be a bitch; it takes communication with other people for that word to mean anything. A common concern in one's twenties is what one's 'real' self consists of. The reality of the situation is that while it's important to have some sense of a distinction between an 'image' we project socially and how we behave away from company or with closer friends, no one aspect of us is any more real than any other. We're multi-faceted glittering disco balls, bouncing light in all directions, and life is a great big bloody disco. Or something.

Armed with this understanding, we can try to look at our behaviour a bit more objectively. Maybe you are rather quiet socially, and don't make much of an effort to endear yourself to people when you meet them. You wouldn't make a point of telling a host that you enjoyed her party if you didn't like it, and you don't approve when you know that someone's being flattering without really meaning it. You'd probably have to say that a person would have to do a bit of work to get to know you and see that you're more than the understated and quiet person you project.

Well, there's nothing terribly wrong with the above, but all this might seem very different from the outside, or what we can loosely take as 'reality'. People might naturally expect more of an effort from you socially, and may misinterpret your shyness as disinterest, aloofness or dislike. Is that their fault or yours? You could come across as not terribly nice, for no other reason than you're quiet. It takes a lot of back-up skills of dry wit or real charm for plain quietness to be endearing in a social situation. We *all* have great qualities which are there when people *really* get to know us, but even this 'real' self suffers from the same problem of still not necessarily being as engaging or as pleasant as we think it might be.

Essentially, what this comes down to is the importance of social skills. Making a point of being flattering or charming to people isn't being insincere. Perhaps it is if you are being asked for your honest opinion which is, in fact, far from positive, but even then there are ways of giving feedback which are effective and encouraging. A lack of these important social skills is normally a symptom of a lack of confidence, which leads us to the good news. Confidence can be faked. It's not real.

I don't think (and certainly it's helpful to not think) that 'confidence' really exists any more than 'motivation' really exists. If you feel you're under-motivated, consider this: the word is used only by people who say they don't have it. People who are 'motivated' rarely use such a term to describe themselves. They just get on with the task at hand. 'Lack of motivation' is an excuse: it's giving a name to *not* just getting the job done. Forget motivation; just get used to doing things straight away. With confidence, the situation is similar. Firstly, you must realize that confidence doesn't exist as an objective fact. A person in isolation isn't inherently confident or unconfident; we become those things only when we start interacting. Equally, there is no difference worth speaking of between a person who is 'really' confident in a situation and a person who is just behaving so. So we can usefully see confidence as just behaviours and tricks that make us appear in a certain way. Why might we want to appear as confident people? Because in the right measure, it's an enormously attractive quality. And it can make us feel very good. Too much, of course, or too little can be exhausting. The moment someone naturally makes a good impression socially, it's an enormous relief for everyone he or she meets. When you are introduced to someone, don't you immediately decide how much you like them? How enjoyable they are to talk to? If they seem charming and engaging, it's a pleasant relief. It's not insincere, or superficial, it just makes them pleasant to be around.

Now please don't for a moment think that I am speaking from a position of expertise on being charming or even particularly confident. My own issue in this area comes from an uncertainty over whether or not I should expect people to recognize me from the telly. If I feel that they might do, I always make a point to try to be engaging and to leave them with a decent impression of me, for reasons I've already given. But unless they display a clear sign of recognition, I presume they don't know me and that it's safe to appear bored and boring and mumbly if that's how I'm feeling. I've been out with real stars who know that when they walk into a room everyone will recognize them. Therefore they can switch 'on' and work the room a bit, shaking hands with people who speak to them. It would be ridiculously presumptuous for me to start doing that. I can imagine the 'Who does he think he is?' comments being muttered in quiet corners. However, I'm always a little embarrassed to find out that a person serving me in a shop when I was feeling tired *did* know me after all, and that I might have made a poor impression. All too infrequently is this feeling compensated for by getting the goods in question at a reasonable 'celebrity' discount.

Equally, like many cantankerous and incontinent old ladies, I really don't like parties much and get very claustrophobic after an hour or so in bustling company, unless I'm lucky to fall into a genuinely interesting conversation with someone. I'm sure you're the same – I don't know anyone who actually enjoys parties for their own sake, aside from the hosts. By no means do I regularly brighten up a room with super-confident behaviour. But I secretly admire people who do. And the fact is that it takes very little to shift into a confident state.

Firstly, what is your self-image? Andy, my writing partner, has an extraordinary ability to bring high energy, enormous humour and charisma into pretty much any social situation. He is remarkable. Much of this comes from a flattering self-image and enormous levels of self-belief. I was fascinated to find out that although he is undoubtedly a short guy, he sees himself as tall. Conversely, a six foot four friend of mine who tends to feel more awkward socially told me he always imagines people are taller than he is, and is constantly surprised by photographs that show him looming over their heads. Somehow the daily behaviour of physically looking up or down at everyone they meet had been lost on these chaps due to their self-images.

It takes little reflection to see that our self-images are arbitrary, and far more likely to be born out of our insecurities than our strengths. And what exactly is a self-image? Far from being abstract, let's take it for what it is: the image you make in your head of yourself when you picture who you are. You might have an overriding self-image you refer to most of the time, and plenty of other ways of seeing yourself that are specific to certain situations: at home, meeting people, at work and so on. Pinpoint a couple now; take a moment to see what comes to mind. Note what appears in your head when you think of yourself. Who makes the decision as to what those pictures or mini mind-movies contain? You've probably left those to create themselves, and a lot of unhelpful bits of information have got stuck in there. Should you bother to change what's in those pictures?

The fact is that spending a few minutes playing with the content and look of those pictures can lead to worthwhile and even dramatic changes in your life. The way you see yourself defines the limitations you place on your behaviour. It's rather straightforward. People who are able to give up smoking overnight, for example, are very likely to be the ones who decide to see themselves as a non-smoker, and then behave in that new and exciting way, not worrying if they occasionally slip up; rather than the people who merely 'try not to smoke' and set up a stressful challenge that presupposes eventual failure.

Decide on a self-image you would like. Picture a version of yourself that is realistic but exciting. It's pointless imagining a super-hero version of yourself which is completely unattainable, but be sure to make it something that really appeals. Now, in the same way that you can look at a person and tell that they ooze confidence, make sure that this image of you radiates the qualities you would like to have more of. Design this self-image, and make it detailed. See this new 'you' interacting in new ways that delight you, and not having to deal with the issues you may have faced in the past. Make it a good one.

Now that you have the contents of the picture in place, you need to make sure that you are representing it to yourself in the most appealing way. You want to emotionally engage in this picture so that it makes you drool, not just have it as a rather distant snapshot. So, remembering the ways in which you can control these mental images, try out combinations of the following to see what works best:

1. Make it large, like a picture on a sixty-foot IMAX screen.
2. Make the colours rich and intense.
3. Turn up the brightness.
4. Try bringing it in closer.
5. Add *sizzle*. Let the picture be pushing out of the screen with vitality.
6. Add a soundtrack. Mentally play a theme tune or song that fills you with confidence, or the appropriate emotion for the picture.

Wallow in it, and add anything that makes it even better. Maybe the approving voices of certain friends help. Imagine key figures being impressed with you, and let that in turn affect the picture. Once you can really feel its appeal with every fibre of you, try the following trick. Imagine that the image in front of you has thick rubber bands attached to the corners, which are in turn anchored behind you. The picture is then slowly pulled away from you, and stretches on those rubber bands. As it is taken off into the distance, it feels like you've got a giant catapult aimed right at you. Have the picture locked in place, but be aware of the extreme tension in those stretched rubber bands.

Now, bring up in front of you an image of something that has traditionally made you feel under-confident. Think of a situation where you would benefit from this new self-image. Picture whatever you would see or think of that would normally trigger bad feelings.

As soon as they begin to creep up, have that negative picture quickly shrink down to nothing, as you release the catapult and zoom the self-image right up in front of you. Let it sizzle into place and drastically change the bad feelings for good. Note the changes, then clear the screen, reset the self-image at a distance and do it again. Be careful to make the exchange only one way: in other words, don't pull the self-image back into its high-tension start position. Just start each time with it already there. That way, your mind only sees it go the one way – towards you.

You need only do this five times or so, then test it and find that it happens automatically. If you try to get the bad feelings back by thinking about the old trigger, it's really very hard to do so. You've learned to naturally associate the old trigger with this new self-image. This can be very useful if you are becoming a non-smoker: make a great image of yourself as a non-smoker and have that triggered by the image of a cigarette, or whatever the most potent triggers are for you.

This is an NLP technique known as the 'swish' pattern, again created by Bandler. While it's far from being the be all and end all of personal change, it can be helpful, if you can be bothered to sit down and go through it. Again, it's more useful to have someone else talk you through it, and preferably someone who is energetic enough to help you create and experience the necessary feelings that need to be attached to the various parts of it. And it works not because it's a special technique, but rather because it apes very closely what would happen if you *naturally* felt self-confident in that situation, or if you just started to feel good there instead of bad. Plenty of people are fully able to make these shifts without recourse to a prescribed technique. The value of methods such as this, I feel, lies not in the techniques themselves but the fact that they tend to undo the general feeling that we have to be 'stuck' in unhelpful patterns of thought. When divorced from the exaggerated claims made by the NLPers, tricks like these can be useful.

Of course it is becoming over-fond of such techniques that can lead to the peculiar madness of that scene. With its appeal of bypassing the content of problems entirely, to look instead only at changing a process from feeling bad to good, it can encourage a mentality of disengagement and lack of responsibility for one's actions. I remember a fanatical NLP friend of mine talking to his daughter, who had reached boiling point with him for not helping her deal 'normally' with some problem. She grew angry at his continual process-related questions, when all she wanted was a bit of real-world sympathy and a chat. She shouted at him, and really put her finger on many of the frustrating and ridiculous excesses he was guilty of. His answer was, 'Good. Now, how do you *know* you feel anger about that? What are you picturing in your head?' Immediately it was her 'limitation', not his ludicrous behaviour, which was to blame. Another high-flying NLPer had been through a series of short, bad relationships and was telling me that after the last one fell apart he did some 'brainwork' to start feeling good again, and now he was off to meet someone else. Perhaps a bit of real introspection and questioning of deeper issues might have done him a bigger favour than just, presumably, perpetuating a bad pattern.

Self-help techniques can be enormously rewarding for some people, and self-evident for others. Gurus such as Tony Robbins make fortunes from motivational courses that are both amazing and sinister, but which boil down to an age-old and obvious adage: *just get on with it*. It's about *do or don't do*. In social life we are defined by our actions, not by our motives; our thoughts or intentions mean very little unless they lead to action. It's how we behave, or even sometimes how much we make the effort to be nice, that makes the difference. An obvious but much-missed point.

Confusion and Self-defence

We should all go together to a magic convention. They are extraordinary events, at once both unintentionally hysterical and staggeringly depressing. One year I was attending such a convention in Llandudno and was walking back to my hotel in the early hours of the morning. I had quite long hair at the time, as well as the Emperor Ming goatee, and was wearing a velvet jacket, waistcoat and fob watch; in those days I thought I had an old-world dapper charm, when in fact I looked like a gay time-traveller. As I headed back to my hotel with the inexplicably Scottish name, I found myself heading towards a young couple coming in the opposite direction. They were both quite drunk and arguing loudly. By the time I realized that they were going to be troublesome it was too late to cross the road and get out of the way. As they approached me, I might have caught the guy's eye (a mistake if I did), because I was suddenly aware of the horrible words 'What the fuck are you looking at?' shouted at me from suddenly very close range with the force and pent-up anger of a very aggressive Welsh drunk. Peripherally I saw the girl walk off down the road and leave us.

There's an old Wing Chun Kung Fu technique I would normally have snapped into without thought: in the face of aggression, you lie on the floor in the fetal position and sob, kissing the toecap of your aggressor's shoe. However, having given thought to the use of confusion techniques to disarm aggressors, I was able to put some of my theory into practice. This brief thought process happened against the backdrop of a clear, vivid and brightly coloured mental image of my person lying beaten *and* stabbed in a mangled confusion by the side of the road. So I made my body relax and my face friendly and warm, and I said, 'The wall outside my house isn't four foot high.'

He paused for a moment. 'What?!'

'The wall outside my house isn't four foot high. But I lived in Spain for a bit and you should *see* the walls there – enormous, right up here!' I gestured with my hand to clarify how high I meant.

Now, you're going to thank me for this, so bear with me. Here's what has happened. He has come at me with a huge amount of adrenalin and force, and his question 'What are you looking at?', like any intimidating question, is designed to put him squarely in the position of aggressor. No direct answer to his question can change that. My confident and friendly answer about the walls makes absolute sense within itself, but is completely out of context. This guy has to work out what I'm talking about, and in doing so he becomes enormously confused. By offering him more of the same (talking about Spain), he feels he might be afforded some relief from the confusion, but such clarification doesn't come. He is wrong-footed, confused and no longer in control. He experiences something of an 'adrenalin dump', which leaves him useless.

The state of bewilderment he was in would also have rendered him highly suggestible. The use of disorientating techniques to amplify a person's responsiveness to suggestion is a classic ploy of talented persuaders. A politician knows that if he fires a set of confusing statistics at listeners, followed by a 'summing up', they are more likely to believe that concluding statement, rather than if he had offered it without the deluge of too-much-to-take-in information first. A salesman knows sometimes to overload a client with information to enhance how open they will be to a direction that follows. In effect, we are offered relief from the confusion and we happily do what we're told. Until our normal equilibrium returns, we are putty in our manipulator's hands. My plan, then, was to render this guy heavily suggestible so that I could deliver something like, 'It's OK, I don't know if you'll notice yet whether it was your right or left foot that stuck hard to the ground first, but you'll certainly be relieved after a couple of minutes of trying so hard in vain to unstick your feet to find that they eventually come unstuck . . .' Layers of presupposition that his feet would stick to the floor would be lapped up as relief from the confusion, and I'd be able to leave while he struggled to free himself.

As it turned out, though, such lengths were unnecessary. After I told him about the Spanish walls, I added, 'But here, they're tiny! Look at these ones!' And I pointed out a tiny three-brick-high wall around the garden right next to us. He looked at the wall, and that movement told me that I now had the upper hand. He looked back at me, rather slumped in himself by now, let out a long 'Oh, fu-u-u-ck . . .' and crumpled, hanging his head hopelessly. To my delight and surprise, he started telling me the story of his evening; I remember something about his girlfriend bottling someone at a party, or similar. He sat down on the kerb, distraught and broken, and I sat next to him and listened for a while, offering sympathetic noises and understanding. When I left, he thanked me.

It was an extraordinary event, and I was pleased that the technique, fine in theory, had worked so well in practice. So I offer this to you as something for the back of your mind for when you find yourself in a nasty situation with an aggressor. A good friend of mine, James, told me of a harrowing time he had had on a platform in a tube station when he and his friend were surrounded by a group of intimidating kids who insisted they hand over their phones and wallets. A nasty game was being played where the kids were acting in an oddly friendly but persistent manner, as if nothing was untoward, yet at the same time flashing a knife. It was clearly a frustrating and intimidating experience. Their game works because the person being attacked gets caught up in trying to respond to the aggressors' questions and loses all control or dignity. There were plenty of other people around on the platform, and many of them would have been aware of what was going on. Of course they did nothing. Ultimately James held his ground (though his friend handed over his belongings as he was broken down by the relentless demands to do so) and got away with a nasty punch in the back as he boarded the train, but alternative ways of dealing with the situation, based on my Llandudno experience, have occupied me since.

Imagine, for example, if James or his friend had responded very differently. Rather than being drawn into the situation, James cheerfully pipes up, 'I used to have this pencil case in primary school that looked like a calculator, but the point was that it wasn't, it was just a pencil case. Can you believe that the headmistress told me I couldn't bring it into school *just because it looked like a calculator*? It wasn't, it couldn't do anything at all!'* Clearly the response of the main kid in control of the group won't be, 'That's ridiculous of her, but give me your money.' He and the group will be disarmed, just as my aggressor on the street was, and not know what to say. What they *will* know is that their game of intimidation isn't working with this guy. What if James continued with, 'She used to make us sing this stupid song every morning which I *hated* . . . hang on, how did it go?' and then launched into a song? Loud enough to make the gang extremely self-conscious (not to mention James)?

While hopefully there'd be no need to go as far as to start singing, the logic is simple. You are casually and unthreateningly bypassing their intimidation by simply playing your own incompatible game. Delivered with a cheery tone of voice and the attitude that they should understand exactly what you are talking about, you are neither being intimidated by them nor challenging them. I

*Yes, true memory from primary school.

would recommend that you have in your mind a few obscure song lyrics to recite, or something clear in your head that you feel you can use. I'm sure there will be the occasional unfortunate time when the level of aggression from a perpetrator is so unthinking that this technique would be redundant, but it is a very workable way of extricating yourself from most unpleasant interactions of this kind.

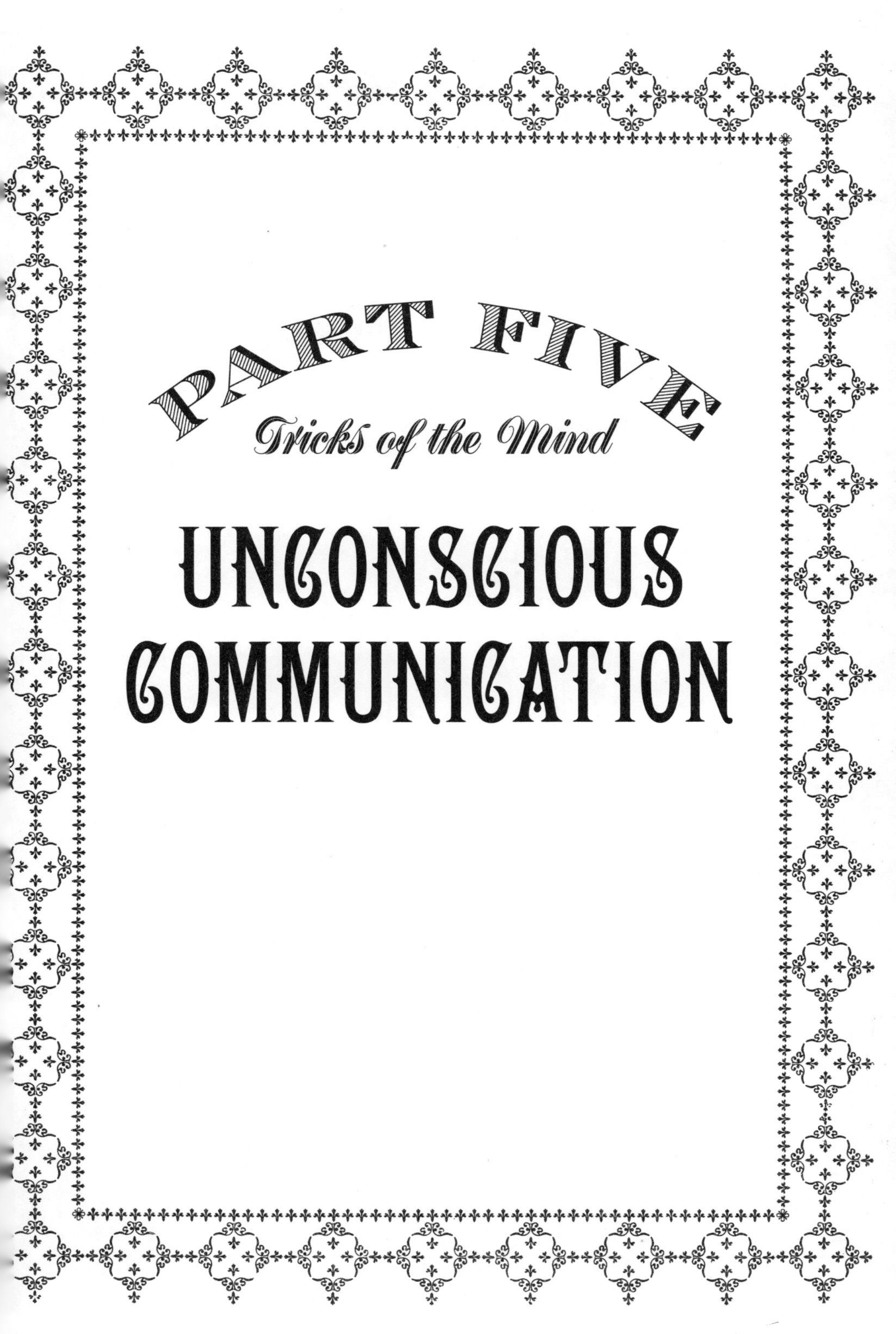

PART FIVE

Tricks of the Mind

UNCONSCIOUS COMMUNICATION

UNCONSCIOUS COMMUNICATION

I by no means consider myself to be particularly well known outside a small group of oftentimes disturbed Channel 4 viewers (sorry, '4'; never 'Channel 4'), but there are times when I get to have a taste of what real fame would be like. I find the thought quite frightening. At the time of writing, I have just turned down an offer to move to the BBC primarily because the thought of being much better known at the moment is a genuine turn-off for me. I have had a couple of sincerely unpleasant stalkers, and numerous obsessed persons exhaustively attending live shows night after night or constantly writing under the misapprehension that we have some sort of romantic involvement. Some are genuinely disturbed schizophrenics who have created rich, consuming fantasies – not necessarily pleasant ones – in which I play a major part as romantic hero or villain.

Beyond that, and beyond the contrastingly pleasant fees, there are the genuine confusions and mixed comforts that come from being perceived as a 'celebrity', minor or otherwise. Because I am nowhere near the league of huge BBC or Hollywood names, I am caught off-guard when people decide to shout at me in the street or, in the case of a few misguided schoolgirls, occasionally scream in excitement. I have *literally* no idea what to do. If a person comes up and says hello, or is interested in purchasing an autograph, then that is a flattering piece of social interaction and all's tickety-boo. But imagine, for example, you have been thrust into my violently glamorous lifestyle and have been invited to a film premiere. You are looking forward to the movie, and to the notion of seeing it before your friends, but when you turn up you see there is a red carpet and a crowd of loud, screaming people clamouring to catch a glimpse of the stars. Nothing in your life can make you relate to the screaming, even though you know that these people have no interest in you and are certainly not screaming in your direction. Compared to any American, or anyone who appears on 35mm film stock, you are of no importance. You guess that a percentage of them will know who you are and might shout your name. But, and I hope this doesn't sound churlish, what do you do? Do you wander over anyway and sign autographs just in case? No, clearly not, for who knows who you are, or cares? So do you just go over and sign things for the odd person who shouts your name? Well, perhaps, but then when do you stop? When do you walk away from the line and decide that you're now scribbling your moniker for people who have absolutely no idea who you are, beyond a vague sense that you might be Paul McKenna? And then you're back to the first problem.

I have in the past tried to find alternative routes into cinemas at such events. At the royal premiere of *The Lion, the Witch and the Wardrobe*, I suspected that the Albert Hall would yield an appropriate side entrance for me while the likes of Annie Lennox and Dawn French graced the carpet with all the star status it invites. I was, however, politely prevented from trying to sneak round the back and re-directed down the glitzy route, where I was pathetic enough actually to pretend to be on my mobile as I walked past everyone. I actually put my phone to my head and had a pretend conversation.

That way, I figured, I didn't have to think about the shouting, and no-one would be upset if they *did* shout and I didn't come over. I'm pathetic.

This is not false modesty on my part. Equally, I know that most of you wouldn't be seen dead screaming at film stars from behind a barrier. I also know that if you court modest popularity with television work you have to take on board the weirdnesses of it as well as the advantages, so I'm not criticizing anything other than my own confused C-list response to it all. Somehow, the rather two-dimensional version of any television presenter which blares at people once a week from their screens and leaps through the air of their private homes and into the backs of their faces creates the illusion to certain unpolished minds that they actually know that presenter and have a relationship with him or her. This is the trick upon which much of popular success relies.

One aspect of this understandable misapprehension which I often hear is the idea that because of what I do on TV, I must be constantly 'reading' people; seeing through every façade and quietly identifying people's real motives based on their body language. I didn't realize that so many people must think this until I recently tried to hire a personal trainer. Most of them declined, as they were worried that I'd do 'mind-tricks' on them. To do what? Make me exercise less? More? I am often asked in interviews if I am able to 'switch off', as if my perceived 'abilities' are some sort of curse. I know it's entirely a product of the image I project through the shows, and I secretly wish I could live up to it and be more mysterious and dazzlingly confident in such situations. Invariably, I've found out, I get described by journalists as 'surprisingly nervous', 'intense' or even 'geeky'. This is probably in part due to the fact that I don't like interviews very much, and also that probably the interviewer expects someone rather more controlling and impressive. That and the fact that I'm probably nervous, intense and geeky. I don't know.

I neither constantly 'read' people, nor am I always judging their secret motives. I have to come up with ideas to perform pretty much all the time, and the thought of performing or playing to character when I don't have to is not a pleasant one. When I am working, I mix psychology with conjuring, either often masquerading as the other, so you'd be wrong to decide that the tricks, tests and stunts rely on no more than a superhuman understanding of non-verbal and unconscious communication. However, it is impossible to work in the area I do without developing a good knowledge of such things, and to utilize them as part of the tool kit. I obviously have an interest in them; so I will happily offer my thoughts as long as you realize that my shows, with all the deception and exaggeration they entail, should not be viewed as examples of what an understanding of mere body language alone can create.

LEARNING TO READ PEOPLE

The first thing to take on board is that the real point to learning a sensitivity to unconscious behaviour is that it is enormously helpful if you find yourself in conversation with someone who is boring. As people are normally more than happy to talk about themselves for long periods, you can be assured that just by asking a few questions to keep them chatting away you'll be rewarded with a great opportunity to practise and improve your own responsiveness. You may have no great interest in *what* they say, but at least you'll be hooked by *how* they say it.

There is a big challenge to get through before you even start. Anyone can 'people watch', and those who say they are fond of doing so are generally as insulting and blind to other people as those awful types who say they 'collect interesting people', or that you'll love so-and-so because she's 'absolutely mad'. You might wish to enquire as to which aspect of her schizophrenia you should aim to find particularly charismatic, but for me, these sorts of statements hark back to the idea of casting oneself squarely as the central protagonist in one's life-play, and everyone else as amusing bit-parts. While this sort of thing is undoubtedly part of being human, so also is the balancing urge to try to see others as real, three-dimensional entities, not to repulsively pigeon-hole them or treat them as objects. If your motive for 'reading' people is to decide that they are a certain sort of person, then you must first shake yourself out of this nonsense. Personalities fluctuate. Where we are extrovert in one situation, we will be introvert in another. You may know a person as a reliable type, but you never experience her when you're not around, when she may be quite different.

Handwriting analyses and personality readings fall apart at this first hurdle when they make bold statements about personalities. Personally, I think that anyone who has been rejected for a job application on the basis of a handwriting analysis has serious cause for complaint. You might as well be refused on astrological grounds. Graphology, despite its impressive rules, deconstructions and a plausible surface logic, is no more an accurate diagnostic tool than a dotty old palm-reader working from a tent on Blackpool promenade. This is why a graphologist will tell you that he can detect certain traits (such as honesty and sociability) in the same way that any vague statements can be made to fit anyone, but that the most basic, specific, verifiable facts, like whether the writer is male or female, cannot be gleaned from a handwriting analysis.*

*Although, as with psychic reading, plenty of specific guesses will be made and then credited to the system if they happen to hit. If they miss, they are forgotten.

The fact that personality is fluid, and that anyone with whom you interact is responding to you and therefore affected by you, means that reductionist, simplistic diagnoses about personality based on body language or any other tool must be avoided. They'll simply be wrong. Equally, your own preconceptions about a person must be disregarded. If you feel that a person is dishonest or egocentric, you will look for body language that supports such traits. Developing a genuine responsiveness to non-verbal communication demands a level of detachment, objectivity and rigour; otherwise you will simply end up coming to false conclusions, which may seriously damage your relationships. Real objectivity in such matters is, of course, pretty much impossible. There will always be a level of personal opinion involved, but realizing the importance of removing preconceptions from the equation is terribly important.

A fact that is often missed or glossed over in popular books on body language is the importance of first identifying a *constant*. This means that in order to understand what behaviours are significant one must often first understand how the person normally behaves in a less significant scenario. For example, if a person has an itchy nose and has been scratching it on and off for a while, it would be silly to read his nose-scratching as a sign of deception if it then coincides with his answering a pertinent question. Equally, other environmental issues might cause potentially confusing symptoms, such as when a person folds his arms because he is merely cold, rather than feeling defensive. While this may seem obvious, it is a really important starting point. Because of this, it is often crucial first to understand a person's normal behaviour and then to look for clusters of body language symptoms, rather than to ascribe importance to symptoms that occur in isolation. This is particularly important when looking at lying signals, which we will consider next.

SPOTTING LIES AND GIVEAWAY TELLS

Perhaps more than any other area of body language, it is the identification of deception that attracts most interest, and with it the largest number of daft theories and misconceptions. The most common misconception is that *people break eye-contact when they lie.* Nonsense: people break eye-contact all the time. Our eyes move all over the place to help us retrieve information. In fact, a person who unnaturally holds eye-contact is far more likely to be lying, and probably operating under the same misconception, thinking that if he breaks it he'll appear deceptive.

How ingrained this common misunderstanding is hit home to me after a hypnosis show one evening. I sat a student in front of the audience, which had remained for a question and answer session, and asked her a few questions about her day. I told her to lie once but to try not to give away on which occasion she had lied. I picked out the lie and asked the audience what she had done differently. One person suggested that she had not been able to keep eye-contact when she had lied, whereas she had kept eye-contact for all the other answers. I asked the rest of the group if they agreed with that theory, and there was general approval. In reality, as I then explained, the time she lied was the *only* occasion that she *kept* eye-contact. In response to all the other questions, she naturally shifted her gaze to find the information she was looking for. Yet the students remembered they had seen the exact opposite, purely because of their expectation.

The NLP thinking that the eyes will either look straight ahead or move up and to the right instead of to the left when the subject is inventing a mental image rather than genuinely recalling one has, I think, value with some people when considered in the limited context of asking visual questions. However, many other people also betray nothing of the sort in their eye movements. Any NLPers getting in a twist are advised to put it to the test by asking the same set of visual questions to different people who are unaware of what's being tested. Many people don't exhibit the pattern. We have already looked at some of the complications of testing such a theory, such as how one knows for sure that a simple visual response is being triggered. But if one just looks for sudden and reliable *changes* in eye movement as a response to significant visually geared questions, rather than being fixed to the idea that up-and-right means a lie (which is ludicrously simplistic), then my hunch is that noting these changes may well be a helpful tool, if the person exhibits such changes and they are supported by other reliable symptoms in a cluster. I make this point tentatively, as I am aware that no serious research has supported the original NLP claim.

There are certainly many unreliable 'gimmicks' for spotting porkies which are best left to folk wisdom. My own approach to looking for lies is part of a wider attitude and method, which I shall try to describe here. I don't suppose that my approach is particularly original, but it seems to work for me. Firstly, it is necessary to watch a person in a state of disengagement. This can either be because I have a specific agenda in mind – for example, I am looking for signs of deception or perhaps even helping someone to resolve a problem – or because I just wish to pay them this sort of attention. The point of 'disengaging' is not to get too caught up in the content of what is being said, but to be able to take note of the unconscious language (both verbal and non-verbal) the person is offering me.

There are three ways to spot deceit: by looking at non-verbal language, verbal language, and by measuring small physiological responses such as increases in blood-pressure, heart-rate and sweating of the palms. This third option is left to the polygraph, which is often mistakenly called a lie detector. It isn't: it merely measures these small changes, which could of course be produced by a nervous or frustrated suspect for any number of perfectly innocent reasons. The polygraph reading must therefore be combined with the skills of the examiner in handling the interviewee and interpreting the reading before any conclusion can be reached as to whether the subject is lying. However, this necessarily subjective interpretation, and other procedural criticisms which are often aired, make the accuracy of a polygraph test a matter of great debate. Researchers have tested to see whether the polygraph is as effective as its defenders claim. In one undercover test, they had four polygraphers on four different days each test four employees of a company to see which of them had stolen a valuable camera. However, each polygrapher was told prior to the test that one employee was under particular suspicion (a different employee was used every time). The idea was to see whether or not this piece of information would sway the results of the polygraph test. In fact, no camera had been stolen and all the examined subjects were telling the truth in denying the theft. Yet each time, the polygrapher in question confidently identified the 'suspected' employee as the guilty party.

Polygraphs aside, the techniques left for the rest of us to identify lies correspond to the first two methods: non-verbal and verbal language. In other words, our body language and the way we speak. We will have a look at both here. Within these two areas, it is worth bearing in mind that there are three processes which a person might experience when lying. Knowing these processes will help you look for signs of one or more of them leaking out into the person's words or behaviour. The three processes to bear in mind are as follows:

1 : Emotional Processes.
2 : Content Complexity Processes.
3 : Controlling Processes.

Emotional Processes refers to the emotions which can leak out during deception. The most common emotions experienced by a liar are guilt, fear and excitement. I may feel guilty about lying; I might fear the consequences of my lie if, for example, the stakes are high; I might be excited about lying, especially if there are other people around who know the truth and might be amused by my bold lie. This last emotion is referred to as 'duping delight'.

Content Complexity Processes come from the fact that lying can be cognitively quite an involved task: for example, it will often become more difficult to maintain a convincing lie if you are questioned more and more on the subject in question. Equally if we are taken by surprise, it is often quite difficult to lie. The result is that you have to think rapidly or just more than normal, and this fact might well leak out in your behaviour.

Controlling Processes are those which we carry out to hide the signs which we think might give away our lie. In other words, we try and behave normally, and this will usually involve unnatural or incongruent behaviour which can be spotted.

I feel that the key to reading body language is to understand that you are looking for key *changes*, not simple, specific 'tells' that mean a certain thing. So in order to be able to effectively read a person, or spot a lie, you must first establish what his 'normal' behaviour is, in order to appreciate any deviance from it.

Establishing a Baseline

Without this appreciation of the person's 'normal' behaviour, it is impossible to note important changes. For example, if a person is already swinging his foot back and forth, it may be the *ceasing* of the swinging that suggests a significant response to a question. Once you have a baseline, you can then spot changes, such as moments of increased stress, without becoming obsessed with what numerous particular gestures are supposed to mean.

How do you establish a baseline? Well, with people you are close to, you may already have a good idea of how they behave. With others, you can establish this by chatting about insignificant matters, and watching how they behave. Note the natural rhythms and relaxed gestures the person makes, and seek to ensure that he is comfortable with you. Any odd behaviour on your part will contaminate the process and yield an unreliable result. The list of key areas in the next section will guide you as to where it's important to pay attention. Once you have done that, understanding how shifts might occur in each area is an important factor in learning how he is reacting to the conversation on emotional and intellectual levels.

I would suggest you take each of the following points in isolation and practise noticing each in turn, before you start watching people as a whole. These are the things I will tend to pay attention to when I have reason to be processing in this way.

Key Areas of Unconscious Communication

HEAD AND FACE

Surprisingly, given how most people think they can 'read' the faces of people they know well, this is often the worst place to look for tell-tale signs of what's going on beneath the words being used. Generally people are quite good at controlling their facial expressions and you have to be quick to catch flickers of their *real* state which might occasionally come through, such as a momentary look of anger or fear before a smile, or other tiny 'micro-expressions' which can often only be reliably spotted with the aid of video playback or extensive training. Equally, a person might be saying that he feels very strongly about something, but if his face does not have etched upon it the expression of the relevant feeling with the same depth as he purports to feel it, he may be speaking insincerely. It is very difficult to consciously produce all the genuine signs of emotion on the face. For example, a person pretending to be angry will find it hard to voluntarily narrow his lips, a sign of real anger.

The commonly asserted view that a smile is not real unless the eyes are involved is true, but there is more to the story. Paul Ekman, a major pioneer in the area of facial cues, has conducted many experiments which show how conflicting emotions such as anger or disgust may creep momentarily into a fake smile. Two muscles are involved in the production of a real 'enjoyment' smile, or smiles with 'Duchenne's marker' (named after the scientist, who in 1862 first drew attention to the difference between real and fake smiles): the zygomatic major (which pulls up the lip corners towards the cheekbone) and the orbicularis oculi (which raises the cheek and crinkles the skin around the eye socket). Please write those down in your notebooks and use them to show off at parties. Ekman and his colleagues' research called for smiles not to be treated as a single entity, but to be broken down into different types. Ekman and Friesen were the first to differentiate in this way in 1969; before that it was not believed that the face could betray concealed emotions. Further research has found that the Duchenne marker is only one of several distinguishing features of a real enjoyment smile. For example, the zygomatic major action (the lip movement) is generally shorter in the case of real smiles than with faked smiles (i.e., between 0.5 and 4 seconds). So believe a quick smile over a long one. Also, Ekman has reliably shown that Duchenne smiles correlate directly to the signs of enjoyment as measured by EEG: in other words, the smile makes you feel good and feeling good makes you smile.

Since Ekman developed the exhaustive Facial Action Coding System to measure and label combinations of facial movements, his research has shown how much we give away without realizing it. However, without the aid of extensive training or specialist equipment, these 'leakages' are generally too quick to spot. Also, as he suggests himself, we may often prefer to be taken in by a fake smile or a similar expression of concealment rather than deal with the consequences of detecting a lie, so many signs that should be detected in real time are undoubtedly ignored.

Ekman's work really shows that our faces will always betray what we genuinely feel. This is because there is a direct link between our emotions and our physiology: each affects the other. No such direct links exist between our emotions and our words, which is why we can produce the words of a lie with relative ease but must struggle to stop our physiology from giving us away. Our emotions activate muscles in the face, which means that we must try to suppress those fleeting micro-expressions if we are to hide our true feelings. Commonly, those emotions will arise unexpectedly and then be controlled. For example, a suspect during an interview might suddenly become fearful when he realizes that the police know more than he imagined. At that moment, a fearful expression is very likely to appear on his face. He will of course try to suppress his fear, and Ekman's research shows that we can indeed suppress these expressions within one twenty-fifth of a second after they appear. If the interviewer blinks, he will miss it. But a freeze-frame of the first moment when the suspect realized he was in trouble will often show the frightened face which reveals the suspect's guilt.

Through various experiments aimed to detect lies about people's political beliefs and whether or not they stole money, Ekman has shown that an observer trained in the FACS can detect up to 80 per cent of truths and lies. This is a very successful result, when compared to the results of most professionals in the field of spotting deceit, which, as we will see, are very low.

HANDS

Hand movements are fascinating to watch, particularly when the speaker is talking about a subject in an animated way. Often the hands will give valuable clues as to how the person perceives his relationship to the subject he is talking about, and how he weighs up different options; they may even leak a vital clue as to what's really on his mind. For example, consider the gesture of pointing at oneself while talking. This might be a full-finger point, or a gesture with the palm of the hand towards the chest. The former is more common when the speaker is annoyed or particularly animated. Obviously this gesture is a signal that the speaker is referring to himself. However, it may occur in such a way that betrays the fact that the speaker sees himself in a role he does not consciously mean to communicate. For example, imagine he is talking about a problem at work or in a relationship, and as he says 'I don't know what the source of the problem is', he gestures at himself. This might suggest that he unconsciously feels *he* is the source of the issue, in which case he may well be.

Alternatively, the speaker may point to other people without realizing it, and in doing so give away his true feelings about some aspect of his relationship with another person or people. This might even relate to people who are not present. For example, I once attended a meeting in which one chap, David, was sat with another chap, Simon, to his right. I did not know David, but it was important to me that he got along with Simon and me, as there was a business relationship I hoped would flourish there. Simon, however, was being rather abrasive, and I was concerned that he might be irritating David. A few days later I met David and we spoke about the meeting. I noted at one point he said something like 'I'm sure there will be one or two obstacles to overcome', and as he did so he gestured with his right hand, pointing softly towards where Simon had been sitting in relation to him at the previous meeting. He did this entirely unconsciously, and it seemed to be a signal that Simon was that obstacle. While it wasn't conclusive on its own, it meant that I could then mention Simon later on and watch for reliable, subtle abreactions to his name. When he did respond reliably with tension to Simon's name, it meant I could then deal with the concern. This was a situation where it wouldn't have been appropriate for David to talk to me about Simon and the fact that he found him annoying, yet his feelings could certainly have jeopardized a good working relationship.

The 'weighing' gesture can sometimes give a clue as to which way a person's mind is working. For example, the speaker may talk about how he isn't sure whether to carry out option A or option B, and in expressing his indecision may mime 'weighing up' the options as if his hands were a pair of scales. Generally it's clear which hand refers to which option as he'll introduce the hands one at a time as he verbalizes the choices. This is demonstrating 'On the one hand . . . and on the other' quite nicely for you. If you see this, you should pay attention to whether or not he treats one side as 'weightier' than the other. Or you may well find that the speaker's next gesture shows you that he has already settled his decision. For example, he continues with 'I don't know which one I'll go with' and in saying so clearly drops one hand down, or shifts to one side, demonstrating that the weightier choice on that side is the preferred one to him. Such a movement would suggest that he has already made up his mind, although he may not consciously realize it yet.

Hands also have a habit of showing you how the person represents subject matter to himself spatially. For example, despite his words, he may show you non-verbally that the problem he is dealing with is so 'in his face' that it stops him from seeing a solution (he waves his hands in front of his face as he refers to a bad situation). Or at the other extreme he may show that he is rather detached from an issue by placing it at arms' length, even though his words may purport to demonstrate emotional involvement. Absent-minded gestures can be enormously revealing.

Sometimes these 'illustrating movements' that contradict a person's story can be quite specific. I remember talking to a friend about how he had found a suicide note and a wallet containing money on the Clifton Suspension Bridge in Bristol. He was reporting to me the extraordinary events of the previous night: a suicide had taken place earlier and he had been the first to look for and discover the poor chap who had jumped. He was quite animated, a state that lent itself to quite a lot of gesturing. As he spoke, for example, about rummaging through the undergrowth, he mimed exactly that with his hands. He described picking up the wallet that had been left on the bridge to check the identity of the deceased, and his hands made soft gestures that clearly constituted an absent-minded mime of going through the cards and cash in the wallet. However, I noticed that as he told me that he then 'got rid of it' (suggesting verbally that he either threw it off the bridge or left it on the bridge), he actually mimed putting the wallet in his inside coat pocket. It was a 'soft' and incomplete half-mime, but it quite clearly told a different story to his words. Of course I picked him up on it later, and he admitted to pocketing the wallet. But he had been utterly unaware that he had made any gesture at all.

If a hand comes to the mouth or nose while the speaker answers a significant question, this may indeed be a sign of deception, as is well known. It is as if the speaker is trying to block the words from coming out. As we will see, though, it is dangerous to read into any gesture that occurs in isolation.

Another clear signal, which is very common and often denotes stress, rising frustration or a desire to leave, is the drumming of the fingers on the leg or the arm of a chair. If you see a conversational partner start this sort of behaviour, it usually suggests that he does not want to continue the conversation. At this point he certainly won't be paying attention to what you have to say to him. Try changing tack, or realize that the conversation has come to an end. This would not necessarily denote a lie, but it would certainly signal discomfort if read alongside other signals.

However, this is not to say that liars typically fidget. This, like the idea that they break eye-contact, does not seem to stand up in tests. While these illustrating movements mentioned above might indeed give away something of importance, you should also look out for a general decrease in these gestures as well as in the number of subtle hand and finger movements. This is likely to be a type of controlling process, where the liar is trying to control any odd movements which he feels might give him away.

FEET AND LEGS

Drumming can also occur with the feet. While standing up, person may start tapping his feet as a sign that he wants to get away. While sitting cross-legged, he may be seen to start swinging his uppermost leg, or tapping away with his foot at an imaginary pedal. Watch also for sudden crossing, re-crossing or uncrossing of feet when significant subjects are brought up. Such signs of discomfort are worth noting to see if the subject in question is a cause for concern. As we pay least attention to our lower bodies when trying to promote a self-image, there is often much to be gleaned from this area. A person may sound disinterested in you, but if her feet are a little turned out towards you, especially when coupled with a slight turn of the hands which also exposes her wrists in your direction, the chances are that she is actually very open to you indeed. Equally, a business associate may be smiling and chatting comfortably with you but may have her legs crossed away from you and her right arm holding her cigarette right across her body, the barrier inadvertently suggesting that her interest is insincere or her real attitude more careful than her attempted image of openness.

In another situation, a seated person may suddenly stretch out his legs and lean back in his chair. At the risk of sounding obvious, this is a probable sign of disinterest in what you have to say. This may be coupled with a folding of the arms, or even a folding of the arms coupled with a balling of the fists: these signify much stronger rejection, or probable deception if accompanied by an incongruent answer. The reason why some of these examples seem more obvious is that, by paying less attention to such things, people tend to give their feelings away in much bolder ways.

BLINKING

These tiny movements (presuming that the person does not need glasses) seem to correlate to the amount of mental stress we are experiencing, and the frequency of our blinking shows the speed with which we are processing information. This is a sign of content complexity processes – the second of our three processes tends to occur in lying. In a normal conversation where the other person is attuned to you, he will blink at roughly the same rate as you, often at moments when you pause in your speech. When he has to engage in a lot of cognitive work in his head – for example, to work out a lie – that blink rate will normally increase.

SHOULDERS

A person who is in easy rapport with you will very often mirror your body position, which means that if he is stood in front of you, his shoulders should be parallel to your own. If you bring up a subject with which he is not comfortable, or if he disagrees with you, he may express this by turning his shoulders away from you a little. If he makes this movement while *he himself* is talking, it may well suggest that he is uncomfortable with his own statement and may be lying. A shoulder-shrug may also escape from a person when he is talking to you: again this may signify a lack of conviction in his own statements.

While these are examples of the type of signals to attune oneself to, these should clearly not be viewed in isolation. Imagine that all the non-verbal language of the person is a surface representation of the many cognitive and emotional processes going on inside him. Stan Walters, in his 2000 book *The Truth About Lying*, suggests the idea of a car dashboard, and likens the person's behaviours to the various readouts, such as speedometer, tachometer and so on. The behaviours are merely surface representations of hidden processes. In the same way that a look across the dashboard of your car can tell you that everything is working in harmony, so too can a check of a person's body language symptoms tell you whether everything is in order, or if there is conflict. Areas of conflict can then be tested and dealt with.

When deception is being specifically looked for, there are particular verbal signs one should be aware of. In fact, it has been suggested that people may pay so much attention to not giving themselves away through their actions that they forget to be careful with their words. Make a mental note of the following verbal giveaways.

METAPHORICAL LANGUAGE

This is verbal but largely unconscious language, and may offer all sorts of clues as to what is going on in the person's mind. If a person says, for example, that he needs to 'get on top of' a problem, this will probably tie in with how he perceives it in relation to himself, i.e. he'll picture it as *above* himself. Understanding this means that if you can get him to shift that image so that he mentally looks down on it, he will probably feel far more in control. Paying attention to his choice of words is enormously important in understanding how a person represents to himself the things he is talking about. We have spoken already about the advantages during sales pitches of knowing whether the customer has, say, an *image* of what he wants rather than being concerned primarily with sound, feel or quality, and how the key predicates he uses in his speech will often give away the representation he makes to himself of what he desires. Listen out for words or expressions that betray a person's real feelings that may not match their projected attitude.

BRIEF EXPLANATIONS

Although a person will probably become a little long-winded when lying, he will conversely tend to be rather superficial in his descriptions of significant events. Embellishments are suddenly skipped over, and details ignored. Time slips might occur, rather like the child who says 'We were just looking at it and then it broke.' If you ask a liar to expand upon his story, the chances are that you'll get a repeat of what you've just heard, rather than an offering of more details.

NOT USING 'I'

A liar will normally be reluctant to refer to himself, whereas in normal conversation we refer to ourselves a lot. Look out for less use of 'I', 'my', 'me' and so on, as well as an increase in references to what 'everyone' or 'no-one' does or thinks, what 'always' happens, and so on, which generalize away from his own particular involvement in the story and place a distance between him and the lie.

TANGENTIAL ANSWERS

Here, the liar is pedantically quibbling over an irrelevant aspect of an accusation you have made or a question you have asked. This is very common with children in its most obvious form, and can be very frustrating.

> Why do you always have to be defensive?
> I'm not 'always' defensive.

> I bet you just barged in and took it without asking.
> Barge in? You're the one who barges about.

This seems to be an attempt on the part of the liar to shift the argument to a less troublesome area. Sometimes this strange quibbling will lead to very odd answers that seem to make little sense, such as Clinton's famous response, 'That depends on what the meaning of "is" is' when questioned about his relationship with Monica Lewinsky.

'I'M BEING HONEST'

Worried that they may not be believed, liars often overcompensate by qualifying the lie with an unnecessary 'Honestly . . .', or 'You won't believe this, but . . .', and so on.

SLOWING DOWN

Because a liar has to juggle different thoughts with one another, and because one cannot process more than one thought at a time, there is a tendency for a person's speech to slow down when he is not telling the truth. His language may also become a little stiffer and more formal, and there will be more slips of the tongue and pauses in speech, albeit ones that may be filled with little sounds like 'er' and 'um'. However, it is any marked change in speed which is the important thing to notice. If a person naturally talks rather slowly and suddenly speeds up in response to a pertinent question, you may want to find out why that is. Overall, there is a 'smoothing' of speech when telling a lengthy lie – a sort of 'preparedness' that does not correspond to our normal verbal pattern.

PITCH

Voices tend to be higher and louder than normal when we want to draw attention to what we are saying, and lower and quieter when we want to show withdrawal or distance from the issue. A person saying that he is not bothered by an issue may be lying if his voice pitch has risen. A change in pitch, again, is more important than a theory about whether high or low denotes stress.

Undoubtedly this seems far from simple; perhaps you are even disappointed that I cannot offer you a straightforward system. The truth is that different people lie in different ways, and there are simply no single behaviours which all people share when deceiving. It's very difficult to tell. Terrifyingly, tests have shown that professional lie-catchers (such as the police) are as poor as college students at spotting lies, although the professionals are more confident in their decisions. The success rates for both groups each average out at around 55 per cent, which is only a smidgeon over what you'd get for guessing. That's a remarkable and worrying fact. (It seems that only members of the Secret Service are better than students at detecting deceit).

However, that's no reason not to have fun practising. As already mentioned, it is vital that you do not look for individual shifts and then read into them. The key is to be able to spot clusters of behaviours, verbal and/or non-verbal, and to disregard symptoms that occur in isolation. If you believe you have spotted a deceptive or uncomfortable response to a subject, change the subject to a less significant matter and see if the person returns to a more comfortable state. Then when you return to the problem question, check to see if another cluster occurs. It may not consist of the same behaviours, which is why you need to be open to spotting *any* shifts from the baseline which seem significant. This process of returning to the seemingly significant area and testing for similar reactions is terribly important. You are checking to make sure that the shifts you have picked up on are genuine unconscious responses to your questions or statements, rather than unimportant body shifts due to physical discomfort or other environmental annoyances. Finally, there is the danger that in watching the person's non-verbal behaviour and asking questions in a pointed way you will seem rather predatory and will therefore through your manner be inadvertently causing the very signs of defensiveness or stress you are picking up on. You must bear in mind that people often react more to the *way* in which they are being spoken to than to the specific topic of discussion. The more comfortable you can make the person feel, the more accurately – and the more easily – you will be able to read him.

TEST YOUR ACUITY

Try the following game with a friend, and see how well you do. Firstly, sit her opposite you and make sure that she does not know what you will be looking for. Don't tell her you'll be looking for lies just yet. Explain that you will ask her a few questions about her last house and that she is to answer honestly.

Now ask specifically visual questions. The following are good examples, as they necessitate the recall of images:

1 : What colour was the front door?
2 : What was the view from the kitchen window?
3 : What would you see in the hallway when you walked in?
4 : What pictures do you remember seeing on the walls of the house?
5 : What was the wallpaper in your parents' bedroom?

And so on. Ask two or three of these questions, and see if the person's eyes flicker across each time to a particular place. If they do, make a note of where that is. Otherwise, watch for any other subtle signs. Bear in mind that a complete lack of movement may in itself be a sign of truth-telling in this person for the purposes of the game.

Once you have been able to establish a 'baseline' like this, you can move on to the next part. Tell your friend that you will ask her some more questions, and that she is to lie to any one of them. She must lie convincingly, and you will try to tell her when she is doing so. Continue to ask those sorts of visual memory questions. Avoid any questions that may elicit strong feelings or auditory recall, as this may interfere with the primarily visual processing you are hoping for.

If you noticed a clear eye movement when she was telling the truth, now look for the one eye movement that does not match the others. Perhaps she looks over to the other side when she lies. Perhaps she maintains eye-contact, fearing that looking away might be a sign of a lie. Perhaps her eyes flicker downwards. Or maybe her eyes go to a similar place, but just not quite the same one. Personally, if this last example occurs I would hazard a guess that the invented information, although a lie, was actually a real memory, *just not from her house*. Perhaps she has thought of a friend's or a relative's house instead when forming the lie.

Also – especially if there are no changes in eye movements – be on the lookout for any other signals. Perhaps, for example, there is a movement of the fingers on the lie that was not there for the truthful answers, or no movement despite being present every other time. Perhaps the person gestures when lying, and keeps still at all other times, or vice-versa. If you wish, you can move away from visual questions and ask more emotional questions, inviting your friend to lie about her feelings at one point.

An understanding of the descriptions given in this chapter will help you know what to look for, although the changes may be easier to spot in normal relaxed conversation than in the artificial and brief exchange afforded by this kind of game. Finally, bear in mind that you will need to try this many times before getting an honest sense of how good you are at it. Luckily, it's fun to try.

SIGNS OF TRUTHFULNESS

Sometimes it is easier to identify signs that a story is true rather than look for elusive lying tells. German psychologists have developed the popular *Statement Validity Assessment* to be used in cases of alleged sexual offences to children, to determine the credibility of the child's testimony. At the heart of the SVA is a nineteen-point list which forms the *criteria-based content analysis* phase of the assessment. Here we see a number of signs which point to a credible testimony which are of use to us here. If someone is telling you a story which you believe may not be true, it is worth being aware of some of these points. Aldert Vrij discusses the system in his book *Detecting Lies and Deceit,* which is where I first came across it. Since then I have found myself using it as a checklist when listening to people's stories. The list also represents a lovely insight into the sorts of patterns we all fall into when relating events. Here are the most valuable criteria from the system:

1. *Unstructured production*. Truthful stories, unless they have been told many times, tend to involve all sorts of jumping forwards and backwards across the timeline of the narrative. A person will get so far into a story and commonly have to backtrack to give background information on something which he realizes is about to come up. While we tend to feel we've ruined a story by doing this, it is in fact an extremely common pattern. Equally, a person may well tell the story not from the start but rather by explaining the essential point

they want to communicate first before then filling in the background and providing the narrative. The chronology will most likely be all over the place, especially if the story is emotive and relatively fresh.

2. *Quantity of details.* The richer the details, the more likely the story is to be true. As we have already discussed, a typical liar will not elaborate on details when questioned about the specifics of an event. He'll just tend to repeat himself. An openness to providing additional information is a good sign of truthfulness.
3. *Contextual embedding.* This occurs when the person places events within the context of his daily life rather than as isolated events which sound like they could have occurred in a vacuum. For example, 'I was just sitting outside in the garden to relax a bit after cleaning the kitchen – the sun had just come out and I didn't fancy watching *Countdown* which I normally would, so I thought I'd sit on the patio for a bit.' These contextual references tend not to appear when the story is a fake.
4. *Descriptions of interactions.* Truthful stories are more likely to involve details about how the person interacted with other key characters. For example, 'I asked him what he was doing there, and he laughed weirdly – so I felt a bit threatened and backed off a bit.'
5. *Reproduction of speech.* Few liars will reproduce parts of a dialogue in their stories, preferring instead to report what was said rather than *say* it in the story. For example, 'I said, "Don't do that you'll mess it up,"' is more likely to point to a true story than 'I told him not to do it or he'd mess it up.'
6. *Unexpected complications during the incident.* If the story contains neither interruptions nor unexpected events that interfere with its flow, it's less likely to be true.

7. *Unusual details.* These are details offered along the way that stand out. For example, the fact that a person in the story had a gold tooth. Details may be superfluous to the main flow of the story.
8. *Accurately reported details misunderstood.* Classically, this would involve a child too young to understand sexual activity talking about a perpetrator's sexual actions in naïve terms. But it can happen in other contexts; an event might be referred to where its meaning was lost on the person relating the story, but is understood by the interviewer.
9. *Accounts of subjective mental state.* Here we would expect the person to refer to how she was feeling at different times in the story, or what thoughts were going through her head.
10. *Attribution of the perpetrator's mental state.* Here, the person describes how another character in the story seemed to be feeling. For example, 'He was clearly annoyed because he took his glasses off and raised his voice.'
11. *Spontaneous corrections.* Little corrections or dropped-in additions make a story more convincing. Here are both: 'He was using his laptop to write – he had one of those little Sony Vaios – and sat there for hours and only ever ordered a coffee. Well, no, he did get a muffin at one point, but he was there for ages.'
12. *Admitting lack of memory.* A truth-teller has no need to worry about spontaneously admitting lapses of memory or details he cannot remember whilst telling the story. It would be quite normal for him to say something like, 'Can't remember why we were there but we were all staying at this hotel.' However, this criterion is not fulfilled by giving an answer such as 'I don't know' to a direct question.
13. *Raising doubts about one's own testimony.* The truthful person

might admit that certain parts of the story might be wrong or misremembered.

14. *Self-deprecation.* Here the person refers to details which might incriminate himself or make himself look foolish. E.g., 'That was my own fault, I knew I shouldn't have left him alone.' Sometimes this may extend to pardoning the guilty party in the story altogether.

There are of course still reasons why these criteria may be present when a lie is told, or be absent in a truthful report. Therefore, in a criminal context, these criteria must be cross-referred with a second 'validity check-list' that looks at the characteristics of the interviewees, the pressures upon them and the style of questioning in the interviews themselves before being seen as at all conclusive. So again, take care before jumping to conclusions. Spotting lies is a fascinating but extraordinarily tricky skill.

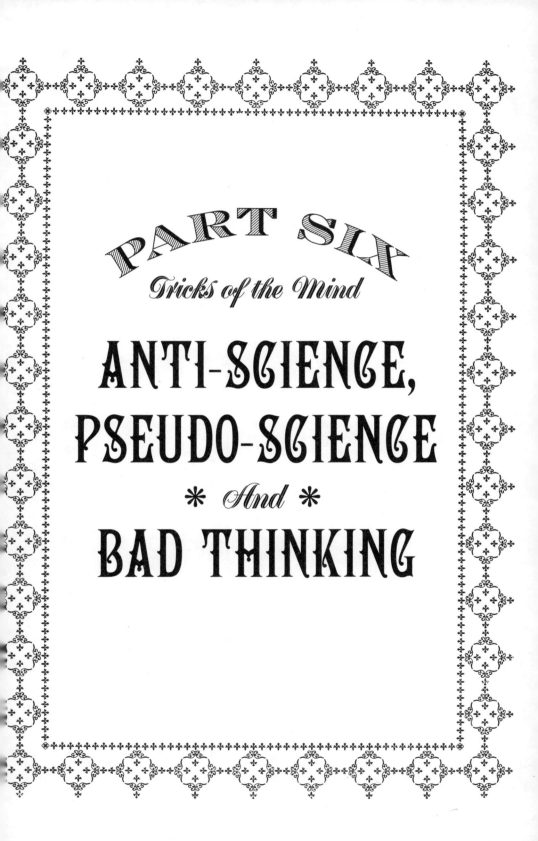

Tricks of the Mind

ANTI-SCIENCE, PSEUDO-SCIENCE * And * BAD THINKING

THINKING TRAPS

Imagine there is a terrible disease reported, and although it affects only one in ten thousand people, it is absolutely lethal. You are worried about it, so you decide to undergo a medical test to see if you have the disease. Now, no medical test is ever 100 per cent accurate, but your doctor explains that this one is known to be 99 per cent accurate, regardless of whether or not you have the disease (in other words, it will deliver a correct positive or negative result 99 per cent of the time). You decide to take the test. You're a little nervous, but you think it's a sensible thing to do. A blood sample is taken, and you're told the results will be sent to you in the post.

A week later the envelope arrives from the testing centre. You open it up, and read the contents. Staring you in the face is the answer you dreaded: the results are positive. The test has indicated that you have the lethal disease. You are devastated.

And you are right to be, aren't you?

Just for a moment, review the scenario above and ask yourself what may seem like a very easy question: how likely are you to have the disease? Please decide on an answer before reading any further. If you are unsure, just settle on an estimate.

I imagine most of you have re-read the above and confirmed that the answer must be that you are 99 per cent likely to have the disease. Those of you made suspicious by my request to reconsider your answer may have been nervous about committing to that percentage, but would certainly commit to saying that you are far more likely than not to have the disease. Only a few of you, trained in statistics, will know the correct answer. From the information given above, you should not be concerned about the positive test results. You are *less than 1 per cent* likely to have the disease.

That's right – although the test is 99 per cent accurate, you are less than 1 per cent likely to have the disease. The key to unlocking this counter-intuitive fact lies in one piece of information you may have missed, or at least not properly factored in: the disease hits only one in ten thousand people. So your positive test result, with its 99 per cent accuracy, could mean that you are one of the 99 per cent of people who have been correctly told that they have the disease, or you could be one of the 1 per cent of people who *don't* have the disease but who have been wrongly told that they *do*. (Remember that the test is 99 per cent accurate, regardless of whether or not you have the disease.) So, are you more likely to be one of the correctly diagnosed people with the disease, or one of the wrongly diagnosed people without it?

The disease strikes only one in ten thousand. So, forgetting the test for a moment, you can immediately see that you are far more likely (to the tune of 9,999:1) *not* to have the disease. Now, let's imagine that a million people take the test. Only a hundred or so of those will actually have the disease. Ninety-nine out of those hundred will be correctly diagnosed as having it, because the test is 99 per cent accurate. On the other hand, 999,900 people won't have the disease, but 1 per cent (or 9,999 of them) will be wrongly diagnosed as having it. So are you one of those ninety-nine who have it, or one of those 9,999 who don't? You're over one hundred times more likely to be in the second, safe, category.

The last fifteen years or so have seen a genuine attempt by cognitive scientists to research our fascinating tendency to fall prey to cognitive illusions, which are mental traps as persistent as optical illusions. The problem above is not just a clever puzzle, it is a potentially devastating real-life possibility and speaks volumes about our inability to understand probability and risk.

I toss a coin seven times, and record whether it lands heads (H) or tails (T). For my own perverse enjoyment, I write down the following list and give it to you. It shows three results, but only one of them is the real outcome. Which is most likely to be the real result?

1. HHHHHHH
2. TTTTTTH
3. HTTHTHH

Make a mental note of your answer. Be honest.

The answer is that each combination is as likely as any other. A coin is no more likely to land on any one specific combination of heads and tails than it is to land on any other, including the same way up every time. This is because the coin has no memory; each throw will yield a fifty-fifty result of H or T. However, we are seduced by the fact that the third option looks more 'typical'. In the same way, who would dream of choosing the following lottery numbers: 1, 2, 3, 4, 5 and 6? Yet the chance of this sequence being the winning combination is as likely as any less obvious sequence you may choose.

This confusion of 'probable' and 'typical' leads to the famous 'gambler's fallacy'. I have sat at the roulette wheel and watched suited, impressive, Chinese pros meticulously note down the results of wheel spins to decide which colour is most likely to come up next.

Clearly, if the ball has landed in black five times in a row, it would seem sensible to bet on red. Simply not true! While it is the case that in an *infinite* number of spins the colours would be expected to even out, the colours may only roughly balance over a *very large number*, and certainly are not required to balance over a short number of spins.

Another common obstacle stands in the way of our rationality. The cognitive researcher Massimo Piattelli-Palmarini offered the following game. Firstly, give yourself five seconds to come up with a rough answer to the following multiplication in your head. You won't have enough time to work out a proper answer, so hazard a guess:

2 x 3 x 4 x 5 x 6 x 7 x 8

Please note your answer, and have a few other people try it too. Note their answers as well.

Next, find some more people of the same intellectual level and have them offer an answer to the following, with the same restriction of five seconds:

8 x 7 x 6 x 5 x 4 x 3 x 2

As Piattelli-Palmarini perspicaciously points out, the second set of results will be significantly greater than the first. How can that be? Looking at both, we know that the answers must be the same, but somehow the second sequence yields higher estimates.

That's not all, though. Compare the estimates, your own and those of your friends, to the real answer. The correct answer is . . . 40,320. Did you find your estimates were much, much lower than the truth? The answer lies in the fact that we begin to multiply the numbers (2 x 3 x 4 . . .) and then, once we have an estimate at this point, we find it very hard to stray far enough from it. It's enormously difficult to let numbers boldly multiply in our heads. We root ourselves somehow to figures we have in our minds, and get stuck. It's even been shown that if a trial lawyer suggests a sentence of a number of months for a criminal, the judge is very likely to think close to that figure when arriving at his decision, even though he may appear to disregard it. Where suggested numbers are higher, judges return with higher sentences themselves. It's as if we set ourselves a yardstick once we hear or see a number and can't stray very far from it. This is a common cognitive pitfall known as *anchoring*. If an enormous sheet of newspaper was folded over on itself a hundred times (let's imagine that's possible), how thick would the eventual wad of paper be? The thickness of a brick? A shoe box? As Sam Harris points out, to prove a similar point about intuition in his excellent book *The End of Faith*, the correct answer is that the resulting object would be 'as thick as the known universe'. Again, we anchor ourselves to the initial smaller measurements.

Ask anyone if they weigh up probabilities in a rational and level-headed way, and you're likely to get a proudly affirmative answer. Yet we are somehow wired to make these sorts of mistakes, despite the fact that we know better. It's almost as if we know certain information, but just can't bring ourselves to use it.

Now, consider the following:

> Harry was very creative as a child and loved attention. He didn't always feel 'part of the gang' and this led to a desire to try to impress others with his talents. He went through school rather self-obsessed, and tried his hand at any creative field. He really enjoyed any opportunity to give a presentation or to show off in front of an audience.

Take a look at the following statements regarding Harry as an adult, and place them in order of most likely to least likely:

1 : Harry is an accountant.
2 : Harry is a professional actor.
3 : Harry enjoys going to classical concerts.
4 : Harry is a professional actor and enjoys going to classical concerts.

Please go ahead and mark them in the order you think is appropriate, before reading any further.

Did you decide Harry was more likely to be an actor than an accountant? Mistake number one. There are many, many more accountants in the UK than professional actors. Can accountants not be self-assured and good speakers? Because the description fitted your sense of how a 'typical' actor might describe his background, you were blinded to making a sensible estimate.

Did you decide that number four was more likely than number three? Stop and think: how can 'Harry is a professional actor and enjoys going to classical concerts' *ever* be more likely than just 'Harry enjoys going to classical concerts'? In number four, Harry could do *anything* as a job. The probability of two pieces of information being true is necessarily lower than that of just one of them being true. It sounds obvious now, but we still tend to blindly choose the necessarily *less* likely option as the *more* likely.

Imagine I have snuck a loaded die (I use the correct and irritating singular of the word 'dice') into one of Las Vegas's fine casini. The die is cleverly weighted to provide a bias towards rolling a six. I would expect it to roll a six most of the time, but not all. I roll it a few times and log the results. Decide which of the following is more likely:

1. 3, 1, 6, 2, 5
2. 6, 3, 1, 6, 2, 5

By now you are catching on, but it's so tempting to say the second option, isn't it? Yet the second option is *necessarily* less likely than the first, for the reasons given in the previous example. It is, you will note, the same as the first sequence, *plus* the extra condition of rolling a six at the start. It can only be less likely, as in the first example, when *any* number could be rolled first. If you prefer, you can remove the six from the start of the second result and place it at the end, so the two lines look more similar – you will still be tempted to say that the second result is more likely.

We are hopeless!

If you really want to start a fight, may I suggest the following classic example of counter-intuition? Known now as the 'Monty Hall Problem', its first appearance was probably the one presented in Bertrand's *Calcul des probabilités* (1889), where it was known as Bertrand's Box Paradox. Famously, it was presented to the 'Ask Marilyn' advice column in *Parade* magazine in 1990, and the answer given in the column, though correct, sparked a storm of controversy. Brilliantly, Marilyn proved a lot of mathematicians wrong. Here is my version of the problem, as featured on TV, with which I have caused many bitter arguments:

> I show you three ring boxes and one very expensive ring which you are trying to win. While your back is turned, I place the ring into one of the ring boxes. I know which one it goes into, but you don't. Then you turn back round and I explain the game. I will ask you to guess in which box I have placed the ring. You can point to any box of the three to make your choice. Then, before asking you to commit, I will open one of the remaining boxes which I

know does not contain the ring. I'll show you that box is empty, and remove it from the game. Then I shall ask you whether you want to stick with the box you have chosen, or whether you would rather switch to the final, remaining box. If you choose the correct box, you keep the ring.

Should you stick, or switch?

What would you do? Do you gain anything by switching? People have very different answers to the problem, but the most common is that they would stick. Somehow it feels right. After all, if it's only fifty-fifty at the end, why switch? Surely it's more frustrating to change and then find you were right the first time?

The answer is, *you should always switch*. You are always twice as likely to win the ring if you do so. In fact, the chances increase from one-third to two-thirds by changing. It isn't fifty-fifty.

If this seems ludicrous or just plain wrong to you, let me explain in a few different ways, so that you can pick the explanation you can most easily follow. Firstly, rest assured that this stumps all sorts of bright, intelligent people and even mathematicians, if they don't know it.

Look at it like this. Let's say I will always put the ring in box C. 'C' is our winning box. Two out of three times, you'll first choose A or B and be wrong. That means that two out of three times, if you think about it, I have no choice which of the remaining two to open and remove, as one of the two boxes you leave for me to choose between will be the winning box C. If you choose A, I *must* open B and leave C, and if you choose B, I *must* open A and leave C. In both cases, I am avoiding the winning box. In both cases, you should switch to the one I avoid because it will be the winning box. On the rarer occasion (one out of three) when you unknowingly pick the winning box C straight away, I can then open either A or B, and of course you shouldn't switch. But that's only in one out of three cases, the time you happen to get it right on the first go. Please read that again.

If you still want to see those final two boxes as fifty-fifty, imagine it this way. Let's pretend there were a hundred boxes, not three. When you make your first choice, it clearly has a one in a hundred chance of being right – *very* unlikely. Now – and imagine this is happening – I reveal as empty ninety-eight other boxes, leaving yours and one other one (in, say, the thirty-seventh position) closed. Now, bearing in mind I *know* which box has the ring in it, isn't it much more likely that the one I've chosen to leave closed (number thirty-seven) contains the ring, rather than the one you chose in a one in a hundred chance? The two boxes don't look fifty-fifty now, do they? Your first choice is still very unlikely, and number thirty-seven seems much more probable. That's because your first choice in this example would have a 1 per cent (one in a hundred) chance of being right, which means the only other possibility (the final box) must necessarily have a 99 per cent chance of being right. The two have to add up to a 100 per cent chance, as we know it's in one of them. Similarly, in the three-box game, your first choice has a one-third chance of containing the ring, quite naturally, and that means that the final box I leave for you must have a *two*-thirds chance.

You are assured that the answer is exactly as explained. Enjoy the fruits of bringing the problem up in company.

You might argue that this last example is an interesting thought-exercise, or even a theme for a bewilderingly successful game show, but rather divorced from real life. The fact remains that cognitive traps make us unwittingly prone to drastic misunderstandings of probability, and this can undoubtedly lead people, including doctors and jurors, to make terrible decisions.

In an earlier chapter, you learned that the way in which you view images in your head makes a huge difference to the extent to which you can connect with them. That leads to one of the biggest causes of the sort of irrational thinking we are discussing. If something can be easily pictured, it feels more real and immediate than something that does not convert itself into such a powerful picture. Somehow the rolls of the loaded die which included a couple of sixes *looked* more real, and we *felt* it as more likely even though we knew they couldn't be. Equally, a drug that promises to reduce the mortality rate of a disease from 10 to 0 per cent seems much more worthy of investment than one that reduces the mortality rate of a different disease from 40 to 30 per cent, even though each will do as much good as the other. We look at pictures and read reports of rail crashes and play out terrible sequences in our heads, deciding it's dangerous to travel, yet we are twice as likely to have an aeroplane crash into our house (1 in 250,000) than we are to die in a rail accident (1 in 500,000).* We are in an area where emotion rules over reason, and the results can be damaging.

SCIENCE AND RELATIVISM

In Bristol I used to live by the Clifton Suspension Bridge, which the more finely honed of you may know. At each end there is a huge, monolithic brick tower in the vague shape of a looming, bulgy letter 'A', and each of these As has its own little serif in the form of a platform across the top. In Brunel's original plans, there was to be sat on each tower a giant golden sphinx, facing across to the other side of the gorge. I think this was by all accounts a superb idea, but the

*From Dick Taverne's *The March of Unreason*.

top-hatted fellow had to abandon the project because of a lack of funds, and the bridge was completed only after his early death at the age of fifty-three. Perhaps he desired something more dramatic after completing the more prosaic college campus at Uxbridge, but sadly the twin gilt hybrids were never realized. The bridge now sits sphinxless. For fans of the Victorian Bristol school of artists, it's interesting to note that earlier landscapes which prematurely incorporated the envisioned finished bridge naturally but wrongly included these two sphinxes.

I always felt that the loss of the big lion-women was a real letdown. There is something so bold about the idea of them, so permanent and optimistic in their statement. Nowadays we shy from making such clear statements about anything, for we are terrified of oppressing somebody somewhere. We don't build extravagantly, and we don't speak extravagantly. Language itself has become seen as an oppressor. We forgo the proud pomp of a Crystal Palace for the anaemic and apologetic temporariness of a Millennium Dome.

It's all about post-colonial guilt. In the 1960s, an anthropologist named Clifford Geertz paved the way for multiculturalism by being the first and foremost to talk about tribal cultures on their own terms, rather than as exotic and primitive curiosities. The key here was to see that the values of a different culture were no more or less valid than those of another – a real step away from the distasteful colonial ethos. In time, as we slipped into post-modernism, a fetish developed for *all* truth being relative. Our 'truths' and 'meanings' were seen as simply products of our own value systems, and to suggest that one belief was somehow better or more valid than another was at best deemed old-fashioned and sweet; at worst it was treated by certain commentators and self-styled intellectuals as a symbolic rape. This relativism – both the extreme opposite of fundamentalism and yet an effective means of promoting dangerous and unfounded ideology by disregarding the value of evidence – was typically enshrouded in layers of purposefully obscure language, as if exhaustingly impenetrable wording was necessary proof of superior thought. Much of the sociological literature on the subject reads as an exercise in auto-erotic asphyxiation.

As this hermeneutic hysteria became embedded in our psyche, science began to develop a bad name. Scientific knowledge came to be seen as just another example of subjective and personal meanings, this time happening to belong to the scientists and a mere product of their value system. It was seen as neither more nor less valid than the most unscientific beliefs held by an eccentric New Ager. And this may not seem unfair to you: certainly to point out that a scientist has her set of beliefs in just the same way that a psychic healer has hers, and that one mustn't call one valid and the other invalid, seems to be a fair and enlightened approach. In the same breath, one might add that the atheist is surely as religious as the Christian, in that he has adopted a set of beliefs to which he chooses to rigorously adhere. While it's temptingly clever to make that claim, it is a nonsensical statement; no more logical than to say that a Christian is a type of atheist. Having a set of beliefs about religion is not the same as being a religious True Believer.

What, then, of objectivity? If truth is all relative, where does that leave us? Does nothing exist outside our own values and perceptions? Is the wall behind me still there even though I can't see it? Was there ever a wall? While this is maybe a fascinating thought-exercise for student philosophers, I'm perhaps naively happy to work with the more useful model that the wall is very likely still to be there even though I can't see it, and act accordingly (like not running backwards into it). Equally, as mentioned by the rather terrific and refreshing author Dick Taverne (whom I like to imagine named after an Olde Gaye Pubbe), I imagine that most post-modern theorists are happy to accept the fact that science has some real-world objective validity when they put their trust in the aeroplanes that take them to their conferences.

There is, of course, much that is sensible, useful and preferable in seeing people's sense of right and wrong in tandem with their upbringing and learned values. Equally, there are of course scientists and atheists who are flawed like any other human beings and think in heavily blinkered ways. But before we get carried away, there are certain things we must bear in mind.

Firstly, it is the role of the believer to provide evidence for his claims, not the role of the non-believer to prove that the believer is wrong. To return to Bertrand Russell, I cannot prove conclusively that there isn't a teapot orbiting the earth, and I shouldn't have to just because you say there is one. If you believe that and want me to believe it too, it's up to you to show me. And the chances are I'll want better evidence than 'I believe it because I just *know* in my heart there's one out there'. If you don't believe me, try proving any negative and you'll see you soon get stuck. Imagine I want you to believe that there is a green mouse in your house. It's my job to find it and show it to you; you would never be able to prove there was no green mouse there. You could search for it and take everything out of the house, but it could always be hiding somewhere you weren't looking. You can't prove it doesn't exist. As long as you're willing to believe the green mouse is there when you finally have unequivocal evidence that it *is* there, as opposed to someone just telling you it is, then you're not being remotely narrow-minded to presume it isn't or to ask for that evidence. That's healthy scepticism. Show me real-world evidence for your extraordinary claim, and I'll believe you.

Secondly, the scientific method is misunderstood. Pretty much all New Age or anti-science thinking works on the principle of starting with an idea and noticing only evidence that supports it. It is a guaranteed recipe for confirming any belief, and explains the essence of why people are prepared to believe the oddest things. Now, the same accusation is made about science. We imagine the case of a homoeopath, quietly happy with the fact that her 'alternative' methods work very well; meanwhile, science ignores the many success stories she has had with her treatment and just refuses to accept that it can work. Scientists, surely, just have their way of seeing the world, and try to explain everything in their terms. Maybe a scientist has his way of understanding aromatherapy, and the practitioner has her own 'holistic' way. No-one can say that the 'science' explanation is right. Also, 'science' comes down to the work of individual scientists, all of whom are prone to profit motives, corruption or tunnel vision, so how can we possibly accept what they say as objectively true? And isn't it the case that anything science says now will be disproved anyway at some point in the future? So isn't the only thing a scientist can know for sure is that he will eventually be shown to be wrong?

As reasonable as that may sound to some, it shows a real misunderstanding of the point of the scientific method. Until recently, I rather liked the logic of the last question and believed that the only answer to give to them was 'yes'. But I, too, was naive about how science actually works. As we have discussed, we all have it in us to believe most things quite happily. We can convince ourselves of anything if we want to. If I believe that the earth is round but my uncle believes it's flat, who is to say who's right? And how would we show who's right? The answer comes down to one thing: *evidence.*

Whereas non-scientific (and potentially dangerous) thinking starts with a premise and then looks for things that support it, scientific thinking constantly tries to *disprove* itself. That alone makes all the difference in the world. A scientist comes up with a premise: A causes B. Rather than look for all the cases where A causes B to support his premise, he starts trying to disprove that

A causes B. Then, if after rigorous attempts to prove himself wrong it seems to hold up that A does indeed cause B, he'll publish his results. Now it's up for his peers to check and double check his findings. They will probably want to run their own experiments, to see if they replicate the results or disprove for themselves that A causes B. If that scientist has conducted bad experiments, or if his results are shown to be faulty, his reputation will suffer enormously.

That's the aim. Sometimes, time will show that something was missed. Or an unethical, media-hungry scientist might allow hasty results to be publicized by interested parties before releasing them to his peers for this further testing. Or perhaps a scientist will indeed be just looking to confirm his suspicions of something, and somehow that bias might still, despite everything, seep through. In exceptions like these, mistakes are made, and *bad* science is done. But consider the process. While one can make accusations of inevitable and occasional bias, that criticism has to apply at least as heavily to the 'alternative' camp who are not driven by a desire to try to look at it all objectively. Being as generous as possible, we can certainly say that the non-scientific side, with its emphasis on faith, or intuition, or feelings, is going to contain a level of unavoidable bias which should make us think twice before hurling that accusation at the scientific community. The aim of scientific testing is to get *out* of the head of the scientist, with his prejudices and values, and to see what seems to happen reliably in the world *regardless* of personal conviction or ideology. The scientific method is the antithesis of the relativists' notion that it's all about personal values, or that scientific knowledge is just the same as any set of beliefs.

Here's another way of looking at it. Science is unusual in that it is cumulative. It is a system built over time, wherein useful information is retained and ideas that simply don't stand up are discarded, based on the confirmation of knowledge through testing. Science, like technology, is inherently progressive and by definition represents the model that can be shown to work best. If something works, it becomes science. If a piece of 'alternative' medicine can be shown to work reliably, it ceases to become alternative. It just becomes medicine.

This is tremendously important to understand, as we live in a time when misguided aspects of relativist thinking are still around us and unscientific, scaremongering stories are popular with the media. Scientists are painted as the corrupt hacks of evil big business, and as proper thought is too easily drowned beneath waves of misinformed public feeling, we often forget the importance of evidence-based fact.

Worry about science

Bear with me a little longer, I'm ranting, I know. It's this misunderstanding and unfashionableness of science which bugs me, and on which I need to dwell for another moment as I shall be talking much about scientific approaches in the rest of this section. The Enlightenment brought with it optimism about science which has now been replaced with a certain amount of fear. We now worry that it is stepping into areas where it shouldn't, and we listen to scientists and religious leaders arguing on television over contentious developments . Although we are healthier and happier than before, we no longer have that spirit of experimentation and curiosity. The popularity of the 'Precautionary Principle', used by Green lobbyists and prevalent in the press, is a clear example of that worry. It is an argument to prevent new policies from coming into practice which environmental lobbyists feel could be harmful to the environment. Very commonly one sees it used against controversial issues such as GM crops. The principle, although a little difficult to tie down, essentially states that if there is any risk of danger involved in the implementation of a new policy, then the policy should be scrapped. Better safe than sorry.

While this can often be a sensible argument, we forget that nothing can ever be shown to be entirely without risk. No scientist could state such a thing with certainty; instead, he has to make more reserved statements about the likelihood of possible risks. Also, the argument might hide a preference for blind ideology over evidence. Taverne, who you really should read, referred to a question asked of Lord Melchett (not, I understand, the character from *Blackadder Goes Forth* but rather the director of Greenpeace in 1999) by a House of Lords Select Committee looking into GM crops:

> **Question**: 'Your opposition to the release of GMOs, that is an absolute and definite opposition . . . not one that is dependent on further scientific research?'
> **Answer**: 'It is a permanent and definite and complete opposition.'

Such logic dispenses with any curiosity that is vital for the progress of science. Often it can be very dangerous. Rachel Carson famously wrote *The Silent Spring* in 1962, and in it 'exposed' the environmental dangers of the pesticide DDT. She claimed it caused cancer of the liver, and offered anecdotal evidence of other damage to health. For many years in Bristol I was informally lectured by an organic-obsessed neighbour on the evils of pesticides. Clearly DDT was the great, moustachioed, cat-stroking, chair-swivelling Evil One of them all, compared to which all other bad pesticides were mere shabby-coated, fingerless-gloved villains sat on upturned whisky-crates behind a fence playing gin-rummy in an episode of *The Red Hand Gang*. I was amazed to read in Taverne's book that no tests have ever been replicated to show that DDT damages the health of human beings. However, DDT *is* a fantastically effective way of preventing the spread of malaria. Between the late 1940s and 1970, DDT prevented around fifty million human deaths from the fever.

In 1963 there were seventeen cases of malaria in Sri Lanka, and in 1968, after DDT was banned, there were over a million. There are still a million or so deaths a year from malaria. Over-reaction, mindless precaution and politics have been responsible for this vast number of deaths. In Taverne's words, a total ban would be 'a victory for the conscience of the rich world, invoked without regard for facts, at the expense of the lives of the inarticulate poor'.

The easy relationship between anti-science groups (including many environmental lobbies) and the media (hungry for frightening stories) is a powerful tool for spreading worry. In 1998 there were some headline-grabbing stories in the UK regarding a possible link between MMR immunity jabs for babies and the onset of autism. The MMR jab is vital for preventing epidemics of measles, mumps and rubella, measles being the most worrying. On the basis of these newspaper reports a huge number of new parents refused to allow their babies to receive the jab, not wishing to take the risk. In fact, the story was yet another result of the media enjoying science scare-stories, encouraged into sensationalism by an anti-vaccination group's pressure and their own natural desire to boost paper sales. The scare story came from a single paediatrician who observed twelve autistic children with bowel disease and hypothesized that the autism in eight of them might have its origins in the bowel disease, which in turn might have been connected to the measles virus in the MMR vaccine. In fact, when the possible link to autism was later tested across the world, with *millions* of children, it was seen to be entirely unfounded. There was no link, no support for the single doctor's hypothesis, and it was even pointed out that the noted rise in autism cases happened *before* the MMR vaccine was introduced. The paediatrician, who was funded by a pressure group eager to find a link between the vaccine and autism, is now under investigation. That part, however, is not an interesting media story, and a large number of people made a dangerous but understandably over-cautious decision because a seed of fear had been irresponsibly planted. The media hype did not reflect the fact that the publicized testing was 'small-scale, inconclusive, preliminary and riddled with supposition', as the leading paediatricians and childhood vaccination experts are now trying to make clear in a bid to stop the media from raising more doubts. We are now in the dangerous situation where *all* children are being put at risk because of the resulting drop in vaccination levels to well below what's needed to protect the population at large. In their open letter in 2006 following a massive increase in childhood deaths from measles, the experts said, 'Unless this is rectified urgently, and children are immunized, there will be further outbreaks and we will see more unnecessary deaths.'

I am more than happy to admit that we do not necessarily progress or improve as a human race alongside the leaps and bounds of science and knowledge. The idea that we do is an aspect of humanism that comes from the Enlightenment, and can be very wrong. (Those of you who read the modern philosopher John Gray will know his compelling argument that the Enlightenment thinkers merely replaced God with science, and that the resulting humanism falls just as foul to another illusion of salvation, albeit through science rather than through Faith. Gray's image of the Taliban leader ordering terrorist attacks on his mobile phone is a memorable image of how technological advances don't bring us any closer to utopian harmony, or a secular Kingdom of Heaven.) Our tendency to abuse and exploit the knowledge we have for nasty ends of course necessitates a system where checks and controls need to be in place as our technology runs far ahead of our morality. We should, of course, be sensibly concerned.

However, somewhere in the prevalence of media sensationalism and the rich world's conscience, many of the quiet facts of science and evidence have been met with disfavour or simply ignored. And one area of hugely unscientific rhetoric is the belief in the supernatural and a faith in 'alternative' medicine, where, again, the still small voice of reason is often seen as negative or irrelevant. Given that my work takes me close to these areas, we'll take a look at them now. I might rant a bit more – forgive me if I do.

BELIEF IN THE SUPERNATURAL AND PSEUDO-SCIENCE

If you were good enough to try the cognitive challenges at the start of the chapter, you'll know that we are often very badly equipped to get our heads around issues of probability and likelihood. Irrespective of our intelligence, we all fall prey to similar traps when it comes to trying to think rationally. If we are appreciating a piece of music, or finding ourselves falling in love, there may be value in pooh-poohing rationality and opting for rampant sentimentality. However, we can take it as a given that finding areas of life where scientific language may not be the best medium to describe our experiences does not devalue it as the most useful model for working out what reliably happens in the world.

If a person, for example, has received some homoeopathic or 'alternative' remedy for a problem and now feels better, or if she goes to see a psychic and feels contented afterwards, then we might argue that all is well and there's no reason to 'debunk' the vehicle of her therapy. Should we deny such people their comfort? Personally, I have no desire to detract from the happiness or satisfaction people have derived from such interventions, unless they bring the case to me as an argument (normally along the lines of 'how do you explain *that*, then?'). I don't think it's any of my business what people believe in, unless it affects me in some way or leads to dangerous fundamentalism. I know that there are rarely simple answers to many of life's perplexing issues, and that whatever truth there is will probably consist of an enormous number of contradictions. I don't find it easy to align myself with any one political ideology for that reason: I just can't imagine any one side of an issue is going to be comprehensive.

However, the issue of belief in the supernatural has been of great interest to me since I first questioned my identity as a Christian. Also, because so many people do profess a belief in the paranormal or New Age remedies, and some of those people are interested in a genuine discussion of possible explanations other than supernatural ones, I shall share my thoughts on the subject here.

Andy, my creative partner who I have mentioned before, often finds himself having a similar discussion with people who believe in such things. He first tells them something which I now offer to you if you are also a believer.

> Let's absolutely presume that your explanation is correct. No-one's contesting it or attacking it and I'm not going to try to prove it wrong. OK? Now, let's put that in an imaginary box so it's safe. Now that we know it's safe, let's have a look at some other possibilities, which might explain things in a different way. Just out of interest. Then you can decide whether it makes more sense to consider those other options first, before going for what's in the box. That's up to you.

David Hume, the eighteenth-century philosopher, arrived at a very important maxim regarding supernatural claims. It is as follows: 'No testimony is sufficient to establish a miracle, unless the testimony be of such a kind that its falsehood would be more miraculous than the fact which it endeavours to establish.' In other words, is it more likely that the person making the extraordinary claim is deceived, or that the claim is true? The two can be weighed up. Extraordinary claims require extraordinary proof. This is terribly important. What tends to happen instead is that extraordinary claims lead to extraordinary conviction. We tend to think that the depth of our personal experience of the extraordinary thing in question, be it God or healing crystals, is evidence of the veracity of the claim. It really isn't; it's just evidence of how much we are prepared to believe in something (without proof). Attached to this understanding is the fact that if you believe in something extraordinary, you cannot insist that non-believers prove you wrong in an argument. It's *your* job to do the proving. We're back to the problem of trying to prove a negative. Imagine, for example, that a grown man is arguing that there is a Father Christmas. It's not up to everyone else to prove that there isn't, in order to decide the matter of whether he exists. He'd better have extraordinary proof to support his extraordinary claim.

Put another way, 'what can be asserted without evidence, can also be dismissed without evidence.'*

Confirmation Bias: Looking for What we Know

One tendency that gets in the way of us making the best decisions with regard to these sorts of belief systems is that of *confirmation bias*. Imagine you have heard that Dave (who you don't know) is an extrovert, and you wish to find out whether this is true. You're

*From Christopher Hitchens, the journalist and commentator on Iraq. Attacking the irrational religious beliefs behind terrorism, Sam Harris gives this quote in *The End of Faith* and adds, 'let us pray that billions of us soon believe him.'

allowed to ask him some yes/no questions about his behaviour. What sort of questions would you ask? Just give that some thought for a moment; get a sense of the line of questioning you would take. I would imagine you might ask the following sorts of questions:

Do you like to go to parties?
Do you enjoy being around people?

These questions are typical, as shown in experiments that look at confirmation bias. The point is, if you ask these sorts of questions of Dave, you will likely walk away convinced that he is an extrovert. Dave will seem to fit the description you have of him. In tests, experimenters give two sets of people opposing descriptions of Dave and have them go in and ask what they like in order to test the conflicting hypotheses they've been given. Sometimes the questioners are requested to ask only questions that require a yes or no answer; sometimes Dave is told to answer yes to everything. What invariably happens is that both groups ask questions that support their hypothesis, and both come out with their hypothesis confirmed. The group that was told that Dave was an introvert will be as convinced as the group who was told that he was outgoing. All because we tend to ask only questions that will confirm our suspicions.

Here's another way of looking at it, which shows how subtle this tendency is. Imagine I have four cards, and each card has a letter on one side and a number on the other. I lay them out for you so that the following sides face you in a row:

A D 3 7

Now I tell you the following rule, and it may be true or false: if there is an A on one side of the card, there is a 3 on the other side. Got that? Good. Now, I'd like you to decide which cards, and *only* which cards, you need to turn over to decide whether that rule is true or false. Think it through, think it through . . . go on . . .

Most people answer just A, or A and 3.

Well, the statement says that if there's an A on one side, there must be a 3 on the other. So it makes sense to turn the A over to see if there's a 3. If there isn't, the rule must be false. But we would also have to turn over the 7 to see if the rule applied. There could be an A on the back of the 7, and then the rule would be false. Turning 3 over, however, gives us nothing, as the rule does not say that if there's a 3 there has to be an A (only that if there's an A there has to be a 3). In other words, if there were an A or a Z on the back, it wouldn't prove or disprove the rule. So the correct answer is A and 7.

Very few people choose the 7 because people tend to look for things that confirm, not disprove, what they've been told. Turning the A and 3 are ways of confirming the hypothesis, and this is what most people want to do. They want to see if the A has a 3 and if the 3 has an A. They don't think of trying to disprove the rule by seeing if there is a card with an A on one side but a different number on the reverse. Similarly, people will ask Dave all the questions that set out to confirm what they've been told about him, not to try questions that really test what they've been told by attempting to disprove it.

In one classic experiment, two groups of students were arranged, one made of people who believed in the death penalty as an effective crime deterrent, and one opposed to it. Both were given two studies of the efficacy of the penalty, one for and one against. They were asked to evaluate the studies. Both groups were predictably more critical of the study that opposed their view, and more interestingly decided that the study with which they agreed was 'better conducted' and 'more convincing'. Again, we look for what supports our hypothesis. We are not dispassionate judges where we already have a belief, however tenuous, in place. To look at things objectively and step outside of our beliefs can be almost impossible. For any of us, that is, not just believers in the paranormal.

The all-too-common extreme, though, of this sort of bias is circular reasoning. This is the fallacy of the True Believer. The True Believer is impervious to real-world evidence because he just ignores anything that doesn't fit his belief system. Instead, he notices everything that matches and supports his beliefs, and inevitably comes to hold those beliefs at a very profound level. They can become absolutely part of his identity. It is this that brings together the religious, the psychic, the cynic (as opposed to the open sceptic) and the narrow-minded of all kinds. It is something I encountered a lot among my fellow Christians. At one level it can be seen in the circular discussion which goes as follows:

'Why do you believe in the Bible?'
'Because it's God's Word.'
'And why do you believe in God?'
'Because of what it says in the Bible.'

At a less obvious level, it can be seen in the following common exchange:

'Why do you believe Christianity is true?'
'Because I have the experience of a personal relationship with God.'
'So how do you know you're not fooling yourself?'
'Because I *know* that it's real.'

Even as an enthusiastic believer myself I could see this kind of tautology at work, and over time I realized that it is common to all forms of True Belief, regardless of the particular belief in question. The fact is, it's enormously difficult – and you need to be fantastically brave – to overcome the circularity of your own ideologies. But just because our identity might be tied up with what we believe, it doesn't make that belief any more correct. One wishes that True Believers of any sort would learn a little modesty in their convictions.

Extraordinary Coincidences and Psychic Phone Calls

How many people would you have to get together in a room before it was likely that two of them shared the same birthday? Heads down; work silently on your answers please. Estimates are allowed. 'Likely' means 'over 50 per cent probability'.

Would you believe that you need only twenty-three people to reach over 50 per cent probability? In fact, a room of thirty people will make the coincidence pretty likely (70 per cent). The secret lies in the fact that we are talking about *any* birthday matching, not one specific birthday. What feels very unlikely may not be that rare an occurrence. And this is not just a cute maths problem: it ties in with everyday examples of supposedly extraordinary things. Sometimes the answer to 'Wow, what are the chances of that?' is 'Really not so extraordinary'. It may seem an amazing coincidence to bump into a friend in the middle of a big city, but in fact once you realize that you'd have been amazed if that had happened with *any* friend *anywhere* in the city, the chances get much larger very quickly.

Particularly worthy of note is the illusion of extraordinary coincidence which occurs when someone calls you on the telephone shortly after you've been thinking about them. How wonderful to think that we have achieved some sort of psychic communication with a friend! This illusion is particularly seductive as it allows us to feel that we have some sort of supernatural control over events, or perhaps that some sort of astral plane exists where our thoughts about a person remotely inspire the idea of contact. These are fun and appealing thoughts. Personally, I find the wider and more honest picture very appealing, as it shows me what wonderful creatures we must be to interpret events in this way. In fact, we think about people all the time. How many people might go through our minds in a day? If not one of them *ever* called us a little while after we'd thought about them, then *that* would be truly extraordinary. Yet, true to our delightful form, we have no reason to remember all the times we thought of people and they *didn't* call; we only notice the coincidences.

Now, if you are someone who believes that these things happen for a more esoteric reason, you will then have the irresistible opportunity to rearrange events to prove that a psychic event occurred. For example, you won't just remember that this person passed through your mind earlier that day, you'll remember that you felt a special connection with them, or even felt that they would ring. The time between thinking of them and the call in question will be shortened in your mind. The coincidence will be supported to the point that it becomes inexplicable, in the same way that our magic spectator misremembers the trick to create a great story that doesn't cast him as a fool. If you are in any doubt, there is a simple way to see whether this is a genuinely psychic phenomenon. Choose a person unlikely to ring you and spend a dedicated period of time concentrating on an image of them or willing them to ring. Repeat this and see if it produces reliable results. Or even one result.

What of downright amazing coincidences? How can anyone 'explain' those utterly remarkable events we hear about from time to time? In one television routine, I told (well, slightly adapted to involve the protagonist's wife) the apparently true story of a car repairman who was out on call in the middle of nowhere. His work finished, he was walking back to his truck to go home. As he walked past a telephone box it started ringing, and he went in to answer it. The caller knew his name, and began talking to him about a business appointment he had the next day. The repairman, confused, recognized the voice: it was his secretary. He asked her how on earth she had known to call the payphone. She answered that she had called him on his new mobile. He explained to her that in fact she had called a phone box which he had just been walking past in the middle of nowhere. She insisted that she had called his mobile, and checked the piece of paper she had the number written down on. It was then she realized her mistake: she had accidentally dialled his payroll number, which she had written down on the same piece of paper. The payroll number happened to be the number of the telephone box which he just happened to be walking past at that time.

Now, I presume the story is essentially true, though I have no doubt that some embellishment has been added. I heard it from someone (a respectable scientist and sceptical investigator into the paranormal) who had heard the repairman talk about it on a daytime magazine programme. And what's good enough for Richard and Judith is good enough for me. Possibly this is not a coincidence tale that strongly suggests a psychic event, beyond some notion of 'synchronicity'. But it is this sort of amazing tale, or any other you would like to substitute, which can so easily provoke a 'now you can't just call *that* coincidence' response from those who would look for a paranormal explanation. Indeed, it would seem that to say 'It's just a coincidence' is more ridiculous than to 'admit' that some supernatural agency must be at work. Isn't that the case? Am I not clutching at straws in order *not* to see something other-worldly at work here?

Well, consider this. You have, I understand, a one in fourteen million chance of winning the lottery. It's extraordinarily unlikely that you'd win. As you might gather from a previous statistic, you are on average *fifty-six* times more likely to have an aeroplane crash into the roof of your house than to win the lottery. However, somebody somewhere wins. That part *isn't* unlikely. That's almost a given. So if I said to you, 'Go on then, science-boy, explain how someone can win when it's fourteen million to one against them,' you'd look at me oddly and say there was nothing to explain. It would be different if someone were able to predict exactly *who* would win before the numbers were drawn, but the fact that someone somewhere will win is perfectly straightforward. There's no mystery. The incredible 'coincidence' of a set of numbers being the winning set will happen to someone, somewhere.

I don't know what the odds were of that phone ringing as that guy walked past, but I imagine they were pretty tiny. Whatever the probability, strange events like this will come together somewhere, to someone. In the same way that the lottery winner is amazed at her luck, so too these coincidences are extraordinary when they happen to *us*. But it's not extraordinary that they *happen*, somewhere, to someone. And that stands even if the lottery winner in question says she chose the numbers because they came to her in a dream. Most people have their own esoteric reasons for choosing particular numbers. She will probably feel that the dream was a premonition. To her it will be a confirmation that such extraordinary things can be foretold. And what a great experience for her! But to the rest of the world, including all the other lottery players who 'dreamt' numbers, had them appear in a vision, or used special, lucky numerological or 'foolproof' gambling systems, nothing extraordinary has happened. Someone was going to win, and next week it will be someone else. And those bizarre, one-in-a-million coincidences that seem impossible to explain are going to happen somewhere to someone. Occasionally they'll happen to you. Most of the time they won't really be as amazing as they may appear at first glance, as in the previous examples. But where they really are extremely unlikely, you can remember that such things have to happen to someone. The only amazing thing is how it feels to happen to *you*. So savour the experience, but the only reason to say that the event must have paranormal origins is if you're ultimately unable to step outside your own excitement.

Before we continue, if it seemed dry, or soulless, to point out how straightforward such an amazing thing might seem when viewed from another angle, then that's quite an understandable initial reaction. Certainly these tales of extraordinary coincidences are juicy and enjoyable, and a shift to a more rational approach demands a shift from feeling to thought. That's an important move to make when you wish to make sense of something or see how it ticks, which I can only imagine should be a concern of anyone who wishes to be taken seriously when deciding to believe in something important. But there are True Believers who refuse to, or cannot, make that move to detached thinking and find such an approach necessarily joyless. They miss that we can *all* feel that initial joy at such anecdotes and events, but only some of us get to experience another level of joy which is warmed by its closer proximity to the truth. We need to live by our hearts as well as our brains to engage most wonderfully with this world: sadly there is often a proud refusal amongst True Believers to engage with the latter.

Anecdotes and Fact

Betray anything approaching a sceptical attitude to anyone who is still happy to talk to you and you will be answered with a great story of some very convincing demonstration of psychic healing or New

Age therapy, or even the occasional ghost story. These are always stories of successes; one never hears of the healer that couldn't find the problem, or the therapy that proved worthless. After all, why would such non-stories be told?

We are wonderfully, blissfully cocooned in our own worlds. We cast ourselves in the role of the most fascinating hero or heroine in the plays of our lives, and we interact with secondary roles, forgetting that we are ourselves only bit-parts in the sweeping, five-act Wagnerian epics of other people's lives. Naturally and blamelessly we attribute far more importance to events that happen in our own lives, which we can feel and represent to ourselves vividly, than those which happen to other people. Don't we in most conversations follow another person's story just waiting to come back with one of our own when they've finished? Can we listen to someone talking about his or her parents without relating their tale to our own? Our wealth of experience is all we have to make sense of what we hear and see. In fact, our ability to form rapid generalizations from our own one-off experiences is absolutely vital: we needed to touch only one or two hot-plates at home when we were gurgling babbies to learn that they hurt and therefore they probably all hurt in other people's houses too. It's vital we all relate things back to ourselves in this way.

Yet if we are anything other than the most arrogant adults, we learn to balance the impact of personal experience with an understanding of *it might just be me*. We have a terrible time in a hotel, but continually hear great reports of it from other people. It doesn't mean we remember it any more fondly, but we realize we might have been unlucky. I loathed the film *The Shawshank Redemption*: I found it trite, cliché-ridden and in every way like the worst kind of predictable TV movie I would hesitate to make Robert Kilroy-Silk sit and watch. And any of you people out there who are now cheering and waving this thin volume above your heads with the giddy delight that comes from the surging feeling of long-awaited validation will realize that we stand few and far between. The film was hugely successful and seems to rank among the all-time favourites of people who don't appear at first glance to be deaf-blind or simply retarded. So while I am more than happy to rant about its overworn, insulting and otiose sentiment to anyone who mentions the film, I begrudgingly have to qualify my lividness with the reluctant caveat, 'But everyone else seems to love it so maybe it's just me.'

Phrases like 'maybe it's just me', 'maybe I just got lucky', 'it might have just been a coincidence' and so on are rarely offered in defence alongside positive experiences. While similar qualifications are often given so that one doesn't seem like a misery-guts when telling of a loathed film or a bad hotel, we understandably don't want to detract from a fascinating or wonderful experience by admitting the same possibility, that it might have just been a one-off. But when it comes to making decisions about huge belief systems or cosmic forces, a dose of this modest and wider perspective is certainly a useful thing.

For example, a friend was telling me the other day that his mother had been attending a reiki course. He had gone to see her and had hurt his thumb the day before. He didn't tell her about the thumb, but she passed her hands over him to do a reiki diagnosis. He told me that when she got to his thumb she was able to tell he had a problem there. This was clearly an impressive feat, and it left my friend rather convinced by the efficacy of the process. (She didn't, however, manage to heal him, for the record.) He had a couple of similar stories, neither of which related to his mother but which were interesting and not dissimilar to others I had heard. While I would have no desire to detract from the personal enjoyment he'll derive from such memories, such reports are worth deconstructing for the sake of our discussion here. The main problem is this: we only have a story, and therefore it will be subject to deletions, exaggerations, edits and wonky memories. Taking these on board, we can suggest a series of valid possibilities. While some of them may seem a little wearily dry, let's not forget Hume's lesson that extraordinary claims do require extraordinary proof:

1. His mum knows him well, and might very possibly have been able to tell if he had exhibited some tension around his bad thumb. This doesn't seem unlikely at all. She could have picked up (consciously or unconsciously) on it at any point, either during the diagnosis or beforehand (in which case her expectation might have provided a 'feeling' which was then 'confirmed' during the passing of hands over him). In which case, all kudos to her for being perceptive.
2. She might have mentioned a few troublesome points here and there, or stopped at different places. Because of the all-too-human pattern finding and selective memory traps we've been discussing, my friend remembers only the thumb. In this instance, his story is a much more simplified version of what actually happened.
3. Some other way via the relationship between son and mother, with the former unconsciously telegraphing his hurt thumb through tension, attention and movement, and the mother perceptively searching for such signals, and maybe with a bit of selective memory on his part they arrive at the diagnosis. Impressive and fascinating, but nothing to do with the theory behind reiki.
4. She got lucky.
5. Reiki is absolutely real, and there really is a cosmic energy flow the healer is able to channel. It absolutely works, and science simply refuses to accept that.

I don't mean the last option to sound sarcastic. But perhaps there are fascinating and enlightening reasons contained in options one to four as to why the diagnosis was right in this instance, without having to believe in a special cosmic energy. The obvious fact is that there's no way of telling. A True Believer in reiki would tell me just to accept the story as solid evidence; stop trying to clutch at the straws of reductionist, over-analytical western science. A genuinely open-minded person, on the other hand, would say, 'Yes, it could be any one of those things, and they're all worth looking into.' And with an anecdote, there's really no further to go. Should my friend reject the appealing sentiment of his experience with his mother? I don't think so. But should he decide to believe in reiki based on that experience? Well, that's up to him, but it would probably be sensible to put it in perspective. Let's not forget that his mother didn't heal the thumb; she just pointed out that there was something wrong with it. Had she just said, out of the blue over coffee, 'Is there something wrong with your thumb?', would he have found that as impressive? Short of having a series of people come to her with different ailments (which they themselves were unaware of so as not to unconsciously telegraph their conditions to her), and seeing how well she did overall, there is no way of telling which of the above options applies. What we can do, however, is look at evidence outside this one scenario and ask whether or not there is any real evidence for reiki.

I am reminded of a story told to me by another friend as evidence of psychic ability. A friend of his was a policeman, and he had attended a social event thrown by the force – a Policemen's Ball, I suppose. Also attending was a psychic who had apparently been used by the police. (At this point I should add that many psychics make such claims all the time. Normally it's a lie, or perhaps they have called the police offering help. It shouldn't be taken as evidence that any more than a tiny number of policemen, if any, have taken psychics seriously.) She approached this friend-of-my-friend at the end of the event and shook his hand. As she did so, she closed her eyes and appeared to go into a trance. 'You'd better go,' she said. 'Henrietta's getting cold.' She opened her eyes and looked at him. 'Who's Henrietta?' she asked.

Henrietta, it turned out, was the pet name the policeman had for his car, which was parked outside. It had started snowing, and sure enough, his car was getting cold. The story was told to me with an air of 'explain *that*, then', as the policeman in question had been hugely impressed. He had told it many times in the years after the event, and one person who had heard it was now telling me.

I don't ever want to 'explain *that*' from any story, when a story is all I'm hearing. Here, I was listening to a story of a story. However, it made me think of the importance of presentation, which we discussed in relation to conjuring. In the same way that the reiki-practising mother might have just asked about her son's thumb and there would have been no story, so too this 'psychic' (who of course I'm happier to think was an out-and-out fake) might simply have said, 'Apparently you call your car Henrietta.' In that instance, the response would have been, 'Right, who told you that?', as undoubtedly a number of policemen attending would have been aware that he had a pet name for his car. A non-event. But because she rolled her eyes and appeared to go into a trance as she shook his hand, the same fact – that she knew the pet name of his car – suddenly appears inexplicable. And if she had just been told or had just overheard that he called his car by that name, note how much more effective it was to appear to know less than she did. To say 'I sense your car is called Henrietta – she's getting cold' might make the policeman suspicious that she had been told. The display of ignorance in asking 'Who's Henrietta?', however, controls the policeman's response ('My car – how on earth . . . ?') and bypasses his suspicion. Regardless of what really happened, the *way* she said it could have been enough to turn a non-event into a lifelong memory of something impossible, even to cause a shift in his personal beliefs. What would have made the difference? *Showmanship*.

As for what really happened, who knows? It's just an anecdote. And that is, I believe, the only way to respond to such stories. They are usually engaging and impressive tales when viewed from the perspective of the story-teller, in the same way that the lottery win is miraculous when viewed from the perspective of the winner. But anecdotes are not evidence of anything. One person's experience says nothing about the reliability of the thing in question, and isn't it all about reliability? Too much can get distorted in the remembering and telling of the story. These sorts of stories should be seen as raising interesting possibilities worth investigating; you shouldn't just credulously believe them if you want to be taken seriously. You don't have to be a scientist to think like that. Surely it's just about intelligence and scuriosity.

Another friend, deeply into the ways of the psychic, told me he put crystals in his plant pots to make them grow better. Now, anyone who is happy to say that sort of thing in public must be ready for a bit of ridicule outside his circle of fellow True Believers. So presumably he'd want to make sure he wasn't talking nonsense. Assuming he would have been fully aware that there are plenty of other factors that contribute to a plant's growth, would it not have been just simple curiosity to put a couple of pots with the same plant next to each other in the same window, water them at the same time, but put crystals in one and not in the other? He could privately do that to see whether the crystals made any difference. Am I really being so harsh to think that someone might just try that? Just to see? And if there was a big difference, then maybe do it a few times to see if it was repeatable? Isn't that just curiosity? That's much easier than home-testing a reiki-trained mother. But, of course, this just isn't done. No-one from the New Age community wants to test these things.

Luckily, scientists don't turn a blind eye to such things. They *do* want to see if these things work, as science is only about embracing what works, and moving on. So they do construct very fair tests to see if the New Age theory is what does the trick. They test with large numbers of people, and in a way that eliminates all bias. Perhaps unsurprisingly, the results show that the mystic elements – the oils, the crystals, the healing energy – are never what do the trick. But to many people anecdotes and personal experience are far more seductive than real-world evidence and fact. Proper evidence and fact are dismissed as irrelevant when dealing with 'holistic' subjects. Dismissed, that is, apart from when holistic practitioners happily supply anecdotal evidence in favour of their claims and misleading pseudo-scientific 'factual' models of energy. Science is dismissed both as 'Western' and irrelevant, yet also clung to when it can be taken out of context to lend any validity to New Age claims.

Scientific language does not make a science any more than anecdotes do, but it does allow the inquisitive listener to check on facts. For example, I once tried to get a sense of what the theory behind crystal power was from a practitioner. She told me that crystals have a particular atomic frequency that causes them to vibrate, or have an energy. This vibration then either sits in unison with the atomic vibration of another object (a plant, a person, or another crystal) to lend its power to that object, or it does not. Talk of atomic vibrations was, to me, a little easier to understand than talk of mystical energies, so I asked a scientist friend if her theory made any sense. The answer was a clear 'no'. A misunderstanding of GCSE physics is no basis for making non-imaginary, real-world claims.

Superstitious Thinking

In 1948, a man called B. F. Skinner put hungry pigeons into glass boxes. We've all done it. He had a feeder attached to each box through which pigeon food (fag ends and sick, presumably – I've never been sure) was dropped every fifteen seconds. The pigeons were observed for a while to see what would happen.

While research assistants hid behind one-way mirrors and made fun of the birds, congratulating each other on their hysterical but offensive club-footed, retarded, help-I'm-trapped-inside-a-box pigeon impressions, the birds themselves developed some interesting behaviours. As these fat, grey, warbling, puffed-up, disease-spreading scientists watched, they noticed that the pigeons were trying to work out what had to be done to release the food. Although the food was arriving entirely independently of their actions, an early drop would inevitably occur at the same time the bird made a particular gesture, such as bobbing its head or pecking at the roof of the box. The bird seemed to presume that this action had caused the arrival of the food, so each pigeon began to act out a ritual inside its box consisting of repeated actions misguidedly designed to trigger more food. Some would walk around in circles, others would peck repeatedly in the corner, and so on.

The birds, clearly, were stupid. Idiot pigeons. But there is more that we can learn from this than the nature of avian ignorance. Clearly the birds thought they were exercising control over their rewards. Their strange rituals were analogous to the superstitious rituals of human beings. Imagine, for example, a gambler's lucky charm, or a superstitious student's fortuitous pen. Clearly these objects don't really affect the game or the exam result, but it takes only one or two occasions where there has been a coincidence of desired results in the presence of the item for many people to start thinking, 'I'll bring it just in case.' We imagine a link between the arbitrary object and the reward we have been given in the past – the strange circling and the food that has dropped into our box. Presuming, that is, that the same conditioning works with human beings. Surely we wouldn't be so silly?

Following initial scepticism of Skinner's conclusions, Stuart Vyse follows the trail of similar experiments with people in his 1997 book *Believing in Magic*. Firstly, it was tried with children. In Wagner and Morris's experiment of 1987, kids aged between three and six were asked to choose a toy they would like to win. They were then placed in an observed room with a large mechanical clown. If that wasn't terrifying enough for the kids, long-term trauma was ensured by the following procedure: the clown dispensed a marble from its bright red, tooth-filled mouth at regular or random intervals and the kid was told to collect as many marbles as he could to win the prize he had chosen. Although it's not mentioned in the literature, I like to imagine that once the disturbed child had plucked up the courage actually to go near enough to take the marble, the clown (actually a scientist in a costume) would leap up and chase it around the room screaming and laughing.

The perverse judgements made by scientists of what children find appealing placed neatly to one side for the moment, the kids were asked to do this for eight minutes a day for six days. The results were remarkably similar to Skinner's. The children also seemed to presume that they had some sort of control over the dispensing of the marbles, and after a few minutes they could be observed going through their own rituals, repeatedly and over several sessions. Some would jump up and down, some would consistently smile or grimace, and others would kiss the clown on the nose. Again, superstitious patterns of behaviour had resulted from the coincidence of a desired event with the presence of a piece of behaviour. Rather than just sit and wait for the rewards, both children and pigeons acted out a kind of magical ritual that they believed caused them to get what they wanted.

And adults? Certainly. Koichi Ono, a Japanese psychologist, set up one of my favourite experiments where subjects were asked to sit at a desk on which were placed three coloured levers. In front of the subjects on the partition wall behind the desk was a signal light and electronic counter, which was apparently to keep track of points. Each session lasted forty minutes, and the subject was told to earn as many points as possible, though it was not explained how she was expected to do that. In fact, the points display on the counter had nothing to do with the levers on the desk, and was designed just to display new points at various intervals independently of anything the subject might do.

Wonderfully, the adult subjects fell into similar behavioural traps as the children and pigeons. After a while the Japanese volunteers could be seen repeating elaborate or simple combinations of lever-pulls, banging the sides of the partition, or even jumping up to touch the ceiling until exhaustion set in. Because of the same 'temporal contiguity' (i.e. happening at the same time) of arbitrary action and reward, essentially 'superstitious' behaviours invariably resulted.

What also comes from these and other experiments is the interesting fact that many subjects report that they stick to their superstitious theories *despite* the fact that much of the time they clearly don't work. In those cases, they rationalize the failure to produce the desired result as a mistake on their part, rather than step back and question the validity of the theory.

We like to feel we are in control. We like to repeatedly press the button for the lift or for the traffic-light crossing as if that will hasten the arrival of the lift or the halting of the traffic. We find ways of making our behaviour seem to matter in areas where it simply makes no difference. We win at poker while wearing certain clothes or having carried out certain behaviours prior to the game, and we decide that those clothes or behaviours are necessary to aid future wins. Or, we use an ineffective and overpriced New Age remedy when ill, find that we quickly get better, and decide that the remedy caused the improvement. Our innate and important capacity to look for patterns makes us terrible at thinking in terms of coincidence or randomness, and we become like Skinner's pigeons, needlessly twirling and tapping in a largely indifferent universe.

ALTERNATIVE MEDICINE

In London, I have a neighbour, Mike. (That's not his real name, to spare him any embarrassment. His real name is Guy.) Mike had a girlfriend who, being an actress, was rather into the sorts of 'remedies' we've been talking about. Mike, however, being of a drier constitution, was not. When he went through a heavily depressed period, his girlfriend convinced him to dispense with his scepticism and let a friend of the couple try some reiki healing on him. He was feeling so utterly listless and worthless that he decided he might as well try it.

A while after his session, I spoke to Mike about the healing. It seemed very out of character for him to have tried it, and of course I was eager to hear of his experience. As ever, I really wanted to hear some miraculous tale that would make me a believer. (I once saw and learned what I thought was a genuine demonstration of chi energy and was excited for days. However, it turned out to be a rather simple trick I wasn't even aware I was doing. I was hugely disappointed.) Mike's story of the reiki session was very striking. He said he had never felt as abused and exploited in his life. There he was, he said, at his lowest point, being subjected to what he felt was the worst sort of insidiously self-indulgent, ego-driven rubbish. He felt used in the worst way, all to boost what he saw at that moment as the practitioner's co-dependent, dysfunctional sense of self that needed the title 'healer' to feel worthwhile. He likened it, memorably, to the idea of lying in bed as a kid and having an uncle come in and masturbate on him.

Strong and angry words. I relate this here not as an attack on the healer, who I'm sure is a well-meaning man. But the events did make both Mike and me think about how easily one can succumb to nonsense when one is most needy, and about the morality of those modern-day snake-oil industries that exploit the clutch-at-any-straw weakness of the desperate. It is a foul thing to be ill, and we happily accept spurious offers of remedies we would otherwise laugh at. In the harmfully fascinating and constantly sexy world of the television industry, one cannot walk into a production office and sneeze without a hundred beaded wrists reaching into colourful beaded bags to fish around among the beads for Echinacea or some similar herbal nonsense. (On that subject, the popular herbal cold remedy Echinacea has recently been subjected to fair tests to see if it has any effect other than as a placebo. It does not. Put that in your chakra and heal it.) Runners, researchers, production assistants, producers and even otherwise conservative location managers all have their pet remedies for colds and period pains, regardless of gender; I'm sure if I complained of a tumour they would sweep pens, chocolates and furry toys from a desktop, fling me flat thereupon and perform psychic surgery right there in the office, amid the chit-chat daytime lunacy of the plasma TVs and the faint aroma of decaf lattes and brought-in sushi. Silliness abounds.

Probably because we live in a time when everything is made very convenient for us, we tend to imagine that something has gone wrong if we are occasionally ill. The language of alternative remedies equates 'wellness' with all that is natural and good, as if our natural state is one of health. Of course, this isn't really true. Nature isn't the idyllic, bland forest glade pictured in disastrous New Age paintings or the front of bubble-bath bottles. It is not a place of universal, peaceful co-existence. Nature is a place of warfare and blind cruelty as much as it offers spectacular beauty. And our health comes and goes: we have good and bad times according to the 'natural' rhythms of life. When a doctor makes us better, he is not restoring us to our 'natural' state, he is just making life more convenient for us for a while.

When dealing with the stock market, part of the trick is to buy shares when a company isn't doing too well. The reason for this is that you know it is likely to start doing better and its share-prices will rise. We would do well to bear this cold but useful analogy in mind when we hear tales of miraculous recoveries from remedies, when there is no real-world evidence of the remedies' efficacy. Most terminal illnesses do not involve a simple daily worsening of symptoms leading to death. They fluctuate: there are relapses and improvements that provide relief from the overall decline. In some cases the illness might even disappear for a very long time. When will a person suffering from such an illness feel desperate enough to resort to unfounded and speculative treatments? When she is at a very low point. This is when she is most likely to try an ineffective treatment out of desperation. However, like anyone at a very bad point on the fluctuating wave of gradual declining health, she is likely to experience a period of improvement in the very near future. Any ineffective treatment taken at that time is likely to be given credit for the improvement, when it most likely played no role at all.

Equally, some practices such as chemotherapy typically result in the patient feeling lousy while undergoing the treatment, but then feeling much better and hopefully with a greatly reduced or vanished tumour some weeks after the course has finished. It's not uncommon for a patient to decide that the chemotherapy must not have worked (because she felt terrible and there was no improvement during the course) and then to try some alternative treatment afterwards which of course promises to be gentle. Then, when the effects of the orthodox treatment kick in after a few weeks, the patient will report feeling great or hopefully even cured. However, this improvement may be unfairly credited to the alternative treatment, which was administered at the same time, and not to the real effects of the chemotherapy. John Diamond, in his heroic and unfinished book *Snake Oil*, written while he himself was dying of cancer and telling of his own journey through the misguiding and dangerous promises of alternative remedies, wrote:

> Using precisely the same logic I could tell you that my nasty chemotherapy had no effect on my own cancer, but that six weeks later, after it was over, and thanks to me sticking to a dietary regime of Nestlé's Build-Up, Stolichnaya and the occasional Havana cigar, I felt a hundred times better than I had under the chemo, and that while at the end of the chemotherapy I still seemed to have some tumour, by the end of the period of Build-Up, vodka and smoking I was cured.

The danger is, of course, that the patient can come to rely on these ineffective remedies at the expense of proven medicine. After all, if traditional methods are not able to stop the terrible decline, why not turn to 'alternative' treatments? And if they seem to work, why not turn to them exclusively? I think it's fair to say that there comes a point during a terminal illness when it is preferable to do *something*, even something medically ineffective, if it provides a psychologically more comfortable alternative to doing nothing.

However, whether that justifies the companies that knowingly make large sums from selling ineffective potions, or the sheer size of the industry, is another matter. In 2000, the amount spent on the alternative medicine business in the UK was £1.6 billion. Whereas pharmaceutical drugs are subjected to rigorous tests before being allowed on the market, 'alternative' products are not. Surely if they are able to make claims that are false or which cannot be substantiated, they too should be subject to regulation?

Aside from alternative treatments offered to terminally ill patients, there are plenty of popular alternative remedies relatively healthy people swear by. Everyone either has or knows someone who has great tales regarding their efficacy. Typically, you may have been suffering from a bad cold, and traditional pills and medicines seemed to be doing no good. A friend of yours recommended a terrific herbal remedy that she used effectively herself, so you decided to give it a go. You start to use it on day two of the cold, and by day three the cold had disappeared. Missing the fact that the cold would have most likely gone anyway after a couple of days, you were impressed, and you've been recommending the herbal remedy to your friends with the same enthusiasm.*

Such remedies have been tested in the fairest way to see whether they actually have any impact compared to a placebo, and time and time again the results show that they do not. How might you test such things fairly? Well, the first thing is to realize that any one single experience is neither here nor there; first we have to gather together a lot of people with a similar condition and see what percentage of them are helped by the alternative remedy. However, it's not quite fair to compare the effects of alternative treatment to

*I am reminded of a woman from a Christian house-group I once attended. She was telling us about how she had dealt with getting a cold. She had sat on her bed and shouted, 'No, Satan, I will not have this cold. In the name of Jesus I tell you to get out. Get out!' Stern stuff. 'And do you know,' she continued, 'after a few days it was gone.'

no treatment at all, because of the interference of this placebo response. So half the group (the control group) will be given an inactive, ineffective 'sugar pill', or placebo, and the other half will be given the real treatment. Importantly, none of the participants knows if he is in the treatment group or in the control group.

Now, contrary to the exaggerated accusations made by New Agers that scientists are biased and turn a blind eye to the efficacy of their treatments, the scientists take an extra step when conducting these experiments to remove the possibility of their *own* bias consciously or unconsciously affecting the fairness of the test. Science, you remember, is all about getting *out* of the bias of individual people's experiences and into the real world of what actually works. So the tests are 'double-blind', which means that not only do the subjects not know which group they're in, even the *scientists* don't know. Otherwise, they could unfairly weigh the results by misperceiving improvements in the subjects' condition according to their own personal expectations, or unconsciously communicate to the subjects whether or not they are getting the real treatment, which would then upset the fairness of the experiment. Only the computer that randomized the groups into two knows who is who, and it doesn't yield that information until the end.

Now we can look at the two groups. Let's say there was a measurable improvement in the control group, caused only by the expectation of getting better after taking a pill, or because of some natural variability in symptoms. We'd also expect about the same number of subjects from the treatment group to improve for the same reason (the placebo effect), even if none of the claims made by alternative practitioners are true. The question is, do *more* get better in the genuine treatment group? Is it more effective than giving someone a fake pill and telling him it should make him feel better? The answer, time and time again, is 'no'. The results for both groups are always about the same. These remedies, irrespective of the anecdotes we hear, can be safely said to be only effective as a placebo.

I can't think of a fairer test. If it seems complicated, that's because it's very hard to eliminate all possibility of bias. Any other elements to remove bias and promote fairness are constantly sought and welcomed into the procedure. People in the treatment group may be matched one on one with similar people in the control group who have the same condition and are of the same age, for example, to improve the sensitivity of the test.

A common defence made by fans of alternative medicine when they hear that such remedies fail these tests is to say something along the lines of, 'Well, it's not surprising that they fail. This is just science trying to crowbar something into a model which it doesn't fit. These remedies don't fit the evidence-based objective model. They won't work under scientific testing because scientific testing is the wrong way to see if they are effective or not.' A word on this point, as it seems rather an important one. The worthwhile tests to which I refer are designed and usually carried out w*ith the full cooperation of the alternative practitioners*. Scientists are not, for example, reiki practitioners or acupuncturists, so the test can often only work where alternative practitioners are involved. Between the scientists and the practitioners, a test is devised that both groups are happy with. The cry of 'it doesn't fit the scientific model' is *only* sounded when the remedy then fails the test. The test *that everyone had agreed on*. You can bet that were the remedy to pass the test, the defenders of alternative medicine wouldn't be so dismissive. They'd grab hold of it and shout to the heavens that science has proven their claims. Suddenly scientific testing would be seen as valid. It's only irrelevant when the remedy fails. And think for a moment – what does 'doesn't fit the evidence-based objective model' mean anyway? I have heard words like this uttered on many occasions when I mention these tests. Is it being seriously stated – by people who might be dealing with terminally ill patients and recommending their own remedies over, say, chemotherapy – that evidence and objectivity play no part in deciding whether or not the treatments are worthwhile? How can evidence be irrelevant? Maybe, you might argue, that's not what they mean – just that 'objective evidence' isn't appropriate. But if you only work with subjective evidence – anecdotes and personal experiences – how on earth can you decide how effective something is? Surely it's just straightforward intelligence that would have you see the importance of being able to step back and see whether these things *do what they claim with any reliability*, which is basically what objective evidence means and what any worthwhile testing is for. The idea that some other paradigm of evidence exists which is just as 'valid' as objective evidence is easy to say, but I really can't see what it means. Something either works or it doesn't. And there are good and bad ways of testing to see if it works or doesn't. Sincere ways and half-hearted ways. Curious ways and pointless ways.

Because this objection of scientific testing being irrelevant is raised so often, I'm going to repeat myself. The tests are done with the full agreement and cooperation of the practitioners. They themselves agree with the test. They only complain about the nature of the test when it fails to show a result.

Homoeopathy is a very popular alternative remedy which also fails the test. This lack of any unbiased, real-world support for homoeopathy should not surprise us. It was invented in the eighteenth century and is based on the idea of 'like may be cured by like'. Homoeopathic remedies are created by taking dilutions of substances which if taken in much larger doses would cause the very ailment the patient is suffering from. The internal logic of homoeopathy is that the weaker the dose, the more effective it is. Because of this, the remedies are typically diluted to a point where *no trace* of the important substance in question can be found. If none of the vital substance is there, how can it have any effect? Viewed from any point other than True Belief, it is clearly a ridiculous notion. Yet the placebo effect and a misunderstanding of variability (the ups and downs of illnesses) can make it appear very effective some of the time to some people.

In the case of homoeopathy, the fact that the remedies are diluted to the point where they become pure water makes it very hard to compare them to an inactive placebo. The inactive placebo, surely, would also have to be water. Richard Dawkins, in his foreword to Diamond's *Snake Oil*, makes the point that 'there would be more stray molecules than the desired homoeopathic dose knocking around in water of the highest attainable purity'. Homoeopaths get around this problem of their treatments being necessarily inactive by claiming that the water retains a 'memory' of the original substance. Dawkins responds to this implausible but testable theory:

> Any homoeopath who really believes his theory should be beavering away from dawn to dusk. After all, if the double-blind trials of patient treatments came out reliably and repeatedly positive, he would win a Nobel Prize not only in Medicine but in Physics as well. He would have discovered a brand-new principle of physics, perhaps a new fundamental force in the universe. With such a prospect in view, homoeopaths must surely be falling over each other in their eagerness to be first in the lab, racing like alternative Watsons and Cricks to claim this glittering scientific crown. Er, actually, no, they aren't. Can it be that they don't really believe their theory after all?

In the case of acupuncture, another popular alternative treatment, it is also hard to construct fair double-blind tests. When it comes to sticking needles in a person, there's no 'fake' way of administering them to the control subject, other than to place the needles in places that do not conform to the meridian points set out by practitioners. The problem here is that the person placing the needles into the subject will himself know that he is administering the placebo (as he would have to be an acupuncturist himself to put in needles at supposedly ineffective places), and therefore the double-blind fairness of the test is contaminated. If the person administering the 'fake' acupuncture communicates at any level to the control subject that it isn't for real, the subject's belief is undone and the test becomes redundant. Experiments in the past have shown the importance of preserving this piece of protocol: people are very good at working out, consciously or otherwise, if they are being given the real or sham medicine from the tiniest clues given off by the scientists. A few cases have indeed shown acupuncture to be more effective than placebo administration. In these examples, though, the patients were suffering from conditions known to be placebo-responsive. No difference is found when the tests are for conditions that are not placebo-responsive. From this it can be gleaned that the attempted blinding is not effective, and that there is a placebo response from the real acupuncture that is much stronger than that triggered by the fake administration. As it's only better than placebos when the condition is placebo-responsive, it's fair to say that acupuncture is probably pure placebo.

A friend of mine who had cancer told me of his visit to an applied kinesiologist. In a kinesiology session, the patient extends her arm in front of her and pushes up against the hand of the practitioner, who in turn tries to quickly push the patient's arm down. The patient then digests a series of food substances, and each time tries to stop the kinesiologist's arm from pushing hers down by locking her own. At some point, the patient finds that after taking one of the substances she cannot lock effectively against the arm, and her own is forced to drop. That is the test. Forgetting how ludicrous it sounds for a moment, we are invited to read it as a display of some sort of intolerance to the foodstuff. The patient is then advised to avoid that ingredient, in order to cure or improve her condition. This would maintain a surface plausibility if it were not for the fact that my friend, when being tested with coffee, was not given a small amount on his tongue, as one might expect, but had a sealed jar of Nescafé placed against his chest. There was no contact with the ingredient being tested. Presumably this bizarre practice is common; I noted that Dawkins reported a similar experience in his foreword. It was the coffee that caused the weaker response being looked for, and my friend was told to avoid caffeine. As lame as this sounded, he was still impressed that the coffee jar caused the response of weakness. And it does seem impressive, until we realize that there is no control over how hard the practitioner is pushing. Ever seen the trick where four people try to lift someone out of a chair using only two fingers each? They can't do it, until they act out some sort of ceremony such as pushing down on the seated person's head. Then they try a second time and now they find they can lift him right up in the air. It's a great demonstration, and it works simply because the participants are unconsciously making much more of an effort the second time, when they are led to believe that they can do it. There is way too much room for shifts in effort on the part of the practitioner or the patient for the successful arm-pushing to be taken seriously to mean anything.

So the best way to get around this problem and see if the change in arm strength is really due to the ingredients ingested would be to try a double-blind test. Remove all possibility of people fooling themselves or biasing the results, and see if this potentially great diagnostic tool stands up. The psychologist Ray Hyman tells of such a test, made memorable by the reaction of the practitioner at the end – a great example of the alternative scene's refusal to accept facts contrary to their beliefs. Note how the double-blind procedure works to eliminate the element of anyone knowing what sugar they're getting and unconsciously pushing harder or softer in accordance with what they expect should happen.

> Some years ago I participated in a test of applied kinesiology at Dr. Wallace Sampson's medical office in Mountain View, California. A team of chiropractors came to demonstrate the procedure. Several physician observers and the chiropractors had agreed that the chiropractors would first be free to illustrate applied kinesiology in whatever manner they chose. Afterward, we would try some double-blind tests of their claims.
>
> The chiropractors presented as their major example a demonstration they believed showed that the human body could respond to the difference between glucose (a 'bad' sugar) and fructose (a 'good' sugar). The differential sensitivity was a truism among 'alternative healers', though there was no scientific warrant for it. The chiropractors had volunteers lie on their backs and raise one arm vertically. They then would put a drop of glucose (in a solution of water) on the volunteer's tongue. The chiropractor then tried to push the volunteer's upraised arm down to a horizontal position while the volunteer tried to resist. In almost every case, the volunteer could not resist. The chiropractors stated the volunteer's body recognized glucose as a 'bad' sugar. After the volunteer's mouth was rinsed out and a drop of fructose was placed on the tongue, the volunteer, in just about every test, resisted movement to the horizontal position. The body had recognized fructose as a 'good' sugar.

After lunch a nurse brought us a large number of test tubes, each one coded with a secret number so that we could not tell from the tubes which contained fructose and which contained glucose. The nurse then left the room so that no one in the room during the subsequent testing would consciously know which tubes contained glucose and which fructose. The arm tests were repeated, but this time they were double-blind – neither the volunteer, the chiropractors, nor the onlookers were aware of whether the solution being applied to the volunteer's tongue was glucose or fructose. As in the morning session, sometimes the volunteers were able to resist and other times they were not. We recorded the code number of the solution on each trial. Then the nurse returned with the key to the code. When we determined which trials involved glucose and which involved fructose, there was no connection between ability to resist and whether the volunteer was given the 'good' or the 'bad' sugar.

When these results were announced, the head chiropractor turned to me and said, 'You see, that is why we never do double-blind testing any more. It never works!' At first I thought he was joking. It turned it out he was quite serious. Since he 'knew' that applied kinesiology works, and the best scientific method shows that it does not work, then, in his mind, there must be something wrong with the scientific method.

As I have mentioned before, if an 'alternative' medicine or tool can be shown to work reliably and repeatedly, then it ceases to be 'alternative' and becomes medicine. Science is just another name for what can be shown to work reliably and repeatedly. Indeed, as Diamond and Dawkins and others have pointed out, one can just think of medicines that do work and those that don't. Those are the only two categories of importance, and anything that can be shown to fall into the former becomes scientific. If it becomes scientific, the chances are that it will be investigated to find out what component of the medicine does the trick. That way it can be reproduced in a way that will benefit as many people as possible. However, at this point, because it might not have the word 'natural' on the packet, with all the word's connotations of 'goodness', it feels somehow 'wrong' to the needlessly sentimental alternative consumer. Willow bark, for example, is a classic 'alternative' pain reliever. Scientists saw that it worked reliably and repeatedly, so they looked into what it was about willow bark that caused pain to diminish. They found out (in 1838) that it was the salicylic acid in the bark that did the trick. One synthesized form of this is acetylsalicylic acid, better known as aspirin. There is absolutely no difference between aspirin and the pain-relieving component in willow bark, yet any number of users of alternative medicines will tell you that science won't embrace the healing properties of such things as willow bark, and they refuse to use nasty synthetic aspirin over lovely 'natural' willow. Again, 'orthodox' medicine means nothing other than medicine that can be shown to work reliably.

One very weak defence (though a very effective appeal) of alternative medicine is that it uses principles that have been around for ages in cultures we just don't understand. Well, the fact that a medicine was around hundreds of years ago, is no evidence of its efficacy. The fact that the vast majority of very old treatments can now be seen as ineffective or highly dangerous might even count against it. Those who doubt this might like to try leeches or ask their barber to bleed them next time they feel unwell. As for the appeal of foreign cultures, this is sadly no less sentimental than it has ever been, since charlatans with an eye for the exotic first told tall tales of faraway lands. A look at the underdeveloped parts of the world where these medicines come from shows cultures screaming out for effective Western medicine. As Diamond pointed out, 'A Ugandan dying of AIDS-related tuberculosis doesn't want to be treated with the natural remedies of his forefathers; he wants an aseptic syringe full of antibiotics, and then he wants to join the sixteen-pill-a-day programme which, in the West, would stand a chance of putting his AIDS on hold.' In developed China, where one might imagine that the use of acupuncture and such medicine is common, only 18 per cent of people use such traditional medicines, despite the fact that they are widely available. Diamond continues, 'Traditional remedies are wonderful if you live in the West and need to deal with nothing more pressing than the odd rash, irritable bowel or anxiety attack, and if you have a modern pharmacopoeia to fall back on if things get difficult; they're useless against the diseases which daily kill and maim the inhabitants of the countries from where those remedies come.' The Western defender of alternative medicine is guilty of a profoundly patronizing view of the East if he clings gullibly to such notions of wise cultures steeped in the arcane medicine of their ancestors.

I reiterate, I don't feel any strong desire to preach to people the simple misunderstandings upon which these things are generally based. To each their own, unless they are causing danger to others. But when I read that the already overstretched NHS is dealing with pressure to include homoeopathy as a treatment, I do fuss and fume. When I'm pounced upon by well-meaning but silly people with their special teas and brown pills every time I'm feeling run down, I sometimes want to spank them. As an extreme example, Mike's 'healing' treatment was profoundly humiliating. Though his experience was far worse than most, it does raise the issue of how insidiously insulting well-meant offers of 'help' can be. For people to waste your time during a period of trouble or illness with their own sanctimonious nonsense can sometimes be annoying and unpleasant. From my own experience of offering to pray for friends as a teenager, I am aware of the fact that the helpful True Believer, armed with a disregard for fact and an over-regard for his own beliefs, would never see that.

However, for all of this, I *do* think that these remedies have a value. In fact, quite an important one. First we should look at a much-used term and take on board its importance and its limitations.

The Placebo Effect

If there is a measurable placebo effect caused by alternative medicines, does that not count in their favour? Absolutely, but first one must come to terms with a few facts about the placebo response.

Its importance was discovered around the end of the Second World War by an American anaesthetist, Henry Beecher. He found that he could administer a saline solution instead of morphine to terribly wounded soldiers before an operation and not only would they experience greatly reduced pain, they also wouldn't suffer from the cardiovascular shock that is expected during operations or amputations without a painkiller. Some interest sprang up in the medical community, but Beecher was eager for the full power of the placebo to be recognized, and for its efficacy to be compared to 'real' drugs. Because of his eagerness, his important 1955 paper 'The Powerful Placebo' contained a number of inaccurate interpretations of evidence regarding the efficacy of the placebo, and some spurious statistics which still linger misleadingly in our collective minds today, such as the notion that placebos work on about 30 per cent of people (untrue: they work in one way or another on pretty much all of us).

Dylan Evans, in his intriguing book *Placebo*, noted that the placebo response has been shown to work only in conjunction with certain conditions, contrary to Beecher's assertion that it works for everything. For example, it is enormously effective with pain. In the 1980s, a biochemist was checking the ultrasound equipment used to treat soft-tissue injuries, despite the fact that patients and staff had reported great benefits from the machines. To his surprise he found that some of the machines were not outputting the correct amount of ultrasound, or in the case of one machine, not working at all; yet patients, bizarrely, were still enjoying the benefits of successful treatment. This led to tests with dental patients, where some patients received ultrasound treatment to relieve pain and others only *believed* that they were receiving it when in fact the machine was turned off. Both groups noted the same reduced levels of pain and swelling. Clearly much, if not all, of the treatment was due to the patients' belief that it worked. While pain is undoubtedly a largely subjective affair, swelling certainly is not. The accompanying reduced levels of 'trismus' (the condition where the jaw clenches involuntarily) in the placebo group also pointed to the impressive effect of the placebo on objective, measurable signs as well as subjective ones. Other studies showed the efficacy of the placebo response in cases of ulcers and depression. In the case of depression, one alarming test cited by Evans reported that while the subjects taking real anti-depressants showed a 33 per cent improvement over those taking placebos, the placebo group showed a 200 per cent improvement over a third group who received no treatment at all. Looked at another way, Evans points out, '25% of the improvement shown by those taking anti-depressants is due to spontaneous remission, 50% to the placebo effect, and only a measly 25% to the anti-depressant medication itself'.

Evans argues that the full list of conditions for which placebos prove effective points to the idea that placebos rely on interrupting the 'acute phase response', or inflammation, which occurs in the person (even in cases such as depression, the inflamation response is still present, albeit less obviously). However, the fact that this sort of treatment has no effect in a large number of other conditions, of which cancer is one, points to the danger of over-estimating the placebo effect, or 'mind over matter', when considering alternative medicines. Books that advocate healing yourself of terminal disease through positive thought alone tragically misunderstand the limits of the placebo response. The 'mind', a word synonymous with 'brain activity', can helpfully be seen as another part of the body rather than an entirely separate entity, but the notion that it can magically boost the immune system to knock out any disease is a dangerous one.

The placebo effect has been seen as anything from a sign of gullibility in patients to a complete myth or a super-cure for all ills. While more measuring of the extent of the placebo effect could certainly be carried out (usually clinical tests are drug v. placebo rather than drug v. placebo v. non-treatment), it is clear that it is a fascinating area of rich potential benefit to study in more depth.

So if alternative medicines are routinely shown to owe their efficacy to the placebo, why should they not be embraced? Indeed, in some cases the placebo offered by an alternative therapist might even be more effective than conventional medicine. For example, as Diamond points out, spending half an hour or so with an alternative therapist may involve a massage or some form of touch, a sense of ritual and a clear display of personal interest; one might not get these from a strained GP who can offer you only a few minutes before he coldly scribbles out a prescription. In the case of everyday fatigues, aches and pains, the GP's advice and the alternative therapist's intervention may actually amount to the same thing: relaxation, massage, taking it easy, drinking and smoking less – a kind of 'rubbing it better', as Diamond put it. However, when the GP tells you this, it feels like a dismissal: you probably feel you haven't been taken seriously. When the therapist takes her time, clearly cares and uses all sorts of interesting devices to arrive at essentially similar advice, it feels like a proper answer and something to believe in. Not surprisingly, this may mean that a patient derives more benefit from an alternative therapist's intervention in cases that are responsive to placebo treatment.

I agree with Evans's and Diamond's feelings that if alternative therapists discarded their unfounded claims and exaggerations and accepted that when their therapies work it is due to this quite reliable placebo principle, then the worlds of conventional and complementary medicine could draw much closer together, and each could learn important lessons from the other. Let's not throw the baby out with the natural bath products. Orthodox practitioners should learn from the personal touch and psychological principles that underlie alternative medicine. Equally, sincere and intelligent alternative practitioners who are genuinely interested in being effective should accept the importance of testing medicines rather than relying on hearsay and anecdcote.

The Appeal of the Imaginary

Belief in the paranormal. Isn't it the feeling of a 'largely indifferent universe' that causes this? I think so. A large part of the appeal of religion (after childhood indoctrination has exploited a vulnerable mind) surely comes from the fear of death and nothing beyond, and much of that fear trickles down into superstitious or paranormal beliefs, and the notion that there is something smiling down on us. While I don't personally see any reason to think that there must be such a force at play in order to perceive life and what fills it as quite wonderful, it is arguably a useful model for many people. Also, aside from being psychologically very comforting, the idea of spiritual forces finds its appeal in the fact that it also makes for colourful imagining. This, I think, is an important factor. The ease with which something can be represented to oneself makes a real difference in its emotional impact, as we have previously discussed in relation to the way we create images in our minds. We have already spoken about unscientific scare-mongering in the press. If a newspaper runs an ill-researched story that screams out that such and such a product causes cancer, that awful image lingers in the mind much more vividly than the actual facts of the scientific report, which perhaps stated only that certain chemicals are present in the product which may be carcinogenic but not at the low doses as found in the product. The fact that the chemical may actually be beneficial at this low dose (which is often the case) does not lend itself so easily to bright, clear pictures in the mind, and thus has far less emotional impact than the misleading idea of it containing cancer-causing chemicals.

Similarly, a television programme that shows edited highlights of a medium or psychic giving readings to a tearful audience has far more visceral impact than a debunker on another show deconstructing the techniques of such performers. The message of the debunker will reach some who listen, but the simplicity of what the psychic appears to do makes for clearer, bolder mental representations. We can picture the psychic's perceived skill in our minds, whereas it is harder to picture the various techniques he may actually be using, consciously or otherwise, to create the illusion of paranormal ability. We perceive simple, direct cause and effect, and no amount of deconstruction from sceptics will ever match that in terms of visceral and emotional appeal. And it is rare that our emotions do not win out over intellect.

The other huge issue I perceive is one of identity. Let's imagine our average believer in psychic ability. And let's be nice – fat, failed and forty with a house of cats and no boyfriend is an unhelpful stereotype. To an extent, we might be able to also imagine many evangelical Christians (I think of myself here when I was younger, and I imagine I was not particularly untypical). Both characters will probably have experienced a sense of perhaps not quite fitting in with their peers. They will have friends who share their beliefs, but they will most probably have experienced some ridicule from people outside that group. Like most individuals who don't feel they entirely fit in, they will probably cling quite tightly to their respective sympathizing social group. Equally, they will develop a real sense of identity based on those beliefs. If you do grow up feeling as though you don't quite fit in as a child, it's very easy to decide that you're certainly not going to fit in as an adult. You hang on to your eccentricities and hate the idea of conforming. It's a common pattern. Even if our imaginary True Believer has not had such a childhood, he's likely to sense the peculiarity of his beliefs as an adult and want to stake his identity in those beliefs. It becomes about 'who he is' rather than 'how he behaves'.

It is at this point that he might take pride in a lack of rationality: instead of seeing mindless True Belief as a flawed and possibly dangerous thing, he might flaunt his irrational circular thinking as evidence of how good a believer he is. A real pride comes from this sort of puffing up of feathers. Believers of many sorts are particularly proud of bold and blind faith. Presenting a person in this position with hard evidence that contradicts his most fundamental principles is not going to make him change his beliefs. To do so would be a crisis of identity. He certainly won't be able to argue effectively against good evidence, other than perhaps to avoid the discussion by saying 'it's a question of faith'. It takes a lot more than a philosophical discussion for someone to backtrack on years of difficult or even painful identity-building.

Equally, another person might decide that she is a believer because she has had a convincing experience with a psychic as an adult. She may (God help her) have had a medium pretend to contact a much-loved, recently deceased relative, and found the experience so comforting and moving that it has become a huge part of her life. It would be too painful for her to view the experience as anything other than what the medium sold it as.

Yet another person may have dedicated himself to an alternative therapy for all the best reasons and then invested a lot of his time and money into research and work around it. Again, this person has too much at stake simply to abandon a belief based on real-world evidence. Much easier to disregard the evidence or find fault with it.

Most often it is inappropriate or insensitive to challenge directly a person's belief. Equally, many people think that science inhabits a different world from that of the spirit, and has no right to trespass there. It certainly is a different world, but if one substitutes the word 'science' for 'real-world evidence' then perhaps the relevance of it becomes more apparent. In a world of religious wars and big New Age business, the question of evidence or explanations for these things *is* important. The defining difference, I think, between the two worlds is this: in general terms, True Believers rationalize failures and ignore them, whereas science welcomes failures and uses them to better understand how something works. A person has every right to decide that unbiased, real-world evidence does not interest him, that he is happy to rely on his personal experience or unquestioned authority for what he believes to be true. He can contentedly go down that route as long as he has no wish to be taken seriously in a rational discussion of his beliefs and as long as he's not blowing anyone up because of them. No-one, however, who decides that scientific evidence is not for him and that his own experience or the stories of others is the be all and end all of deciding what's true *ever* has the right to call people searching for reliable, repeatable evidence narrow-minded. That is hypocrisy of the most laughable kind.

MEDIUMS, PSYCHICS AND CHARLATANS

The final night of my 2006 tour took me to the sleepy Welsh village of Swansea, and it was here that our five-strong crew of Peter, Stephen, Mark, Coops and your devoted author were due to spend the night. There are companies that specialize in booking disappointing and noisy hotels for touring shows, Olivier Award-winning or otherwise. We had requested something special for the big last night of the tour and were delighted to find that we were booked into another orange and brown nastiness with a hard bed and a shower that felt like one was receiving a service that might be hesitantly requested from a professional escort but certainly not expected from the Ramada Jarvis first thing in the morning.

While waiting in the bar of the hotel for my ride to the theatre, I found myself watching Joe Pasquale silently hosting *The Price is Right* on the mute television in the corner. There was a time when the comic and I shared the same manager. And if that surprises you, may I add that at the time of writing my manager's other well-known artist is veteran faux-ostrich rider and funny man, Bernie Clifton. As a contestant on the show spun the wheel to the top prize, I felt an arm on my shoulder and caught a faint whiff of afternoon drinking. 'What's the next number then? Eh?' I looked round to see a businessman standing a little too close to me and waving a piece of paper for me to sign. I signed my name and wrote a brief yet witty message for his niece, and he was friendly and happy. 'It's fucking amazing,' he added, the commingling of beery cheer and the endorphin high of that morning's successful paint-balling further loosening his tongue. 'You and Derek Acorah in the same room.'

Somehow the idea of Derek Acorah being sat somewhere in the bar didn't seem conceivable. 'Derek Acorah? Where?' Had this businessman been fully sober, he would have noted that my tone of exaggerated incredulity betrayed a clear note of nervous excitement.

'Over there – there he is,' he continued, and pointed towards a group sat close to me but partially obscured by a brown and orange corporate leisure-pillar.

Ridiculous, I thought. And then I spotted the wide-combed, bleached back of a man's hair and the glint of a gold earring. *That does look like him.*

'That is *not* Derek Acorah,' I laughed, transfixed.

'Yes it is. I'll go and get him. Hey!'

He was already heading across the ten yards of orange and brown carpet which separated me from the guy with the peroxide hair. I tried to call quietly, 'No! Don't!' but he had already reached his target who was talking to a couple of collegues.

A lot of things went through my mind in a very short space of time. One of them was *Christing hell, that is Derek Acorah.* Another was, *Hide!* I considered running (away from the prying fan and into the foyer, as it were). Do I go and speak to him? If I don't, this businessman will tell him that I ran away. He now had his hand on the blond guy's shoulder and was saying, 'Derren Brown's over there and he doesn't believe it's really you.' I have never wanted to kill a man before, but by God I hated that guy for those few seconds. Shitshitshit. Right, I suppose I should go and meet Derek Acorah.

I stepped across, and confusion and panic gave way to profound embarrassment which I tried to shove deep inside me with a confident smile. 'Hello,' I said, and offered my hand. Derek Acorah stood up and took it. The business guy started apologizing for causing any embarrassment. We both told him it was fine. I joked about a big fight kicking off. I wanted to punch the businessman violently in the throat. Derek was polite. I was surprised to learn later that he is fifty-six; he has a rough laddishness to his appearance that makes him seem much younger. He had been talking to a pretty girl who was wearing huge celebrity tan-tinted sunglasses which covered a good third of her face. I said hello to her too and apologized for interrupting.

Acorah said he had been repeatedly told that I had been issuing challenges to him in the press. That I had been saying that I could replicate anything he could do and wanted some sort of showdown. I have never said any such thing and assured him it wasn't true. In fact, if anything, I thought that he had once made such a challenge to *me*. I explained that I hadn't ever seen any of his shows and for that reason was always able to avoid entering into any attacks or name-calling in interviews. When asked by journalists, I told him, I might express my reservations regarding the world of mediumship and psychic ability, but I have never been antagonistic towards him personally at all. I always avoid the subject.

We talked a bit about the press creating this sense of rivalry. I had recently been interviewed for an article about my feelings regarding death and funerals, keeping my answers light-hearted. I was asked about Acorah, and as usual avoided any attack, saying that I had never seen his show. Pushed on the subject, I did talk about my dislike of charlatanism associated with mediums, but was careful to keep it general. Five minutes of chat on and around the subject was reduced in the article to the following exchange:

Q. What are your views on Derek Acorah?

A: I hate everything he stands for and have never seen his show!

Literally. Exclamation mark and all. Excruciating. Next, I was asked who I would haunt if I came back from the dead. It was, I presumed, a joke question, so as we had just been talking about Acorah, I offered the light-hearted answer, 'Derek Acorah. That would scare the shit out of him.' Possibly I was asking for this last answer to be taken out of context, but clearly it had got back to Acorah as part of my apparent antagonism. Several times since I have been referred to in articles as 'Derren Brown, who would like to come back from the dead to haunt Derek Acorah'.

Now here I was in a hotel foyer in Swansea explaining myself to him. He questioned me about the comments, and I was happy to assure him nothing was meant and the press were merely looking for a spin. The pretty girl with the sunglasses stepped in briefly and seemed to miss the point that I had no antagonism, so her producer at the table explained to her again that it came from the press, not me. She said there can only be 'one winner' in such a rivalry. I wasn't sure what she meant. I thought she meant the press, but I presume now she meant Acorah. She insisted that if I just say 'Derek does his thing and I do mine' then the press could not create a rivalry from that. I held back from clarifying that my reservations ran too deep to say anything that bland. Better nothing at all.

We were both enormously civil, and Acorah said he could 'tell from my energy' that I wasn't what he was expecting, and that he was pleased. I continued my reassurances, and general tutting at the press. It turned out he had a show in the same theatre as me the following night. We smiled at this and wished each other a good show. A pause followed, during which we continued to smile and didn't offer each other tickets to our respective performances. This moment was interrupted by a friend who came to tell me that my car had arrived.

On the way to the theatre I wondered if I'd been a terrible coward. I was not only civil, I was deferential. Such an odd meeting. Should I have been more vocal about my 'reservations'? How strongly did I feel about fraudulent mediums? Strongly enough to walk over and be rude to a man I don't know? I was intrigued by the fact that my own apparently strong feelings gave way to the simple social code of being nice. Maybe his did too. Maybe, somewhere in the mudslinging of the psychic/sceptic debate, there's even an unspoken and begrudging whiff of camaraderie between us. A horrible thought.

I have avoided positioning myself squarely as an anti-psychic debunker. Life is too short. Perhaps I don't really care quite enough about the issue. I may not like what people like Acorah do, I may even get heated on the topic if you get me started off the record, but there are finer things in life to be concerned with. I do, however, have a small public profile, and it is my job to express my attitude on the topic from time to time. Attitude is very important, even if it doesn't define you for much of your daily life. It is an important part of being a successful performer. It should be real and honest. But even people with strongly opposing ideologies who have battled it out on a talk show usually enjoy a glass of wine together in the green room afterwards. I always found that odd. I've heard professional sceptics owning up to events they can't explain, and chat-show-circuit psychics joking about some piece of 'psychic nonsense' they have said. Unless you are incapacitated by fanatical views, I guess the charged expression of these beliefs has its place and time, and will sometimes be fierce and other times will wane when standing in a bad hotel lobby in Wales.

What follows, then, is an exploration of the reservations I have relating to the world of psychics and mediums. These things do not consume me, but inasmuch as they relate to some apalling lies that many people are taken in by, I think the topic is worthwhile.

But before we begin . . . A few days after the night in Swansea, the following article appeared in *The Sun*. Its source, as far as I understand, was not Acorah but the PR for the pretty girl with sunglasses, who turned out to be Myleene Klass, a co-presenter on Acorah's new show.

> Rival TV oddballs Derren Brown and Derek Acorah raised spirits – by having a slanging match in a hotel.
>
> Psychic Derek, 56, tackled illusionist Derren, 35, for publicly blasting him.
>
> An onlooker at the Ramada Jarvis Hotel, Swansea, said, 'Derren came over to say hello but Derek looked peeved and asked, "Why are you always slagging me off?"
>
> Derren replied, "That's the way I am. I've never seen your show but I've reservations about you."'
>
> The pair started rowing, but Myleene Klass, Derek's co-host for the new series of Ghost Stories, stepped in.
>
> The insider said, 'Myleene told Derren to leave Derek alone. She said, "You're obviously threatened by him."'
>
> A crowd gathered before a pal pulled away Derren. He triggered the rift by saying recently, 'If I die, I'd like to haunt Derek. I hate everything he stands for.'
>
> Derren is famous for his Russian roulette act and for 'crucifying' Robbie Williams by sticking needles in him.

Perhaps Myleene's penchant for wearing shades indoors prevented her from seeing the bewildering irony of her press release. But hey, at least it made me seem like I stood up for what I believed in. I did get a lot of emails congratulating me.

Cold-reading

Cold-reading is at the heart of the psychic's apparent skill. It is the key to understanding how a psychic is seemingly able to know so much about you. If you have ever had a convincing experience with a psychic, or you know someone who has, this is the non-paranormal explanation of how it all can happen. It is fascinating, powerful and hugely manipulative. It can be used covertly in personal and business relationships as well as for pretending you can talk to the dead or read minds. Knowledge of cold-reading techniques can protect you from abusive scum who would happily exploit you in your most desperate hour to put you in touch with a child you have just lost.

As part of the third series of *Trick of the Mind*, my much-loved, award-winning, landmark television programme, I set about the following experiment. We gathered together a group of five students made up of people who had a mixed attitude to psychic claims. None was a strong believer, but a few were pretty sceptical. I had each of them place in a numbered envelope a traced outline of their hand, along with the time and date of their birth and a small, everyday personal object. This was done anonymously: I had no idea which envelope or contents belonged to which person. I told them that I would, from these items, try to write an accurate personality reading for each of them. I would use astrological and psychometric techniques to get a clear sense of each owner's personality.

After a couple of hours I returned to them with the readings. They identified their own by numbers on the envelopes and were told to read through what I had written and then offer us their thoughts. I explained that some of them would have long readings and others shorter ones, but that I had avoided making woolly general statements and had tried to get into the meat of each personality.

On our travels for filming, we repeated the experiment with Spanish and American students, using a translator for the former group. Each participant, after spending time with his or her reading, was interviewed individually for the camera, and each was asked to give us a sense of how accurate they found it by giving it a mark out of one hundred. One person from each group of five gave it a mark of between forty and fifty. These subjects were not especially impressed with the reading. All the others (twelve out of fifteen), by contrast, were *extremely* impressed. One felt that I had gained access to her private journal and found it all rather too personal. Two other girls echoed the same sentiment and found it very hard to discuss the contents on camera. Many said that they had expected a few vague statements that could apply to anyone, and were shocked at how detailed and personal the reading was. They all gave very high marks for accuracy, and many were in the nineties. One girl gave a mark of 99 per cent.

After these interviews, the students were asked to mix up the readings and hand them out at random to see if they could identify each other from what was written there. As they passed them out, the trick dawned on them: *they had all been given the same reading*. Each was identical, and unrelated to their birthdates, hands or personal objects. The same reading was used for the Americans and translated for the Spaniards. It had been written long before I met any of them.

I am by no means the first to use this sort of demonstration to 'debunk' psychic readings. It is known as the 'Forers Experiment', often used in university courses on parapsychology, though I had the advantage of being able to try it in different countries. I have always found it a rather elegant stunt. When I emailed the stock 'reading' to my producer for her to print out for the show, she was convinced the reading was written for her. In fact, she thought I was playing some sort of trick on her. Later, when we sent it to our Spanish translator, she too fell for it, and thought she was the real victim of the prank.

I made sure that the contents of the reading were not shown on television. The reason for this was simple: if you, my witty, sharp viewer, were to read a few statements from the reading, it would be easy to think, 'Ah, that wouldn't have worked on *me*.' I have decided, though, to reprint the full reading here. Not only does it bump up my word-count, it allows you to read the thing in its entirety, which would not be possible on television given programmers' fear of not keeping up with your supposedly short attention spans and MTV sensibilities. Now, if you like, you can read this with the benefit of hindsight, knowing that it is generic, and decide you would never have fallen for it. Certainly it was written with twenty-somethings in mind, and you may not find it appropriate for you if you are much younger, or indeed already in your naughty autumns. But imagine that you have given your birth details, a drawing of your hand and a personal object to a person you perceive to have real 'psychic' skill, and that you do not expect any duplicity. Read this with an open mind, and see how you respond.

> You are a person prone to bouts of real self-examination. This is in sharp contrast to a striking ability you have developed to appear socially very engaged, even the life and soul of the party; but in a way that only convinces others. You are all too aware of it being a façade.
>
> This means that you will often be at a gathering and find yourself playing a part. While on the one hand you'll be talkative and funny, you'll be detaching yourself to the point where you will find yourself watching everything going on around you and feeling utterly unable to engage. You'll play conversations back to yourself in your head and wonder what that person really meant when he said such-and-such – conversations that other people wouldn't give a second thought to.
>
> How have you learned to deal with this conflict? Through exercising control. You like to show a calm, self-assured, fluid kind of stability (but because this is self-consciously created, it will create bouts of frustrated silliness and a delight in extremes, or at least a delight in being seen to be extreme). You most easily recognize this control in how you are with people around you. You have learned to protect yourself by keeping people at bay. Because in the past you have learned to be disappointed by people (and because there were issues with you adjusting to your sexuality),

you instinctively keep people at arms' length, until *you* decide they are to be allowed over that magic line into your group of close friends. However, once across that line, the problem is that an emotional dependency kicks in which leaves you feeling very hurt or rejected if it appears that they have betrayed that status.

Because you are prone to self-examination, you will be aware of these traits. However, you are unusually able to examine even that self-examination, which means that you have become concerned about what the *real* you is. You have become all too aware of façades, of sides of yourself which you present to the world, and you wonder if you have lost touch with the real and spontaneous you.

You are very creative, and have tried different avenues to utilize that ability. It may not be that you specifically, say, paint; it may be that your creativity shows itself in more subtle ways, but you will certainly find yourself having vivid and well-formed ideas which others will find hard to grasp. You set high standards for yourself, though, and in many ways are a bit of a perfectionist. The problem is, though, that it means you often don't get stuff done, because you are frustrated by the idea of mediocrity and are wearied by the idea of starting something afresh. However, once your brain is engaged you'll find yourself sailing. Very likely this will lead to you having considered writing a novel or some such, but a fear that you won't be able to achieve quite what you want stops you from getting on with it. But you have a real vision for things, which others fall short of. Particularly in your academic/college situation, you are currently fighting against restraints upon your desire to express yourself freely.

Your relationship with your parents (there is a suggestion that one is no longer around, or at least emotionally very absent) is under some strain. You wish to remain fond of them but recent issues are causing frustration – from your side far more than theirs. In fact they seem unaware of your thoughts on the matter. Partly this is because there are ways in which you have been made to feel isolated from certain groups in the past – something of an outsider. Now what is happening is that you are taking that outsider role and defending it to the point of consciously avoiding being part of a group. This will serve you enormously well in your creative and career pursuits. You have an enormous cynicism towards those who prefer to be part of a group or who exhibit any cliquey behaviour, and you always feel a pang of disappointment when you see your 'close' friends seeming to follow that route. Deep down it feels like rejection.

However, for all that introspection, you have developed a sensational, dry sense of humour that makes connections quickly and wittily and will leave you making jokes that go right over the heads of others. You delight in it so much that you'll often rehearse jokes or amusing voices to yourself in order to 'spontaneously' impress others with them. But this is a healthy desire to impress, and although you hate catching yourself at it, it's nothing to be so worried about.

There's an odd feeling also that you should have been born in a different century. You might be able to make more sense of that than I can.

There are some strong monetary shifts taking place at the moment. Both the recent past and what's in store over the next few months represent quite a change.

You have links at the moment with America,* which are quite interesting, and will look to yield worthwhile results. You're naturally a little disorganized. A look around your living space would show a box of photos, unorganized into albums, out-of-date

*This was changed to 'Britain' for our US subjects.

medicines, broken items not thrown out, and notes to yourself which are significantly out of date. Something related to this is that you tend to lack motivation. Because you're resourceful and talented enough to be pretty successful when you put your mind to things, this encourages you to procrastinate and put them off. Equally, you've given up dreams a little easily when your mind flitted elsewhere. There are in your home signs of an excursion into playing a musical instrument, which you have since abandoned, or are finding yourself less interested in. (This may alternatively relate to poetry and creative writing you've briefly tried your hand at and left behind you.) You have a real capacity for deciding that such-and-such a thing (or so-and-so a person) will be the be all and end all of everything and be with you for ever. But you'd rather try and fail, and swing from an extreme to the other, than settle for the little that you see others content with. Conclusion: It's very interesting doing your reading, as you do present something of a conundrum, which won't surprise you. You are certainly bright, but unusually open to life's possibilities – something not normally found among achieving people. I'd say you would do well to be less self-absorbed, as it tends to distance you a little, and to relinquish some of the control you exercise when you present that stylized version of yourself to others. You could let people in a little more, but I am aware that there is a darkness you feel you should hide (much of this is in the personal/relationship/sexual area, and is related to a neediness which you don't like).

You really have an appealing personality – genuinely. Many thanks for doing this, and for offering something far more meaty than most.

Remember that the above was written with no possibility of feedback from the subject assisting me in the readings. It had to be fixed and generic. If you found it remotely applicable to you, bear in mind that this is only a starting-point. In normal situations with psychics, the 'sitter' supplies a wealth of unwitting signals that allow the psychic to give the impression of being very accurate and knowledgeable. We will discuss this process a little later. For now, it can at least be seen that people will happily find a stock reading such as the above powerfully accurate and personal, even though the statements are applicable to a vast number of people, particularly of a certain age group.

The comfort that can be taken from this exercise – and which I made sure the participants on the show understood – is that we all share the same sorts of insecurities. In particular, bright people in their twenties tend to be quite self-involved, wondering what their 'real' self consists of, prone to introspection, and very aware of conflicting aspects of their personalities. Many of the statements above tap into the sorts of universal foibles any of us can find within us, but they are expressed in such a way that they become difficult to refute. For example, throughout the reading I take two opposing personality types (for instance 'introverted' and 'extroverted'), and begin with the undeniable truth that all normal people find themselves fluctuating between one type and another. How we are socially, of course, will never be the same as our more 'private' selves. However, the statement 'You can be quite introverted but then again you can be quite extroverted' wouldn't sound convincing to anyone. Dress it up, however, by tapping into universal experiences of social and private occasions, and include a veiled message of 'You are *really* interesting to be this complex', and the empty truism becomes much more substantial.

This is a basic cold-reading skill. It allows people to read into your statements whatever they like. Many people in our test picked up on the same passage but took it to mean very different things. This is not surprising: despite the sincere tone and verbiage, everything is left wide open. For example, *you are very creative*, but *it may not be that you specifically, say, paint; it may be that your creativity shows itself in more subtle ways*. Like what? Well, it might just mean that you have well-formed ideas others find hard to grasp. If you do paint, it seems like an accurate hit; if you don't paint, you'll flatter yourself that your 'inner' creativity has been recognized. Because a lot of people have at some point written quite criminal poetry or thought of writing a novel, I later talk about 'creative writing' in the knowledge that I am likely to strike a chord with many people. *Equally, you've given up dreams a little easily when your mind flitted elsewhere*. Really? You mean, I think of doing things until I stop thinking of doing them? *You instinctively keep people at arms' length, until you decide they are to be allowed over that magic line into your group of close friends. However, once across that line, the problem is that an emotional dependency kicks in*. Right . . . so you're saying I'm closer to my friends than people I don't know well? Good heavens, man, how do you do that?

By now you will have realized the similarity shared by these sorts of statements and those that appear in newspaper horoscope columns. However, to reiterate, several of the participants in our test said that they were expecting to receive the sort of 'vague and ambiguous' statements that appear in such columns, and were shocked that their readings were 'nothing like that'. It's a very seductive technique.

However, it is nowhere near as convincing as when one is giving a reading to a sitter in one's psychic consulting room. In this scenario, the sitter is already, or is primed to become, a believer. Plenty of people go to see a psychic out of curiosity and swear they never gave anything away. But what the uninitiated thinks of as 'giving himself away' is not the same as what the psychic is looking for, nor does it bear much relation to cold-reading structure. In the same way that a very intelligent and attentive spectator will fall for a well-executed magic trick, so too will a 'sceptical' sitter be quite possibly convinced by a psychic, unless she understands the tricks and techniques of the professional.

Consider the common situation. The sitter arrives. She is (generally) a woman, looking for help and magical solutions. She is open to the idea of paranormal abilities, and has had this psychic recommended to her by a friend who swears by her. Our sitter is invited into the private home of the psychic who is immediately warm, attentive and friendly. Not only is the psychic promising to be a sympathetic ear, she is also offering something undeniably wonderful: the use of magical techniques in areas where the pedestrian opportunities found in the real world have fallen short. The psychic offers the most irresistible promise that one human being can make to another: she will completely understand you. She will see right to the heart of your problem with a special clarity and offer you the solution no-one else can see. All this will be qualified by the psychic's initial statements that she herself cannot always get information exactly; that she will pass on what comes through her and it is up to the sitter to make it fit. The responsibility is not the psychic's, and if it doesn't work, it's not her fault.

In this situation, the psychic has already won the game before she has started. With such a typically willing sitter, she need not give a dazzling display of cold-reading to have a successful session. On stage it is another matter: the bigger names in the industry who conduct psychic or mediumship 'concerts' need a good grasp of the skills to make the evening remotely convincing. The audience will consist partly of 'easy' targets, those people who have lost a loved one and are looking for some sort of contact. But there will also be plenty of sceptically curious spectators who want to see if the famous name is any good at what he says he can do.

Now, as there is little room in a stage situation for picking up on subtle feedback from an audience member in order to take the reading off in a more personalized direction, many of the readings offered tend to be fairly generic. They are the equivalent of the reading I offered the students, but they talk of a lost loved one rather than the subject's own personality. While the stage medium has the disadvantage of little one-on-one discussion to make the reading convincing, this is compensated for by the sheer number of people present. Someone in the room is likely to have lost a person with such-and-such a name; several people over this side of the room will have lost a father; and so on. Once a suitably bereaved and desperate person has responded to a few vagaries thrown out over the audience's heads, a game then commences where it appears that the medium is telling the bereaved private information about the deceased, or indeed about the bereaved herself. The style of these 'readings' will vary from performer to performer, but the structure is invariably similar. The performer will offer a statement for the listener to respond to, and the latter is encouraged to offer more information, which the psychic then takes credit for knowing. The impression is given, to the believer, that the psychic is giving all this information himself, whereas it's generally coming from the bereaved. This will be mixed with a host of statements offered about the deceased or the bereaved person's relationship with the deceased, which like some of the statements in the cold-reading above apply to very many people. Some very specific statements will be thrown out too, which are less likely to hit, but they help with the overall impression that the psychic knows what he is talking about. Everything sounds very unambiguous, but it's a trick.

I have been at quite a few spiritualist meetings in my life as a curious attendee, and I have seen the same cold-reading tricks at work again and again. The following dialogue is a cut-down and sewn-together version of some long readings I have on tape, and represents a rather better 'hit rate' than actually occured or that one might expect from the normal readings to believers. In fact, I have edited out the larger portion of the readings which yielded nothing but failed guesswork and 'no' answers from the audience member. In other words, I have edited this to seem much *better* than it was, not worse. Please bear this in mind. The medium in question was a black-shirted, fast-talking, guy in his twenties who one could easily imagine performing an illusion act or running a mobile wedding disco. He had certainly learned all the speech patterns of the stage medium: he had the old-fashioned, non-threatening northern camp off to a tee, even though off-stage his voice and manner were quite different. The audience was made up of primarily elderly women, but this exchange was with a lady in her forties:

MEDIUM: I'm getting an older gentleman coming through, and he's telling me he wants to connect with someone over here. I'm getting the name James, or Jimmy. Who's that for, please? Let me know if this is for you.

AUDIENCE MEMBER (*a lady in her forties*): Jim. Here.

M: Hello, love. Stand up, yes. He's telling me this is for you. Is this your dad, darling?

AM (*already crying*): Yes, my dad . . .

M: Oh pet, you've done a lot of crying for him, he says. He says cheer up, lass, and he's laughing. He had a great laugh, didn't he, dear?

AM (*nods*)

M: He's saying he was always the life and soul of the party – sometimes you couldn't get a word in, could you, dear? (*agreement*) He passed not too long ago – feels like in the last couple of years, is that right? (*disagreement*) He's telling me you've been saying it *feels* much more recent than it was. I know it was longer ago but it feels closer to you, doesn't it? And he misses you too, dear; he says you were always his special lass. He used to call you that, didn't he? His special little girl? Had a little name for you? Now he's showing me that it was something here that took him (*gestures around the chest area*) and it was quick at the end, wasn't it darling? He's just showing me these things to tell you for proof, so you know it's him, so you know it's real, my love. He had some back trouble too, dear. Tell me yes if I'm right.

AM: Back trouble, yes, he had back pains.

M: Not any more, my love. He says you were always caring for him. Oh, you've found something of his recently, he's showing me something, I can't see what that is. Shiny, something red, what is that? What did you find of his? (*unsure, hesitant response*) Well I don't know, dear, you found it, not me. I'm only passing on what he shows me. Let me know when you remember. I think he's showing me cufflinks.

AM: Oh yes, his cufflinks! I've got them at home!

(*Audience laughs*)

M: He says you shouldn't feel bad about giving them to ... Simon? Is there a Simon? Were you going to give them to someone? Is it your son?

AM: No.

M: He says you've thought about giving them away and you shouldn't feel bad. Is that right?

AM (unsure): Yes.

M: The other spirits here are laughing. They're saying he's still a belligerent old thing. He certainly liked to think he knew the right way to do things, didn't he, dear? Not very good at admitting he was wrong. He's still like that, hasn't changed, not even in spirit. What a strong character. He says you can throw away his glasses. What does that mean?

AM: I kept his glasses.

M: He says they weren't his favourites – he wasn't keen on them.

AM: No.

M: He says you've got some photos of him, but these aren't in an album, dear. Old photos but not in an album. Some of him and an old lady. You've got them in a box. In a cupboard, he's showing them to me.

AM: Yes! That's right.

M: He says you used to look at them more than you do. He likes it when you do, though there's some pictures there he doesn't like. Is it his brother he didn't get on with? Who was Tony, or Terry?

AM: There's a picture with his brother. Don't know a Tony.

M: It's that picture with his brother. He doesn't like it, he's telling me. Find Tony or Terry for me, love, let me know who that is. Something he wants to say.

AM: I think he had a work colleague who might have been Tony.

M: That's right. From work. You're to tell Tony that he has something of his. Something that didn't get sorted out before he passed across . . . You've put something up in your hallway, love, a picture with an animal? (*hesitation*) Or taken something down? Is that a dog, dear?

AM: We had a dog.

M: The dog used to sleep in the hallway, dear, and he says the dog has passed across too. A spaniel, wasn't it? Bit of a mixture, my dear?

AM: Yes.

M: He still sees it now in spirit. Didn't always like it when it was with us here, did he?

AM: No (*laughs*).

At this point the spirit left him and he was able to tell an old lady elsewhere that she had lost her husband, a 'lovely man' who'd had trouble with his eyesight.

How did he know the audience member's father, Jim, had died? He didn't, though she and the audience will remember it like that. He merely threw out the possible names 'James' and 'Jimmy', which could have referred to someone sat in the audience, or the name of someone who had 'crossed over'. When he sees it's a younger woman, he guesses it's her father. I have heard a famous medium on the radio wriggle out of a 'no' response to this guess with the great line, 'No, but he was like a father to you; he was a father in spirit, you see. He saw you like a daughter.' Seamless.

The cufflinks? Well, she's had five years or so, at a guess, to come across something of his. Guessing at colours ('shiny, something red') only makes the hit seem more impressive, and his words sound more accurate. In fact the medium can throw out some very specific bits of information; if the bereaved can't 'find' them, it's her own fault. The medium, after all, is merely channelling. He's just passing on what he's told. Not his fault if the listener can't make something fit.

The back trouble? This is a very common statement made by psychics and mediums, and can generally be made to fit most older people.

The dog? He suggests a 'spaniel' (a very common breed with several varieties), then adds that it could have been a mongrel. From her 'yes', it might have been any cross-breed. But remember, he didn't ever mention her having a dog: he spoke only about a 'picture of an animal' that she might have put up, or taken down at some point in her hallway. Or, I suspect, a picture of anything would have sufficed.

As for the old photos, this is an often-used ploy which I included in my own stock reading. Who doesn't have such things stuck in an old cupboard? And if the audience member says she doesn't, the medium can always insist that she does and tell her to look for them, claiming that one of them is important. Therein lies another ploy: if statements made by the medium don't hit, they can be turned into events that will happen in the future, or which might have happened outside the person's knowledge.

Not surprisingly, people who attend these demonstrations who *aren't* looking for contact but are just going along to be impressed rarely find them very convincing. On television, where many mediums have their home, a couple of hours of readings can be edited right down to twenty minutes of impressive hits. Where the medium has his own TV show, a common technique is for the performer to come out to meet the audience before filming and chat to the guests, asking if anyone is hoping to make contact with anyone in particular. Believing and hopeful audience members happily tell him everything he needs. Later, during filming, he can feed back the information to the same audience members, padded with some guesswork and cold-reading, and it seems that he is giving very impressive readings.

A friend who worked on a television show that featured a psychic as a guest told me a typical story. It is common to have camera rehearsals before filming so that everyone in the production crew is familiar with where the cameras need to point and where everyone needs to be. The psychic was brought in to rehearse her section. She sat with the presenter and went through a tarot-reading for her. The information she gave was standard cold-reading, but the presenter was more than happy to fill in the gaps and tell her that her mother had recently passed away, and other such facts. Then, during filming, they came to this sequence, and the psychic repeated her tarot-reading with the same presenter. Only this time, the psychic told the presenter that her mother had died, and gave a seemingly very impressive reading, using all the information the presenter had told her in rehearsals. The presenter wasn't convinced, of course, but it was her job to look and act amazed. The unwitting viewing audience, of course, would have been mightily impressed.

The technique of working with previously known information is called 'hot-reading'. Some time ago, a very famous medium called Doris Stokes toured with her show. In many ways she was a forerunner of the many well-known stage mediums we have today. Stokes was a tough elderly lady, of showbiz stock, but her appearance of being a docile, grandmotherly septuagenarian lent her huge credibility. Her rosy face graced the cover of various paperbacks in sweet soft-focus, and her concerts were well attended. After she died, one started to hear that she employed stooges at her events to keep them impressive and interesting, but one story, told to me by a woman I met, was a real insight into her now known techniques.

This woman had recently lost a son in a drowning accident, and the local papers had reported the tragedy. Around the same time, Stokes was coming to town, and her press office was preparing the way for her. The woman got a call from Stokes's people, who had presumably come across the story*, saying that the famous medium was aware of her loss and had a message for her from her son; they would like to provide her with a complimentary seat at the event so that Doris could pass it on. The mother asked if Stokes could just pass it on over the phone. That wasn't possible, so she agreed to attend. She was asked to wear something red so that Stokes could identify her.

The lady attended the event and sat in her seat wearing a red jumper. Stokes came out on stage and gave readings to various people

*It came out later that Stokes's team would apparently go through local papers looking for such stories, or otherwise rely on information gleaned from the huge numbers of desperate letters from bereaved people anticipating her arrival in their home town.

in the audience. At one point, when things had dipped a little and she had had a few misses, she turned and pointed out our lady. 'There's a lady over here, she's wearing red, and I'm getting a little boy come through for her who says she's his mummy. Are you there, love?' Dutifully, the lady raised her hand and stood up. 'You lost him . . . he's telling me it was a drowning, is that right?' Yes, that's right. 'His name is Jack, he's telling me.' Yes, that was his name. The audience was astounded. 'He says he loves you and there wasn't anything you could have done. Thank you, love, you can sit back down. Bless you, my dear.' Everyone applauded.

This woman was utterly repulsed and profoundly angered at being exploited so transparently in this way. Her loss had been paraded in front of a thousand people to make a performer look good. A similar thing occurs when psychics appear on television programmes: aside from this technique of speaking to the audience first, they will also often ensure that their own private clients are among the people attending. The poor clients are told to come along to the studio as there may be a message for them from their lost loved one. No mention is made of the fact that the psychic already knows these people and their troubles, yet he can use them in the audience for some apparently very impressive readings. It's a given that the ones most prone to crying will be most likely to be invited.

After a show one evening, I was having a conversation with a chap whose friend owned an old pub in the country. The pub was to feature in a television show with a medium, who was going to talk about or channel the various energies and spirits he found there. People in the town knew about a ghost story and a murder that was part of the pub's history. It was also known that the production crew for the show had been asking the locals for any information pertaining to the story. Clearly it was no effort for the medium, if he wanted, to have found out or been told the details of the pub's grisly history. He only had to ask his own production crew. The filming was carried out, and the medium, as expected, did a great job of picking up on the attending spirits and was able to divine the grisly details of the haunting and the untimely death behind it. 'The problem was,' this chap continued, 'that my mate who owned the pub had made up the murder story and the ghost a few years before to give the pub a bit of colour.' Of course the landlord had gone along with it on the show to promote his pub, but there had never been a murder and he had no doubt the psychic was a fraud. That's the problem with hot-reading: you're going to look silly if you uncover false information.

The defence made by psychics and mediums when pushed on the subject is that it offers comfort to their clients or audiences. In some rare cases, maybe this justifies horrible lies. But if they are indeed lies, who are these psychics to decide that those lies are what people need to hear to make them feel better? Especially when the motives of so many of them are clearly ego-driven rather than genuinely altruistic. And if they are lies, what must these performers think of a public they can only see in terms of gullibility? I was interviewed by a journalist not long ago who had recently interviewed a very famous medium. At one point, the medium's wife referred to her husband's devotees as 'those morons'. The journalist, to my disappointment and probably his own discredit, never printed that part of the story, for fear it would be too contentious.

Mediumship and psychic ability have been around in one form or another for a very long time. They just look and sound different from era to era. For those who care to look, or who think that 'cold-reading' might be something I've made up, there is a tradition of underground literature that teaches these skills to interested parties. One of the better modern books, *The Full Facts Book of*

Cold-Reading, by Ian Rowland, is an excellent and extensive work on the subject. Other publications are more openly geared towards the would-be psychic, and constitute an eye-opening body of work for anyone who has never thought to question the honesty of these performers. Consider the following excerpts from one book, an old, anonymous American publication, *Pages from a Medium's Notebook*, written for people wanting to earn a living as a medium:

> These 'facts of life' we must color – add mysticism, coloring, glamour, tragedy, detail and an element or two – then, too, perform as humans, grasp eagerly this credit of our intelligence, achieve our place in the sun – because, due to the profound effects of our efforts with our client, he in turn tells his neighbour, creating another effect (usually exaggerated) and in turn, another cause – a visit from another human (client.)
>
> There is no such thing as a genuine medium, i.e. a person who can, at will, communicate with departed spirits or obtain messages. Nor is there such a person that can, with accuracy, and repeatedly do so, predict the future events of one's life. Such predictions are not real, but are palmed off as a guise.
>
> Remember, the more worried a person, the more gullible they become. Nervousness is a marked and [*sic*] indication of worry and such can be read in the faces and actions of every person.
>
> When a client comes to see you – you should be mentally superior… do not hesitate, therefore, to assume this superior attitude, tho you need not let it become apparent to your client. It is for your own benefit – not the client!

> Look mentally down upon this poor creature, take your cues and prepare to help them, well realizing that if you do (or don't) give a successful reading, you will get your time fee, but turn thoughts towards giving satisfaction, and helping this brother or sister who in turn will preach the gospel of your fine work and lead other friends into your presence, that they too may leave an offering for the coffers of your bank.
>
> To commercialize spiritualism, you must carry your cause to the people. The most profitable channel is the churches and the meetings. There you come in contact with a hand-picked, receptive audience – aghast and waiting your word . . . That's just a part of the spook racket.

Most people don't take psychics seriously, and may find all this self-evident. But some poor souls take psychics very seriously indeed, and many become reliant on them for advice or a sense of well-being. Perhaps that's their own silly fault. Quite possibly. LBC Radio broadcasts, to their shame, a 'psychic hour' across London every Friday. A friend telephoned me to describe one exchange between the featured medium and some poor soul who had called the station. This is exactly as my friend remembers it, and he swears blind he's not exaggerating for comic effect:

> CALLER: I have a house with a piano. Often at night, we'll suddenly hear a note being played – High C – coming from the piano. We do have a lot of cats,* but it's not any of them as the lid is down. Do you know what that could be?
>
> MEDIUM: Well, there's a couple of things it could be. A friend

*No surprise there.

of mine is a piano-tuner, and he says that often, especially when the weather is getting hot, as it is at the moment, the internal workings of the piano can expand a little and cause a string here and there to pull at its hammer, which will result in a note being sounded. Apparently that can happen.

CALLER (unconvinced): Right, yeah, maybe . . .

MEDIUM: Or, you see, the High C note is a very resonant note energy-wise and will vibrate the chakras in the house, causing the fairies to sing. So it could be that too.

CALLER (delighted): Wow... yes, that sounds right. I mean *perhaps* it could be the strings expanding – sounds a bit far-fetched – but great, thank you, yes, I think you're right. Thank you so much.

Causing the fairies to sing. Exchanges such as this make me wonder how anyone could even begin to take these 'psychics' seriously. It's genuinely funny until you realize that this same brazen cow will presumably offer herself for a reasonable fee to get in touch with a child you may have lost and desperately miss.

I suspect that the reason people prefer to think of these people as mere harmless quacks or genuinely having a special 'gift' is that the alternative is a lie so ugly and exploitative that it's too unpleasant to think about.

One final note, before the fraudulent psychics accuse me of cheating too. I am often dishonest in my techniques, but always honest about my dishonesty. As I say in each show, I mix 'magic, suggestion, psychology, misdirection and showmanship'. I happily admit to cheating, as it's all part of the game. I hope some of the fun for the viewer comes from not knowing what's real and what isn't. I am an entertainer first and foremost, and I am careful not to cross any moral line that would take me into manipulating people's real-life decisions or belief systems. I use cold-reading myself in much of what I do, but in a very different context. Psychics tell you it's real, and invite you to open yourself up at the most intimate level. I tell you it's not real, and invite you to retain some sceptical distance as you enjoy the fun. These are important differences.

More Examples of Cold-reading Trickery

It's interesting to know that cold-reading is rarely a question of reading tiny cues from body language, though openness to non-verbal feedback can certainly help in one-on-one situations. The deception is all linguistic, and here are a few more of my favourite techniques from my own experience of listening to psychics at work, or from reading the instructional literature.

Verbal Forks: The great get-out 'Ah, but he was a father to you in spirit' may seem rather transparent, but this seamless U-turn in a reading happens all the time when a 'no' is encountered from the sitter. For example, the statement 'You do have a bit of a temper that can get you into trouble' could be met with agreement or disagreement. If there is agreement, the psychic can continue, 'It's not unreasonable, but it is something you've become aware of, and something which you've realized that people close to you are hesitant to point out for fear of making you defensive. Your aura shows that it is clearly something you should now look at, as it is blocking many new relationships from developing.' If the original statement is met with disagreement, it can be swerved around thus: 'Not in the sense of shouting or getting stroppy. On the outside you have cultivated an air of reasonableness and detachment. That's a very strong part of you. But inside, when people close to you upset you, it can really make you angry within yourself, and that can lead to hasty actions which you regret later. You'll play conversations to yourself in your head, or find yourself finding it hard to get to sleep because your internal dialogue is running at hyper-speed, as you try to work out something that's annoying you. You look at people who can just flare up and then forget about something with a mixture of derision and slight envy. Your controlled exterior masks some real internal pressure. I have the image of a swan: calm and graceful on the surface, but if people knew the level of intensity and self-critique which goes on beneath, they'd be surprised.' And so the meaning is reversed, and it reads like a more insightful statement rather than a wrong one.

I heard a great exchange with a psychic on an American TV show recently which transparently used this principle. And bear in mind, as ever, we're watching an edited version to make him look good:

> PSYCHIC: The ring you wear, I sense that came from your grandmother.
>
> WOMAN: No.
>
> PSYCHIC: Or from someone who cared for you like a grandmother, though it might not have been your actual grandmother.
>
> WOMAN: No.
>
> PSYCHIC: But your grandmother has given you a ring, yes? Might not be this one, but you have one from her?
>
> WOMAN: No.

There's a fine line between clever forking and desperation.

Specific Guesses: Rowland gives the example 'I'm seeing a blue car outside your door'. If the sitter drives a car that could be described as blue (a potentially rather vague colour description that could range from turquoise to silver-blue), or if next door has a blue car, or if there are contractors at work who have a blue car, or if the sitter *used* to have a blue car, or if a recent visitor has had a blue car, this will be seen as a hit. If not, then the sitter can be told to watch out for one, and it becomes part of a prediction of an important event that will happen in the future. Even something that seems very specific, such as 'I'm getting March as an important month connected with this – early in the month, I think, around the twelfth or so – and a lady with long hair', can read as a prediction of a future event, or a birthday, a death, or the date of any event that might have happened, whether connected to the long-haired lady or not. Once a connection has been found, or an event remembered, the psychic will be credited with having made a very accurate statement, even though nothing has really been said.

Specific Memories: When I have used forms of cold-reading in my own way, I have often referred to memories from a subject's life I could not possibly have known about. Again, these are no more than statements that can be applied to many of us, or experiences many of us will share, but when they hit they can cause huge reactions. For example, 'I'm getting a clear indication of an accident when you were younger, which you have replayed several times in your head since. I see you in water, panicking. You've slipped and fallen somehow and someone pulls you out – is it your dad?' If this doesn't hit, I can turn it into something connected with flooding, or more loosely water-related. A second one is, 'There's an accident from when you were younger. Do you have a brother? He's there, I think. It's a car accident, I think near your home, and I'm seeing a car – I think it's red. I don't think it was anything too serious, but it was horrible at the time.' Again, if this doesn't 'fit', I can back off with any of the details. At worst, I can 'leave it with' the subject to try to remember. This is another common way of passing blame for failure on to the poor person listening.

'Honest' Psychics

What of those well-meaning people who really believe they have a psychic gift? Certainly these people are not just frauds. They don't learn their skills from the sort of literature quoted above. Yet consider these later thoughts from *Pages from a Medium's Notebook*:

> 'Success always attracts success', and again human nature being what it is, no doubt half of the people [in the congregation at a spiritualist church] think they are psychic. They would like to learn the powers and develop the gift (since you have advised all you do) . . . also to earn the money that you represent.
>
> So the medium (I did) starts developing classes. The dupes attend two or three nights a week, learning to develop for mediumship. This will go on as long as they can stand the strain – financial and otherwise. Of course, there is a godly fee for classes. With a class of ten or twenty at $2.00 and up per person . . . IT IS profitable. A lot of students really think (or maybe do) develop [*sic*], at least, their belief – and go forth as mediums – tho I fear no [*sic*] very good ones until at some later time they get wise, and tackle the problem from the angle that I have been discussing all thru this book.

Some among you will remember the early *Mind Control* specials which aired in 2000/01. We filmed a sequence for one of those shows which never went out. The idea was this. I would go to a training college for psychics and see them at work. We would then introduce a person into the room, unknown to both the psychics and me, and I would have each of the psychics give him a reading. Afterwards, I would give my own non-psychic reading (which, unsurprisingly, the subject would find more accurate), and then I would give a reading to several of the psychics present which would hopefully impress them enormously too. End result: I look better than everyone else. Hooray, give him a Bafta.

We turned up to film at the premier psychic college. I was introduced to the Wednesday night circle, a group of ten trainee mystics who regularly met to enhance their skills. Almost all of them were women, but their ages differed widely. Now these people were not performers. Most would never have heard of cold-reading. None seemed obviously interested in being the most impressive person in the room, and none of them, disappointingly, made any attempt to secretly find out anything about our test subject.

The first part of the proceedings consisted of the group offering up a kind of prayer and allowing the various necessary energies into the group. A few of them found that they were already sensing things they should pass on to others in the group. 'Jean, I'm getting that you've been having trouble at work and it's going to get better', and so on. The instructor encouraged them in this for a while, and then we turned our attention to the test subject.

What followed was three hours of gradually losing the will to live. To reiterate, when you see psychics on television, you are watching edited highlights. A recent programme showed various psychics competing for the role of Britain's best psychic, and a magical performer with whom I am friendly was asked to be an observer on the panel. Now, despite the promise of the show to put the psychic contestants through rigorous tests, its ultimate aim was in reality to entertain an audience it presumed to be profoundly thick, with all the bewildering condescension known only to TV producers. Therefore we were not granted any real 'strict conditions' to eliminate conscious or unconscious cheating, and the sceptics on the show (of which my friend was one) were treated as mere boring spoilsports. Watching one sequence where the psychics being tested seemed to be able to divine the contents of an envelope with reasonable accuracy, albeit openly helped along by the smiles and nods of encouragement by another judge, I was intrigued by their successes. I called my friend and asked him about it. Not surprisingly, he said that the two minutes we saw on TV was edited from about an hour of waffling and random guessing at anything from the psychics. Sadly, but unavoidably in a fast-paced show, it was the producers of the programme who decided who was to look best rather than letting us see a fair portrayal of the psychics' dizzyingly ineffectual skills.

Our crew on our own filming day were just trying to stay awake while ten well-meaning but misguided charming psychics offered statements such as: 'I see you on a bus going in the wrong direction. Does that mean anything to you? It might not be a bus. It might be something else, like a relationship.' The test subjects did their best to be polite but fair, and naturally over the course of several hours a few statements unavoidably hit. The student with the long hair was indeed planning on travelling 'to Africa, or Asia, or . . . the world' (a favourite bit of reading). The girl had indeed bought a new bed and was amazed that one of the psychics was able to pick up on that. A few other moments provided some relief in the form of long-awaited but unimpressive agreements from the subjects. Memorably, one exchange went as follows:

PSYCHIC: I sense that you live on your own, or you share a place.
SUBJECT: Erm . . .
PSYCHIC: Yes, definitely on your own, or with other people.
SUBJECT: Can you be more specific?
INSTRUCTOR (angrily interjecting): Do you live alone or share a place? It must be one or the other!
SUBJECT (embarrassed): Well, I kind of live with my parents.
INSTRUCTOR (snapping): Well, then, that's with other people, isn't it? Don't just sit there and not answer, it blocks the energy.

We finished the filming, along with my own (non-psychic) readings. At one point, after I had told one of the group the number of her old house, one of the psychics said to me, 'Why won't you admit that you're reading auras? You clearly are, as the aura stores information like house numbers.' Wow. You'd never need an address book. And this was a teacher at London's primary psychic training college.

We realized that we could never make the piece work. Bearing in mind that no sane person could sit through the whole thing on television without harming himself, it would have to be edited down to its slot of five minutes or so. So should we just show the hits, which would be disproportionately favourable to the psychics, or not include them, or show just one, which would seem to be unfair? The routine was scrapped.

It was clear from watching and listening to these 'honest' psychics that they knew nothing of cold-reading technique. Instead, it seemed a little as if they met every week to stroke each other's egos (they were much more eager to make each other's statements 'fit' than the real-world subjects were) while learning the arts of talking vaguely, apotheosizing intuition and rationalizing failures. Again, it's none of my business if they want to spend their time and money learning a pretend skill, but obvious self-delusion is unavoidably rather sad to witness and one wonders how aware the instructors are of the deception involved and whether they themselves are conscious frauds. Sometimes the line is blurred, but there is a distinct line between someone using linguistic tricks to score lots of 'yes' answers and a person who genuinely feels that they have psychic insight into a person's situation. Of course, the cheats tend to sound better at it.

While it's easy, and important, to hold an exploitative individual to account when he tramples all over the memory of your loved ones in pursuit of money and ego, it's less clear whether there are important issues at stake just because a number of people mistakenly think they are developing psychic powers. Probably it doesn't matter much at all. But there are some issues worth bearing in mind when we come across these 'psychic schools' or individuals who believe they are gifted in this way. Firstly, there is the association with the moral bankruptcy of the vast majority of professional psychics. The novice or believer is unwittingly buying into a world full of charlatans and showbiz skills turned nasty. While that doesn't tar every self-styled psychic with the same brush, it might question the validity of these role models and aspirations. Secondly, there is a social issue. What level-headed person doesn't recoil when an otherwise perfectly charming conversational partner mentions that he is psychic? As tolerant and charming as we are, do we not mentally detach ourselves as if he had said he believed in Father Christmas? I wonder if the answer to all of this is just *believe what you want, of course, but best to keep quiet about it if it's likely to make you sound stupid.* Of course there will always be people interested if you tell them that you can see their aura, because plenty of people will believe anything you tell them, and most people are self-absorbed enough to be interested in what you have to say. But for every one person who is interested there'll be six or seven who have just written you off as a lunatic. And if you think there's a kind of eccentric dignity in that, you're wrong. Heresy doesn't make you right either. The fact that they 'laughed at Galileo' isn't what made him a genius.

Previously I spoke about how hard it is for people to give up beliefs in which they have staked their identity. I would add to that that the believer in supernatural phenomena (psychic, religious or otherwise) also has before him a wealth of easy answers. The world becomes a place that can be explained through whatever cosmic force a believer has chosen. Amazing, tragic or magnificent events can be explained by so-and-so being psychic, the power of energy, the happiness or the vengefulness of God. I remember watching a news report shortly after the tsunami devastated chunks of Asia, and the journalist on screen spoke to a priest who had been helping with the relief effort. He asked the priest a good question, and my ears pricked up: 'Does an event like this shake your faith?' The priest's reply, which I give here as well as I can remember it, was, 'Quite the opposite. Only yesterday I was speaking to a man who had sustained terrible injuries from the tsunami and was dying in hospital. Wonderfully, he came to accept Jesus as his Saviour before he died. So in fact God is working some real miracles here and it's amazing to see.' *What?!* I am sure that the twisted intellectual cowardice shown in that answer was more than compensated for by the priest's efforts in caring for the sick and injured. But how much more impressive would have been a reply that admitted difficulty in understanding it and a lack of easy answers.

Moreover, knowledge and investigation help promote wonder – they do not destroy it. Whatever our tastes, we can generally appreciate such things as music, art or wine better when we understand a bit about them. We read up on our favourite singers or artists because we feel we can appreciate their work better when we know how they think and what they bring to their work. The giddy delight and curiosity that comes from marvelling at the beauty of this universe is deepened, not cheapened, by the laws and facts science gives us to aid our understanding. In a similar way, the psychological tricks at work behind many seemingly paranormal events are truly *more* fascinating than the explanation of other-worldliness precisely because they *are* of this world, and say something about how rich and complex and mysterious we are as human beings to be convinced by such trickery, indeed to want to perpetrate it in the first place. If you are reading this book you will have an interest in the capabilities of the human mind. Nothing cheapens or insults those capabilities more than the insistence that we are psychic. Cheap answers are for cheap thinkers.

I personally don't understand why anyone should need a paranormal realm, or for that matter God, to make this world or this life richer or more mysterious. But I see that there is an ease with which such belief systems provide simple answers and immediate meaning that appeals to the sentiment, and I understand that for many people, particularly those indoctrinated at a young age, such simple answers and easy meaning might be irresistible. Again, though, that irresistibility itself, and the question of why it exists is surely far more fascinating than the make-believe concepts it might lead to in a believer's mind.

I still love the idea of ghosts or angels and am drawn to great stories of the paranormal. I love them because, like anyone, I relish the thrill to the imagination they provoke. The 'unknown' makes us tingle. But these are just stories, and the fact that there is much we do not understand yet does not mean that such things will not be understood at some point. We need first to understand and define the outer limits of what is 'normal' or 'sensory' before we refer to something as 'paranormal' or 'extrasensory'. Until then, to treat something as self-evidently paranormal is to curtail curiosity and the willingness to learn. And by applying easy labels and simple meanings that are satisfying to those who don't like thinking, and patronizing to those who do, such treatment strips us, our minds, our world and our universe of their staggering complexity and richness.

In the words of Douglas Adams (quoted by Richard Dawkins at the start of his wonderful book *The God Delusion*), 'Isn't it enough to see that a garden is beautiful without having to believe there are fairies at the bottom of it too?'

FINAL THOUGHTS

I'll be honest with you, I was concerned. Yesterday afternoon, when I sat down to begin writing this book, alongside watching the entire first series of *Lost*, I was worried that nothing would hold the various chapters together save a cheap binding and a vague sense that they were all connected with the non-arrestable interests of your loyal and unusual-smelling author. I was particularly vexed that my immodest rant on pseudo-science might not prove to be a comfortable bedfellow or easy paramour with such things as improving your memory or vanishing a coin. I would like to think that, despite my consternation, we have together fumbled and hacked our way through the jungle of confusion and ignored the roars and rumblings of discomfiture; slain the polar bears of incertitude and come to accept that no-one will rescue us from this island of discombobulation following our plane crash of whimsically appealing stylistic irregularity. Perhaps, in that sense, when Charlie says, 'Bloody hell, no-one's going to bloody get us off this bloody island,' he's talking about all of us.

Yet somehow we have indeed reached a loose theme: a love of the tricks our mind can play with us. And hopefully we've found a few pointers on how we might take control over reliable principles that lie behind such tricks, or put them to good use. I'm delighted we've come this far, and if some people at your church told you not to read this book, then all the rest of us are very proud of you for being grown up enough to ignore them.

But may I just add one thing.

There is a guy I know who is very good at voices. He can impersonate people quite well and has a knack for vocal sound effects, some of which are quite startling. He's enormously talented and what he does is very impressive. I have a love for impersonation myself and can get away with one or two, so I take a child-like delight in what he can do. And he's a very nice chap.

However, it's hard to have a normal conversation with this guy because he can't stop trying to impress people. His default voice seems not to be his own, but that of Alan Partridge. He cannot leave an answer-phone message without pretending to be someone else. He is his own constant show-reel. He's the 'funny voice' guy. For a while it's very entertaining, but then it becomes tiresome, for as long as faking a smile and offering compliments *can* be merely tiresome. The shame is, he is clearly a very likeable and engaging guy, driven and lively in an infectious way. But in an attempt to be constantly impressive, he borders on the excruciating.

I *know* I've been the 'magic guy'. Like so many magicians, it's easy to become addicted to constantly impressing one's peers and to lose perspective at the same rate that one becomes a rather sad figure. Probably it's only through the performances becoming a job which takes up all my days that much of the romance of the role has been lost for me along with the desire to perform when socializing.

Unavoidably, if the techniques and thoughts in this book are new to you, there will be a tendency to be excited about them, and to want to show off what you have learned. By all means embrace them in this way, for I will have failed if I haven't set your mind at work and given you things to play with. But if you decide that you want to use some of these techniques permanently, and make them part of who you are, then understand the power of withholding. The impact of what is unsaid. Please don't become a geek or a bore. I should never forgive myself.

When any sort of performance hits the right mark, the performer has an uncanny sense of how his audience perceives him. Comics might talk of an interchange of energy between themselves and an audience that allows them to constantly alter their performance to suit the perpetually shifting mood. From my own experience of presenting a long (even grotesquely long) one-man show night after night to audiences made up of wildly different people, I have come to enjoy the game of trying to keep everyone engrossed. One of the most counter-intuitive lessons I learned was what to do if you sense the audience is losing interest. Now, with the spotlights burning through your retinas there is no chance of actually *seeing* the people you're playing to, save the front couple of rows of enthusiastic punters who are your only visual clue.

Because you can't see anyone, your only way of telling how involved they are is through sound. A comedian is most interested in laughs; in my show I expect laughs, silences, murmurs and gasps at hoped-for moments. Sometimes a tiny distraction makes a joke fall flat. Sometimes the acoustics of the theatre make it hard to hear an audience and I play the whole show with the uncomfortable sensation that no-one's enjoying it at all. But by far the most reliable gauge of an audience's interest is the extent to which they cough. A cough is a clear sign that a person has detached a little from the show and is getting fidgety. I have heard that putting on a show is 'the art of stopping people coughing', and I do rather like the idea. How long to hold a moment for, how delivery should be shifted, is dictated to a large extent by a response to the bronchial irritations of a thousand people. And the lesson I quickly learned, which goes against every natural instinct when you are on stage showing off to people, is that if they are losing interest and starting to cough, you must *become quieter*. You may want to talk louder, make bigger gestures and shove yourself more in their faces, but the key is to go small. In doing so, the gathered individuals have to be quiet and focussed in order to hear you, and an unconscious cue goes out into the auditorium that something of interest is occurring.

The artificial and exaggerated form of social interaction in a theatre can give us a clue as to how to apply our showing-off in real life. For a while now I have concerned myself with engaging people's beliefs. A large part of me wishes to have people retain a scepticism about what I do and apply that to other areas in life where our beliefs are manipulated in ugly ways. Meanwhile, the 'performer' part of me that enjoys the dramatic and the mysterious needs to balance that scepticism in the audience with a belief in my skills that hopefully conflicts with the first reaction and creates an interesting ambiguity. Hopefully. To many, I am sure, I am just a smug, bald heap of insufferability. But at least allow me to fool myself.

In that area of playing with beliefs in a theatrical context, another lesson is learned which corresponds to the first: *less is more*. People work *away* from the information you give them. They can only take what you say and apply their own levels of scepticism to it. True, some people unquestioningly believe everything they are told, but such people are normally tucked up at home watching Living TV or busy sending £10 to the person at the top of a list. If you concern yourself with telling or showing people how interesting you are, you will at best provoke a temporary response of polite interest until even that gives way to annoyance. If you let people find it out for themselves, you become a real source of fascination. And if they seem to lose interest, pull back, don't push more.

Be someone who gets this right, and you'll be a rare and special thing. There was a real irony to the NLPers I knew who prided themselves on their communication skills yet because of their need to let everyone know how engaging they were, they were among the least engaging people I have ever known. In one extreme, we see this in the Christian fanatics who stand on the street and preach the word of their Lord, unaware that for every one rare, impressionable soul who might respond positively to their shouting and intrusion there are many hundreds of others in whom they have merely confirmed a belief that all Christians must be nutters. People are too often terrible advertisements for their own beliefs.

So I hope this book will inspire some enthusiasm for a handful of odd facets of our minds. I hope you'll put to good use one or two things I have shown you, and that as you do so you'll remember the importance of real evidence over ideology. And where you choose to communicate these things, I hope you will do so deftly and with intelligence, with a delight in the power of withholding and an appreciation of the potency of a secret. And please, leave the funny voices to everyone else.

CORRESPONDENCE

In January 2002, I received an email from a man who had taken extreme exception to the sequence in an early *Mind Control* special where I had helped a guy win money on a losing ticket at Walthamstow dog track. He had written to Channel 4 and had copied the letter to me. Missing the fact that the racetrack would have clearly been reimbursed after the event, he argued, 'If he would commit a crime such as this on TV what does he do when there are no cameras present? Has he used these skills to bed (or should I say rape) women, break up relationships?' A little later he continues, 'Can you imagine if everyone out their [*sic*] was like Mr Brown? Crime, dishonesty, getting one over on your fellow man? Things such as that would be rampant. The world is already a rubbish enough place to live in without people like this . . . Maybe you can also suggest to Mr Brown that he make an honest living and contribute to the community in a positive way as the rest of us decent law abiding citizens do. The man needs to learn some respect.' I was so flummoxed as to what makes a person write that sort of letter that I hung on to it (which, I suspect, is more than Channel 4 did).

The sort of ill-informed armchair moralizing that pours from the permanently outraged, *Daily Mail*-reading mentality is one of the more revolting and frightening aspects of our society, and if I see any more of it I will have no hesitation in writing a stiff letter to *Points of View* and speaking my mind on the first radio phone-in I come across. But since then I have regularly received correspondence from all sorts of people who have strong feelings about what I do. The content of these often moving letters and emails has been anything from deeply tragic pleas from people who are gravely ill and who see me as their last hope, through to pieces of quite breathtaking hate-mail.

Somewhere in between I have received letters from strangers who genuinely believe we are romantically involved or even married; numerous explanations of my role in Islam; and countless numbers of people responding to what they perceive as psychic messages that I am sending them and threatening to sue accordingly. (No longer do these sorts of letters reach my door or inbox: few make it through the Kafkan (*never* Kafkaesque) strata of my management.) Gifts have arrived too creepy to mention here for fear of encouraging the senders, but if I whispered to you the things that were sent, I guarantee you would feel quite out of sorts all day.

So I thought I would finish the book by offering a few emails and letters of note which I have received, so that you can appreciate the sort of mixed responses my shows spark. I have chosen those which I found interesting, insightful or intriguing, and I would like to thank the correspondents for writing. I have of course preserved their anonymity.

Derren Brown

From: [redacted]
To: <info@derrenbrown.co.uk>
Sent: 28 October 2002 00:35
Subject: a question

Sorry to sound weird here, but does Darren put all of his work down to psychological suggestion? I guess what I'm really asking is - does he think his 'experiments' prove the existence of an extra-temporal energy? I'm not talking about God - I'm talking about non-visible cellular vibration.

Derren Brown

From:
To:
Sent: 11 April 2002 00:58
Subject: To Derren-with love and regret

Can you put your skills to anything other than creating wealth.

Your skills are very much extraordinary, not exceptional.

Some of us possess natural powers of reading through intuition.

Walking the streets of London as a child i saw in my minds eye both danger and safety, and negotiated the two through innate and exceptional abilities.

I read your motives, you were very much the underdog as a child, bullshitting, hiding your inner feelings, easily dominated, perhaps most by your mother, was she German, in the orthodox sense?.

You percieved yourself as small, and sometimes still do but that glint in your adult eye reveals your inner feelings today.

You are no gate keeper.

When will you stop showing off these classical techniques of mind control and prove through your 'self' that you are 'somebody'.

Congratulations on your great con.

Derren Brown

From: [redacted]
To: <info@derrenbrown.co.uk>
Sent: 03 December 2002 14:50

hello...

(sorry for my english ... becuse i'm a forighn student)

i saw many shows about you in the channel 4

and now i want to try this with my self...

i'll come to London on 22 dec from Bournemouth

could tell me if there any show on 22 or 23 becuse i'll leave on 23 Dec

i'd from you (if you could) to show many things you know...

(if you can in your house on sunday... because i'm so shay ... and i want to be alone)

and again i'm sorry if i say some rod

thank you

Add photos to your messages with MSN 8. Get 2 months FREE*.
http://join.msn.com/?page=features/featuredemail

I am APPEALING TO THE HIGH SOCLETY WITH MY ENCHANTED FANTASY ART I WOULD LIKE TO BE A CELEBRITY A STAR I DO NEED AN AGENT TO HELP ME ON THIS I NEED A SPECIAL CARDS TO GO TO THESE EXOTIC PARTYS OF CELEBRTIYS AND THE VERY RICH AND FAMOUS GO TO LIKE ELTON JOHN PARTYS THERE MUST BE SOMEONE WHO IS IN A BIG WAY WHO CAN HELP ME OR CAN THERE FRIENDS OR SOMEONE WHO GOT COTACTS WITH THE ROYAL FAMILY AS I DO WANT TO GO TO AMERICA AS I DO WANT TO BE FAMOUS AND MEET SAM ROBSON WALTON IN AMERICA I WANT THE BIG TIME AND JETSETTERS LIFE THIS IS WHAT I REALLY WANT AS I GOT A LOT TO OFFER PEOPLE AS I FEEL THERE IS MORE OPPORTUNITY FOR ME OVERSEAS FOR A CREATIVE ARTIST AS I TAKE MY SELF VERY SERIOUS AND MY AMBITIONS AS I AM OPEN TO SUGGESTIONS FROM INFLUENTIAL PEOPLE AS IT IS VERY IMPORTANT THESE CONTACTS TO ME AS I LOVE TO BE IN THE LIMELIGHT I WANT GENUINE REPLY PLEASE NO TIME WASTERS .

Derren Brown

From:
To: <info@derrenbrown.co.uk>
Sent: 03 November 2002 01:21
Subject: Derren's home address - is it ...

Really enjoyed the Mind Control evening.

As an experiment, I thought I would not try to allow his home address to be in my mind. Trusting that Derren would have planted clues, or something. No pressure. This is what I got:

14 Westgate Avenue, London SW11

Then 141 Westgate Avenue, London SW11.

Best wishes

Derren Brown

From:
To: <info@derrenbrown.co.uk>
Sent: 12 April 2003 17:29
Subject: Global Symbolism

Dear Sir/Madam

I would most appreciate it if you could ask Derren about the global manifestation of serpent symbolism that is rife everywhere if you look for it.

I was amazed to see this stuff in apparently innocent places like British Telecoms logo for example- the leg+arm is an obvious snake symbol.

I cannot help but think there is something sinister going on.

There are also various other abundant symbols of lighted torches etc.

Could you ask Derren of what he thinks of these and email his thoughts back to me?

Cheers

----
talk21 your FREE portable and private address on the net at http://www.talk21.com

From:

Sent: 07 July 2004 12:03

To:

Subject: God

Derren

I am pleased to say that i have stopped balding and that i have stopped gaining weight and have at last entered the flow of all magic.

My name is and i am in need of your assistance.I do believe you and i have much work to do together.My address is :

Tel:

e mail :

I live in a commune ,so someone else will more than likely answer the phone.I hope God brings us together soon.I look forward to hearing from you.

****

Michael

Thankyou for your e-mail.You have asked for me to be more specific,so i will tell you who i am.I am the Son of God.I am The Lamb and my soul is Jesus Christ.Please pass this infomation on to Derren, i am sure it will be of interest to him.I eagerly await your reply.

Derren Brown

From:
To: <info@derrenbrown.co.uk>
Sent: 30 March 2003 01:29
Subject: when your smiling

Dear Sirs/ ladies,
Sir. i was watching your programme on Channel4. Saturday 29th March.
It was Liberating to see somebody who comprehends the energy of our minds. I loved the way you used the median energies to deliver a non-physical but deadly blow. I Would love to do that to people at times but the all knowing seems to prevent me. I hope someday, in the passage of time we meet. Its nice to see a mind lightning fast and agile.
Yours. With respect,

to some that understand. Animatedclay or stardust with conciousness.

Saturday, January 8, 2005

Dear Mr Brown

You are so clever but such an idiot. And as likely, not for any reason you may think I think. Why? Because you are a negative depressive who has the intelligence to choose not to be. Perversely, you show no more cognizance than any of your knavishly chosen victims. You do everyone, including yourself, a disservice because you add little positivity to humanity.
You take the quiddity of people, the need to be loved, the need not to want to be seen as different and like the worse type of predator, use them for gain before tossing them aside. For your own selfish benefit, that is idiocy. I should like you to distance yourself from your past and grow into manhood. If you do not, you will remain unconscious of your mental retardation. An idiot.

Yours sincerely

Molly Cutpurse

Att: Darren Brown

13.06.04

Dear Darren,

I am sorry. I thought you came to London to challenge me.

I came to your show, the opening night (7.06.04) to show you that I am more powerful and potent than you. When I realised that you did not come to London to challenge me I instantly sent you my master genie to help you on stage. I am sure you felt his presence when he stepped onto the stage.

You can keep him, I am sure he will serve you well.

Darren you are not a Jedi master as the Empire magazine says of you. But you are still an excellent person.

NLP Master Practitioner
Genie Tamer, Trainer
Dr Richard Bandlers Most Potent Student

P.S. Contact me if you want to meet for a drink.

ACKNOWLEDGEMENTS

The following have all, wittingly or otherwise, been a part of this book.

Doug, my editor. Thank you for your honesty and insight and general brilliance. Also, the reader should know that any typographical errors or confusing points of style are the direct responsibility of Doug's team.

Vivien Garrett, Emma Musgrave and Claire Ward at Transworld for putting up with my constant fiddling.

Coops, my PA. For his constant loyalty and delightfulness, when he could be working as an editor or a stage manager. No-one else has a skateboarding PA. They're very special.

Michael Vine, my manager. For his love, and for the remaining 80 per cent of this deal.

Greg Day, my publicist. For looking after me, and for everything (apart from putting me on GMTV after *Russian Roulette*).

Lara Jordan, my friend. I guess our friendship has helped shape my thoughts on some of the things discussed in this book. Thank you for helping me find my own clarity.

Nigel Walk, my oldest friend (he's 108). A great, questioning Christian and my own guide through my years as a believer. Thank you for putting up with my wayward journey.

Also, enormous thanks to:

Andy Nyman, my adorable friend and invaluable collaborator. For filling me with so many brilliant ideas over the years and allowing me to lap up the credit for them. For just everything.

Andrew 'We don't have to be friends' O'Connor, my friend and fellow exec producer. For his thoughts on theatre, and for finding me. Without him, none of you would have heard of me, and no-one would have any interest in these pages. Thank you for not losing faith in me. I learned to make my own fucking tea in the end.

And, as ever, for their influence: my mum and dad, Andrew Newman, Kevin Lygo, Anthony Owen, Stefan Stuckert, Debbie Young, Simon Mills, Jono Smith, *Shooters*, Katie Taylor, Sharon Powers, Adam Adler, Mephisto, Jonathan Goodwin, John Dalston, Jeremy Wooding, Dan MacDonald and Teller. And, of course, the Jersey Police.

SUGGESTED FURTHER READING AND QUOTED PAPERS

MAGIC

Mark Wilson, *Complete Course in Magic*
(Running Press Book Publishers, 1991)
This book got me started in proper conjuring. It's big, and covers everything from close-up tricks with coins and cards to stage illusions you can make at home.

Jean Hugard, *The Royal Road to Card Magic*
(New Dawn Press, 2004)
If you want to begin the journey of learning professional sleight-of-hand, this is the place to start. You'll have to search for it, though: serious magic books are not to be found in Waterstone's. Contact your local magic dealer.

MEMORY

Harry Lorayne, *How to Develop a Super Power Memory* (Frederick Fell, 1996)

This is a classic work which has been reprinted many times since the very quaint 1940s edition that I have at home. Lorayne is a very successful magician and memory expert. This book will cover in more detail the principles I have set out.

Dominic O'Brien, *Learn to Remember* (Chronicle Books, 2000)

O'Brien is probably the top memory expert in the world today and has written many books on the subject. This is a lyrical introduction but perhaps not as useful as his more straightforward *How to Develop a Perfect Memory*, which is now out of print.

Kenneth L. Higbee, *Your Memory* (Marlowe & Co., USA, 2001)

This work offers a balance between memory techniques and a look at the nature of memory itself. Higbee is rather more honest and pragmatic about certain areas of memory improvement which are often glossed over in other books on the subject. Highly recommended.

Frances Yates, *The Art of Memory* (Pimlico, 1992)

This is a lovely work on the history of memory techniques and mnemonics. It offers little in the way of practical advice, but is a fascinating look at a satisfyingly obscure and esoteric subject.

Jonathan D. Spence, *The Memory Palace of Matteo Ricci* (Penguin Books Australia, 1994)

If you are as visibly excited as I am by the notion of memory palaces, then this is the best work on the subject. Not that there are many to choose from. Again, this is not a 'how to' guide as such, but, rather, a rich historical and academic work. Certainly it will inspire you to delve into the rich rewards of the system.

HYPNOSIS AND SUGGESTIBILITY

Graham F. Wagstaff, *Hypnosis: Compliance and Belief* (Saint Martin's Press, 1998)
Wagstaff offers an important behaviourist approach to understanding hypnotism. Although the limits of the behaviourist view are apparent, it's valuable as a coherent argument against the idea of hypnotism being something magical.

Jay Haley, *Jay Haley on Milton H. Erickson* (Brunner Mazel Inc., 1993)
A lovely read about this seemingly extraordinary chap and his methods, though best read with a pinch of salt.

Michael Heap (ed.), *Hypnosis: Current Clinical, Experimental and Forensic Practices* (Croom Helm, 1988)
By no means a light 'how to' book, but contains some good sceptical essays on NLP and Erickson.

NEURO-LINGUISTIC PROGRAMMING

As a general note, I think the early books by Bandler and Grinder are worth reading. Personally, I would avoid much of the later literature by other authors, and also avoid the courses.

Richard Bandler & John Grinder, *Frogs into Princes: Neuro-Linguistic Programming* (Real People Press, 1979)
Required reading for anyone curious about NLP. This is a good book on using NLP to make changes and is fascinating reading.

Richard Bandler & John LaValle, *Persuasion Engineering* (Meta Publications Inc., USA, 1996)
Bandler's enjoyable book on sales techniques. I really like this one.

Richard Bandler & John Grinder, *Trance-Formations* (Real People Press, 1981)
A book on NLP trance-work. Still fun reading, but not a good first book, and only for the enthusiast or would-be practitioner.

Richard Bandler, *Magic in Action* (Meta Publications, 1992)
A book of transcripts of sessions with Bandler and various clients. A knowledge of the techniques may help, but by now you'll be well on the road to imagining that Bandler's far cleverer and deeper than he may be. Yet this is unavoidably interesting reading and Bandler's charisma pours through.

Richard Bandler & John Grinder, *Patterns of the Hypnotic Techniques of Milton H. Erickson* (Meta Publications, USA, 1975)
The work which kicked it all off. Less enjoyable than their later books, and Bandler claims to have dispensed with much of what is written here, but an interesting introduction to Erickson and a classic in the field.

COGNITIVE ILLUSIONS

Massimo Piattelli-Palmarini, *Inevitable Illusions: How Mistakes of Reason Rule our Lives*
(John Wiley & Sons Inc., 1996)
This is a very enjoyable and accessible work on how our minds trick us, and is full of the sort of counter-intuitive examples you have read here concerning rolled dice, tossed coins, diseases and unopened boxes.

Rüdiger Pohl, *Cognitive Illusions*
(Psychology Press, 2004)
Pohl has brought together an anthology of academic work on the subject, and the result is a hugely comprehensive book, if understandably drier than Piattelli-Palmarini. A great text on this very new science.

SCEPTICISM AND SCIENCE

Daniel E. Moerman, *Meaning, Medicine and the 'Placebo Effect'*
(Cambridge University Press, 2002)
This is a take on the placebo effect which includes a study of such things as colour and packaging and the meanings we ascribe to the medicines we take.

Dylan Evans, *Placebo: Mind Over Matter in Modern Medicine*
(HarperCollins, 2004)
I preferred this book. It's a great read and covers the power and limitations of the placebo effect. Worth reading if you have any interest in medicine of any kind.

Dick Taverne, *The March of Unreason: Science, Democracy and the New Fundamentalism* (Oxford University Press, Oxford, 2005)

An excellent and important work that pulls no punches in slamming many areas of the green lobby (rightly so) for its preference for ideology over evidence. Taverne's thesis is that the easy relationship between the media and such pressure groups is a threat to scientific progress and profoundly undemocratic. It looks at the real evidence for and against such unpopular notions as GM crops, and time and time again shows how our fears are a victory of media-manipulated sentiment over reality and reason. A book you'll want to buy for your eco-fundamentalist friends. If they don't read it, the hardback version is heavy enough to hit them over the head with.

PSYCHOLOGICAL EXPERIMENTS

Stanley Milgram, *The Individual in a Social World: Essays and Experiments* (Longman Higher Education, 1977)

This contains the reports on Milgram's famous 'Obedience' experiment which has become synonymous with his name. (For those of you still unfamiliar with him, this is the supposed electrocution experiment we set up in *The Heist.*) Aside from this landmark of social psychology, there are plenty of fascinating ideas and experiments contained in Milgram's work. It's an excellent read and very accessible in tone. There's even a chapter about *Candid Camera*.

Lauren Slater, *Opening Skinner's Box: Great Psychological Experiments of the Twentieth Century* (Bloomsbury, 2004)

It took me a while to like this book: Slater's florid style does not sit easily with the academic nature of her subject. To begin with I found it self-indulgent, speculative and silly, but after a while it really won me over. In particular, her chapter on addiction is surprisingly moving. The book reads like a fiction writer's take on the more notorious experiments of the last hundred years or so, and in that sense brings them all 'to life'. Once you are happy to read the book in this light, it's quite compulsive and lovely reading.

READING UNCONSCIOUS BEHAVIOUR

Malcolm Gladwell, *Blink: The Power of Thinking Without Thinking*
(Penguin, 2006)
I never tire of telling people that when Gladwell came to London I was (so I was told) the one person he asked to meet. *Blink* is a very readable and enjoyable book about making accurate instant judgements, and pulls from a self-consciously diverse range of subjects. Personally, I found it suffered from a lack of scepticism. His readiness to allow his rich imagination to accept the claims of his sources without apparent restraint left me finding the whole thing a bit fluffy and not as challenging as I had hoped it would be. And the validity of my concern is, to my mind, supported by the fact that I was the one person he asked to meet when he came to London.

Aldert Vrij, *Detecting Lies and Deceit*
(John Wiley & Sons, Chichester, 2001)
This is a terrific work on lie-spotting. Vrij is one of the true experts and great experimenters on the subject and his book is rich in detail and bursting with research. Written for professional lie-catchers, as well as students and academics, it is one of relatively few serious books on the subject.

Stan Walters, *The Truth about Lying: Everyday Techniques for Dealing with Deception* (Sourcebooks, 2000)

A more immediately accessible book on spotting lying tells and will therefore be of interest to many, I'm sure. However, this area is so much more tricky and elusive than many popular books on the subject will have you believe.

Peter Collett, *Book of Tells* (Bantam Press, 2004)

A big, light guide to the area of body language and give-away clues. Fun reading for the interested novice.

Paul Ekman & Erika Rosenberg, *What the Face Reveals* (Oxford University Press, USA, 2005)

There's a huge amount to explore, but Ekman and Rosenberg's work on codifying every possible muscular movement of the human face has allowed those trained in the system to develop a seemingly super-human ability to spot micro-expressions; the tiny, fleeting twitches and incongruities that betray our real emotions. This is an academic book rather than a 'learn-at-home' hide, but is great reading for the enthusiast.

Paul Ekman & Wallace V. Friesen, *Unmasking the Face* (Malor Books, 2003)

This is a more accessible starting point to understanding Ekman's work and includes lots of exercises to improve your sensitivity to reading people. Excellent stuff.

RELIGION, SCEPTICISM AND THE PARANORMAL

Richard Dawkins, *The God Delusion* (Bantam Press, 2006)

Occasionally I get asked in interviews what my favourite book is, and until now my answer to this rather tricky question has been *Boswell's London Diaries*. Not any more. Dawkins, no one save a couple of *Times* journalists will be fascinated to hear, has pipped my favourite dandy to the post. My only regret is that Dawkins keeps writing the books and making the TV shows that I want to come up with. *The God Delusion* is a very important defence of atheism, and systematically looks at every aspect of faith and 'proofs' of God's existence. Any brave believer (i.e., not of the cowardly, deaf-blind variety) intelligent enough to want to challenge his faith would be advised to read this book. For many, including those who float around agnosticism or guilty half-belief, it's a big fat life-changing work. For atheists like me, it's an addictive and wonderful read which argues comprehensively and convincingly for the fallacy of religious belief. In a violent age when we should be embarrassed to talk proudly of blind faith, this is an argument which needs to come to the fore without apology or respectful tiptoeing.

Richard Dawkins, *A Devil's Chaplain* (Weidenfeld & Nicolson, 2003)

For those not immediately drawn to Dawkins' well-known scientific works, here is a wonderful collection of essays on various subjects, but underpinned by the joy to be found in this world without recourse to religious or other paranormal beliefs. This was the first book by Dawkins that I read, and it made me a huge fan. His essay about the horror of 9/11 was clearly a springboard for further thoughts which led to *The God Delusion* and the heroic Channel 4 two-parter *Root of all Evil?*

Bertrand Russell, *Sceptical Essays* (Routledge, 1992) and *Why I am not a Christian* (Routledge, 2004)
Classic and powerful reading from the master of rationalism. Required reading on the subject.

Burton L. Mack, *Who Wrote the New Testament?: The Making of the Christian Myth* (HarperCollins, 1995)
A very readable and thorough book on how the New Testament was put together. I started this book as a half-believer and finished with my belief in tatters: once you realize that the Bible isn't history and, therefore, you can't point to the Biblical story of the resurrection as proof of God's reality, it all falls apart. Excellent stuff.

Tim Callahan, *Secret Origins of the Bible* (Millennium Press, USA, 2002)
Interesting and enjoyable work placing the Good Book into a context of comparative mythology, though the Mack book, above, is a better way of getting a good grasp of the necessary history.

Randall Helms, *Gospel Fictions* (Prometheus Books UK, 1990)
A briefer guide to the historical howlers of the New Testament.

Sam Harris, *The End of Faith: Religion, Terror and the Future of Reason* (Free Press, 2006)
An excellent book arguing for the dangers of religious belief in these times, and a great companion to Dawkins' *The God Delusion*. Harris is a terrific writer and the book is compelling, although I

think he ignores many of the reasons why some young Muslims get involved in terrorist activities.

Mark Juergensmeyer, *Terror in the Mind of God: The Global Rise of Religious Violence*
(University of California Press, 2003)
If you like the Harris book and want more, this is a good next book to read on the subject.

Daniel C. Dennett, *Breaking the Spell: Religion as a Natural Phenomenon*
(Allen Lane, 2006)
Great deconstruction of religion, but perhaps not as vivid and addictive as *The God Delusion*.

Michael Shermer, *How We Believe: Science, Skepticism and the Search for God* (Owl Books, New York, 2003) and *Why People Believe Weird Things: Pseudoscience, Superstition and Other Confusions of Our Time*
(W. H. Freeman & Co., 1997)
Shermer is a great writer on the nature of belief and these two books on the subject are worth reading.

Stuart A. Vyse: *Believing in Magic: The Psychology of Superstition*
(Oxford University Press Inc., USA, 2000)
A good alternative to *Why People Believe Weird Things*. Both cover the essentials.

John Diamond, *Snake Oil* (Vintage, 2001)
Written as he was dying of cancer, this is a powerful attack on the

alternative medicine scene which was thrusting itself at Diamond during his final months. It's also an unsentimentally heroic statement from a man refusing to surrender his dignity to an industry which any desperate person would find hard to resist.

Francis Wheen, *How Mumbo-Jumbo Conquered the World: A Short History of Modern Delusions* (HarperPerennial, 2004)
A very enjoyable look at the rise of superstition and irrationality against a socio-political backdrop. Very much recommended.

David Marks, *The Psychology of the Psychic* (Prometheus Books UK, 2000)
Enjoyable reading covering some juicy subjects around pseudo-science and why people believe in such stuff, including much on Geller.

Robert Todd Carroll, *The Skeptic's Dictionary: A Collection of Strange Beliefs, Amusing Deceptions and Dangerous Delusions* (John Wiley & Sons Inc., 2003) and James Randi, *An Encyclopedia of Claims, Frauds and Hoaxes of the Occult and Supernatural* (St Martin's Press, 1997)
Enjoyable resource books on all sorts of pseudo-scientific nonsense.

Ian Rowland, *Full Facts Book of Cold Reading* (2000)
There are a few books about on Cold Reading – the technique generally used by psychics to tell you everything about yourself and your dead relatives – but Rowland's book is the best. Currently available only from his website.

Anonymous, *Confessions of a Medium*
(Micky Hades International, 1976)
You'll need to hunt around for this one. Equally, a search on 'fraudulent mediums' will yield alternatives. Many old books deal with exposing the dark-séance mediums (or 'media', I suppose) of the Victorian era, but Confessions is a 'how-to' guide for the modern fake.

OTHER WORKS CITED

131 Erickson, Milton H. & Rossi, Ernest L., 'The Indirect forms of Suggestion', in Rossi E. L., (ed.) *The Collected Papers of Milton H Erikson on Hypnosis*, vol. 1, New York: Irvington, 1980, pp. 452–77

131 McCue, P., 'Milton H. Erickson: a critical perspective', in Heap, M., (ed.), *Hypnosis: Current clinical, experimental and forensic practices*, Croom Helm, 1988, pp. 257–67

186 Cody, Steven G., *The stability and impact of the primary representational system in neurolinguistic programming: a critical examination*, University of Connecticut dissertation, 1983

231 Lykken, D. T., 'The Case against polygraph testing', in Gale, A., (ed.), *The Polygraph Test: Lies, Truth and Science*, Sage, London, 1988, pp. 111–26

234 Ekman, Paul, 'Why lies fail and what behaviours betray a lie', in Yuille, J. C., (ed.), *Credibility Assessment*, Dordrecht: Kluwer, 1989, pp. 71–82

234 Ekman, Paul, *Telling lies: clues to deceit in the marketplace, politics and marriage*, Guilford Press, New York, 1992, pp. 184–201

234 Ekman, P., & Friesen, W. V., 'Nonverbal leakage and clues to deception', *Psychiatry*, vol. 32, 1969, pp. 88–105

234 Ekman, P., & Friesen W. V., 'Felt, false and miserable smiles', *Journal of Personality and Social Psychology*, vol. 39, no. 6, 1982, pp. 1125–34

236 Frank, M. G.,& Ekman, P., 'The Ability to detect deceit generalizes across different types of high-stake lies', *Journal of Personality and Social Psychology*, vol. 72, no. 6, 1997, pp. 1429–39

245 Ekman, Paul, & O'Sullivan, Maureen, 'Who can catch a liar?', *American Psychologist*, vol. 46, 1991, pp. 913–20

245 dePaulo, B. M., & Pfeifer, R. H., 'On-the-job experience and skill at detecting deception', *Journal of Applied Personal Psychology*, vol. 16, 1986, 249–67

292 Skinner, Burrhus Frederic, ' "Superstition" in the Pigeon', *Journal of Experimental Psychology*, vol. 38, 1948, pp. 168–72

293 Wagner, M. V., & Morris, E. K., ' "Superstitious" ' behaviour in children', *The Psychological Record*, vol. 37, 1987, pp. 471–88

294 Koichi Ono, 'Superstitious behaviour in humans', *Journal of Experimental Analysis of Behaviour*, vol. 47, 1987, pp. 261–71

306 Hyman, Ray, 'The Mischief-Making of Ideomotor Action', *The Scientific Review of Alternative Medicine*, Fall-Winter 1999

PICTURE ACKNOWLEDGEMENTS

Helen Duncan produces a materialization of 'Peggy', 6 January 1933: Mary Evans Picture Library/Harry Price Collection; Helen Duncan produces ectoplasm during a test by Harry Price: Mary Evans Picture Library/Harry Price Collection

Eusapia causes a table to rise, Milan 1892: Mary Evans Picture Library; Ethel Post Parrish: Mary Evans Picture Library

Table levitation demonstration: photo James Cooper

Group of people using a planchett: Fortean Picture Library; portraits of Bertrand Russell and Richard Dawkins by Derren Brown: courtesy Derren Brown; pendulum method of determining the sex of an unborn baby: © Janine Wiedel Photolibrary/Alamy; Derren Brown and Andy Nyman at the Olivier Awards, 2006: courtesy Andy Nyman

Russian Roulette: © Rex Features; shooting *Messiah*: © Chris Yacoubian

INDEX